www.

Sean

Shartell

791

2720

9726

MCAT* 1997–98

Rochelle Rothstein, M.D.
Andrew Koh
Sharon Klotz
Michael Syptak, M.D.
&
the Staff of Kaplan Educational Centers

Simon & Schuster

Published by
Kaplan Educational Centers and Simon & Schuster
1230 Avenue of the Americas
New York, NY 10020

The Kaplan Advantage™ Stress Management System
by Dr. Ed Newman and Bob Verini, copyright © 1996 Kaplan Educational Centers

Special thanks to: Laura Barnes, William Barry, Shira Berman, Adam Bloom, Mike Cantwell, William Dracos, Isabel Geffner, Amparo Graf, Robert Greenberg, Matthew Hart, Alison Holt, Jay Johnson, Jennifer Katz, Gary Krist, Alan Levine, Lee Montag, Bob Moses, Stacie Orell, Scott Prentzas, Phil Schein, Julie Schmidt, Susan Schwartz, Margot Shapiro, Brooke Shirley, Rebecca Small, and Constantine Tamvakopoulos.

Project Editor: Amy Arner Sgarro
Production Coordinator: Gerard Capistrano
Production Editor: Maude Spekes
Interior Design: Krista Pfeiffer
Managing Editor: Kiernan McGuire
Executive Editor: Del Franz

Manufactured in the United States of America
Published Simultaneously in Canada

February 1997

7 6 5 4 3 2

ISSN: 1090–9028
ISBN: 0–684–83673–4

CONTENTS

A Message From All of Us at Kaplan

Welcome to Kaplan. You are preparing for the MCAT with the nation's leader in test preparation. Each year, Kaplan raises students' scores through its courses, books, videos, online services, and digital products. We make the annual investment in research and development necessary to ensure that our materials set the standards for the industry and reflect even the most minor test changes. With more than 167 centers and 1,000 satellite locations across the United States and abroad, Kaplan prepares more than 150,000 students each year for college and graduate admissions tests, professional licensing exams, and language proficiency tests. Kaplan is a wholly owned subsidiary of The Washington Post Company, which also owns *Newsweek* magazine.

Kaplan remains at the forefront of test preparation because of the outstanding team of professionals who create and deliver our products and services. Thanks to all of those who made this book—and your score improvement—possible.

Best of luck with the MCAT!

Stanley Kaplan
Founder

Jonathan Grayer
President and CEO

HOW TO USE THIS BOOK

MCAT 1997–98 is more than just your average test prep guide. In addition to information on all the MCAT question types, this book gives you advice on every major aspect of the test-taking experience, as well as plenty of practice.

Here's how to use the various components of this book.

STEP ONE: READ THE MCAT SECTION

Kaplan's live MCAT course has been the industry standard for decades. We've helped more people get into more medical schools than all the other courses combined. In this section, we've distilled the main techniques and approaches from our course in a clear, easy-to-grasp format. We'll introduce you to the mysteries of the MCAT and show you how to take control of the test-taking experience on all levels:

Level One: Test Content
Specific methods and strategies for MCAT passages and questions.

Level Two: Test Expertise
Item-specific techniques, as well as advice on how to pace yourself over the entire section, and how to choose which questions to answer and which to guess on. The peculiarities of a standardized test can sometimes be used to your advantage. We can teach you how.

Level Three: Test Mentality
The proper test attitude for executing all you've learned.

STEP TWO: TAKE KAPLAN'S FULL-LENGTH MCAT PRACTICE TEST

Having trained in the Kaplan methods, you should then take the full-length Practice Test—a timed, simulated MCAT—as a test run for the real thing. The explanations for every question on the test are included in this book and will enable you to understand your mistakes. Try not to confine your review to the explanations for the questions you've gotten wrong. Instead, read all of the explanations—to reinforce key concepts and to sharpen your skills.

STEP THREE: REVIEW TO SHORE UP WEAK POINTS

Go back to the MCAT chapters and review the sections in which your performance was weak. If you feel that you need more intensive content review, consider buying Kaplan's *MCAT Comprehensive Review*, which covers in detail all the content you need to know to score your best.

STEP FOUR: GET READY FOR THE BIG DAY

Read the Last-Minute Tips and The Kaplan Advantage™ Stress Management section to make sure you're in top shape on test day. Follow these four steps and you can be confident that you'll perform your best on the MCAT.

SPECIAL BONUS: THE ADMISSIONS SECTION

Sure, your MCAT performance is a very important criterion in your application, so the bulk of this book is devoted to test prep. But medical schools base their admissions decisions on far more than just the MCAT. In fact, a host of other parts of your application can make or break your candidacy. So, to give you the very best odds, we provide expert advice to lead you through the parts of the application process before and beyond the MCAT. We'll give you an overview of the entire application process, drawing from our years of helping pre-meds, and outline a step-by-step plan to make your application as strong as it can be. We've also included checklists and schedules to keep you on track.

A SPECIAL NOTE FOR INTERNATIONAL STUDENTS

Competition to get into a U.S. medical school is even stiffer for students who are not United States citizens. In 1995-96, only 118 non-U.S. citizens out of a class of approximately 16,000 entered first-year med school. Most of these attended college in the States prior to applying to med school.

If you're not a U.S. citizen and you're interested in attending med school in the United States, here's what you'll need to get started. Since admission to medical school is so competitive, you may also want to explore the possibility of other health-related programs in the U.S.

- If English is not your first language, start there. Most medical schools will require you to take the TOEFL (Test of English as a Foreign Language) or provide some other evidence that you are proficient in English.
- Plan to take the MCAT; most U.S. medical schools require it.
- Begin the process of applying to medical schools at least eighteen months before the fall of the year you plan to start your studies. Most programs will only have September start dates.
- You will need to obtain an I-20 Certificate of Eligibility in order to receive an F-1 Student Visa to study in the United States.
- If you've already completed medical training outside the United States, get information about taking the United States Medical Licensing Exam (USMLE).

For an overview of the medical school admissions process, see the Appendix of this book. For information about particular schools, including admissions requirements, curriculum, facilities, and other statistics, see Kaplan's guide to all the accredited medical schools in the United States, Getting Into Medical School.

Kaplan's Access America™ Program
If you need more help with the complex process of medical school admissions, you may be interested in Kaplan's Access America program.

Kaplan created Access America to assist international students who want to enter the United States university system. The program was designed for students who have received the bulk of their primary and secondary education outside the U.S. in a language other than English. Access America also has programs for international medical graduates seeking professional certification in the United States. Here's a brief description of some of the help available through Access America.

The TOEFL Plus Program
At the heart of the Access America program is the intensive TOEFL Plus Academic English program. This comprehensive English course prepares students to achieve a high level of proficiency in English in order to successfully complete an academic degree. The TOEFL Plus course combines personalized instruction with guided self-study to help students gain this proficiency in a short period of time. Certificates of Achievement in English are awarded to certify your level of proficiency.

MCAT (Medical College Admissions Test)

If you plan to enter a medical school in the United States, Kaplan can help you prepare for the MCAT. Kaplan also offers professional counseling and advice to help you gain a greater understanding of the American education system. We can help you with every step in the admissions process, from choosing the right medical school, to writing your application, to preparing for an interview.

USMLE (United States Medical Licensing Exam) and Other Medical Licensing

If you have graduated from a medical school outside the U.S. and would like to be FCMFMG-certified and obtain a residency in a United States hospital, Kaplan can help you prepare for all three steps of the USMLE.

If you are a nurse who wishes to practice in the United States, Kaplan can help you prepare for the NCLEX (Nursing Certification and Licensing Exam) or CGFNS (Commission on Graduates of Foreign Nursing Schools) exam. Kaplan can also prepare you with the English and cross-cultural knowledge that will help you become an effective nurse.

Applying to Access America

To get more information, or to apply for admission to any of Kaplan's programs for international students or professionals, you can write to us at

Kaplan Educational Centers
International Admissions Department
888 Seventh Avenue
New York, New York 10019 USA

You can also call us at 1-800-522-7700 from within the United States, or at 01-212-262-4980 outside the United States. Our fax number is 01-212-957-1654. Our E-mail address is world@kaplan.com.

You can also get more information or even apply through the Internet at http://www.kaplan.com/intl.

THE MCAT

Verbal Reasoning

Time	85 minutes
Format	65 multiple-choice questions: approximately 9–10 passages with 6–10 questions each
What it tests	critical reading

Physical Sciences

Time	100 minutes
Format	77 multiple-choice questions: approximately 10–11 passages with 4–8 questions each; 15 stand-alone questions (not passage-based)
What it tests	basic general chemistry concepts, basic physics concepts, analytical reasoning, data interpretation

Writing Sample

Time	60 minutes
Format	2 essay questions (30 minutes per essay)
What it tests	critical thinking, intellectual organization, written communication skills

Biological Sciences

Time	100 minutes
Format	77 multiple-choice questions: approximately 10–11 passages with 4–8 questions each; 15 stand-alone questions (not passage-based)
What it tests	basic biology concepts, basic organic chemistry concepts, analytical reasoning, data interpretation

The sections of the test always appear in the same order:

Morning
Verbal Reasoning
[10-minute break]
Physical Sciences
[60-minute lunch break]

Afternoon
Writing Sample
[10-minute break]
Biological Sciences

SCORING

Each MCAT section receives its own score. Verbal Reasoning, Physical Sciences, and Biological Sciences are each scored on a scale ranging from 1–15, with 15 as the highest. The Writing Sample essays are scored alphabetically on a scale ranging from J to T, with T as the highest. The two essays are each evaluated by two official readers, so four critiques combine to make the alphabetical score.

The number of multiple-choice questions that you answer correctly per section is your "raw score." Your raw score will then be converted to yield the "scaled score"—the one that will fall somewhere in that 1–15 range. These scaled scores are what are reported to medical schools as your MCAT scores.

All multiple-choice questions are worth the same amount—one raw point—and *there's no penalty for guessing*. That means that *you should always fill in an answer for every question, whether you get to that question or not!* This is an important piece of advice, so pay it heed. Never let time run out on any section without filling in an answer for every question on the grid.

Your score report will tell you—and your potential medical schools—not only your scaled scores, but also the national mean score for each section, standard deviations, national scoring profiles for each section, and your percentile ranking.

What's a Good Score?

There's no such thing as a cut-and-dried "good score." Much depends on the strength of the rest of your application (if your transcript is first rate, the

FILL IN THE BLANKS

There's no penalty for a wrong answer on the MCAT, so NEVER LEAVE ANY QUESTION BLANK, even if you have time only for a wild guess.

YOUR PERCENTILE

The percentile figure tells you how many other test takers scored at or below your level. In other words, a percentile figure of 80 means that 80 percent did as well or worse than you did, and that only 20 percent did better.

pressure to strut your stuff on the MCAT isn't as intense) and on where you want to go to school (different schools have different score expectations). Here are a few interesting statistics:

For each MCAT administration, the average scaled scores are approximately 8s for Verbal Reasoning, Physical Sciences, and Biological Sciences, and N for the Writing Sample. You need scores of at least 10–11s to be considered competitive by most medical schools, and if you're aiming for the top you've got to do even better, and score 12s and above.

You don't have to be perfect to do well. For instance, on the AAMC's Practice Test II, you could get as many as four questions wrong in Verbal Reasoning, 21 in Physical Sciences, and 16 in Biological Sciences and still score in the 80th percentile. To score in the 90th percentile, you could get as many as two wrong in Verbal Reasoning, 16 in Physical Sciences, and 11 in Biological Sciences. Even students who receive perfect scaled scores usually get a handful of questions wrong.

It's important to maximize your performance on every question. Just a few questions one way or the other can make a big difference in your scaled score. Here's a look at recent score profiles so you can get an idea of the shape of a typical score distribution.

THE BEST REVENGE

You should make an extra effort to score well on a test section if you did poorly in a corresponding class. So the best revenge for getting a C in physics class is acing the Physical Sciences section of the MCAT.

Verbal Reasoning

Scaled Score	Percent Achieving Score	Percentile Rank Range
13–15	1.0	99.1–99.9
12	3.4	95.7–99.0
11	10.7	85.0–95.6
10	15.1	69.9–84.9
9	18.7	51.2–69.8
8	13.1	38.1–51.1
7	10.6	27.5–38.0
6	13.0	14.4–27.4
5	4.9	09.5–14.3
4	4.5	05.0–09.4
3	2.5	02.5–04.9
2	2.0	00.5–02.4
1	0.4	00.0–00.4

Scaled Score
Mean = 8.0
Standard Deviation = 2.43

Physical Sciences

Scaled Score	Percent Achieving Score	Percentile Rank Range
15	0.1	99.9–99.9
14	1.3	98.7–99.9
13	2.1	96.6–98.6
12	4.4	92.2–96.5
11	7.2	85.0–92.1
10	13.9	71.1–84.9
9	11.7	59.4–71.0
8	18.6	40.8–59.3
7	14.0	26.8–40.7
6	13.4	13.4–26.7
5	8.5	04.8–13.3
4	3.4	01.4–04.7
3	1.2	00.3–01.3
2	0.1	00.1–00.2
1	0.0	00.0–00.0

Scaled Score
Mean = 8.1
Standard Deviation = 2.32

Writing Sample		
Scaled Score	Percent Achieving Score	Percentile Rank Range
T	0.6	99.5–99.9
S	3.2	96.3–99.4
R	9.3	87.0–96.2
Q	12.1	74.9–86.9
P	12.1	62.8–74.8
O	13.1	49.7–62.7
N	12.7	37.1–49.6
M	21.3	15.8–37.0
L	9.5	06.3–15.7
K	4.0	02.3–06.2
J	2.2	00.0–02.2

75th Percentile = Q
50th Percentile = O
25th Percentile = M

Biological Sciences		
Scaled Score	Percent Achieving Score	Percentile Rank Range
15	0.1	99.9–99.9
14	0.5	99.5–99.8
13	2.4	97.2–99.4
12	4.3	92.9–97.1
11	8.8	84.1–92.8
10	16.0	68.1–84.0
9	15.5	52.6–68.0
8	16.0	36.6–52.5
7	12.6	24.0–36.5
6	9.9	14.1–23.9
5	6.3	07.8–14.0
4	4.6	03.2–07.7
3	2.2	01.0–03.1
2	0.7	00.3–00.9
1	0.2	00.0–00.2

Scaled Score
Mean = 8.2
Standard Deviation = 2.39

WHAT THE MCAT REALLY TESTS

It's important to grasp not only the nuts and bolts of the MCAT, so you'll know *what* to do on test day, but also the underlying principles of the test so you'll know *why* you're doing what you're doing on test day. We'll cover the straightforward MCAT facts later. Now it's time to examine the heart and soul of the MCAT, to see what it's really about.

The Myth

Most people preparing for the MCAT fall prey to the myth that the MCAT is a straightforward science test. They think something like this:

> *"It covers the four years of science I had to take in school: biology, chemistry, physics, and organic chemistry. It even has equations. OK, so it has Verbal Reasoning and Writing, but those sections are just to see if we're literate, right? The important stuff is the science. After all, we're going to be doctors."*

Well, here's the little secret no one seems to want you to know: The MCAT is not just a science test; it's also a thinking test. This means that the test is designed to let you demonstrate your thought process, not only your thought content.

The implications are vast. Once you shift your test-taking paradigm to match the MCAT modus operandi, you'll find a new level of confidence and control over the test. You'll begin to work with the nature of the MCAT rather than against it. You'll be more efficient and insightful as you prepare for the test, and you'll be more relaxed on test day. In fact, you'll be able to see the MCAT for what it is rather than for what it's dressed up to be. We want your test day to feel like a visit with a familiar friend instead of an awkward blind date.

The Zen of MCAT

Medical schools do not need to rely on the MCAT to see what you already know. Admission committees can measure your subject-area proficiency using your undergraduate coursework and grades. Schools are most interested in the potential of your mind.

In recent years, many medical schools have shifted pedagogic focus away from an information-heavy curriculum to a concept-based curriculum. There is currently more emphasis placed on problem solving, holistic thinking, and cross-disciplinary study. Be careful not to dismiss this important point, figuring you'll wait to worry about academic trends until you're actually in medical school. This trend affects you right now, because it's reflected in the MCAT. Every good tool matches its task. In this case the tool is the test, used to measure you and other candidates, and the task is to quantify how likely it is that you'll succeed in medical school.

Your intellectual potential—how skillfully you annex new territory into your mental boundaries, how quickly you build "thought highways" between ideas, how confidently and creatively you solve problems—is far more important to admission committees than your ability to recite Young's modulus for every material known to man. The schools assume they can expand your knowledge base. They choose applicants carefully because expansive knowledge is not enough to succeed in medical school or in the profession. There's something more. And it's this "something more" that the MCAT is trying to measure.

Every section on the MCAT tests essentially the same higher-order thinking skills: analytical reasoning, abstract thinking, and problem solving. Most test takers get trapped into thinking they are being tested strictly about biology, chemistry, etcetera. Thus, they approach each section with a new outlook on what's expected. This constant mental gear-shifting can be exhausting, not to mention counterproductive. Instead of per-

DON'T BELIEVE THE HYPE

The MCAT is not just about what you know. It's also about how you think.

SO FAR, SO GOOD

While research on the predictive quality of the new MCAT is ongoing, preliminary results* from twelve schools show that MCAT scores are a slightly better predictor of first-year med school grades than are undergraduate GPAs.

*Academic Medicine, Vol. 69 (5), pp. 394–401, May 1994.

VULCAN MIND MELD

If they could, admissions officers would wander around your mind to see how things work and how your ideas are linked together. Thankfully, they can't; so they make you take the MCAT instead.

ceiving the test as parsed into radically different sections, you need to maintain your focus on the underlying nature of the test: it's designed to test your thinking skills, not your information-recall skills. Each test section thus presents a variation on the same theme.

What About the Science?

With this perspective, you may be left asking the question: "What about the science? What about the content? Don't I need to know the basics?" The answer is a resounding Yes! You must be fluent in the different languages of the test. You cannot do well on the MCAT if you don't know the basics of physics, general chemistry, biology, and organic chemistry. We recommend that you take one year each of biology, general chemistry, organic chemistry, and physics prior to taking the MCAT. However, the key point here is that knowing these basics is just the beginning of doing well on the MCAT. That's a shock to most test takers. They presume that once they recall or relearn their undergraduate science, they are ready to do battle against the MCAT. Wrong! They merely have directions to the battlefield. They lack what they need to beat the test: a copy of the test maker's battle plan!

You won't be drilled on facts and formulas on the MCAT. You'll need to demonstrate ability to reason based on ideas and concepts. The science questions are painted with a broad brush, testing your general understanding.

TAKE CONTROL: THE MCAT MINDSET

In addition to being a thinking test, as we've stressed, the MCAT is a standardized test. As such, it has its own consistent patterns and idiosyncrasies that can actually work in your favor. This is the key to why test preparation works. You have the opportunity to familiarize yourself with those consistent peculiarities, to adopt the proper test-taking mindset.

The MCAT Mindset is something you want to bring to every question, passage, and section you encounter. Being in the MCAT Mindset means reshaping the test-taking experience so that you are in the driver's seat:

- Answer questions *when* you want to—feel free to skip tough but do-able passages and questions, coming back to them only after you've racked up points on easy ones
- Answer questions *how* you want to—use our shortcuts and methods to get points quickly and confidently, even if those methods aren't exactly what the test makers had in mind when they wrote the test.

PIECES OF A LARGER PUZZLE

Don't think of the sections of the MCAT as unrelated timed pieces. Each is a variation on the same theme, since the underlying purpose of each section and of the test as a whole is to evaluate your thinking skills.

CONTENT UNDER PRESSURE

Yes, you do have to know science content, but it's only the launchpad for your preparation.

SO YOU HAVE A MIND LIKE A STEEL TRAP . . .

Memorizing formulas won't boost your score. Understanding fundamental scientific principles will.

The following are some overriding principles of the MCAT Mindset that will be covered in depth in the chapters to come:

- Read actively and critically
- Translate prose into your own words
- Save the toughest questions and passages for last
- Know the test and its components inside and out
- Do MCAT-style problems in each topic area after you've reviewed it
- Allow your confidence to build on itself
- Take full-length practice tests a week or two before the test to break down the mystique of the real experience
- Learn from your mistakes—get the most out of your practice tests
- Look at the MCAT as a challenge, the first step in your medical career, rather than as an arbitrary obstacle

And that's what the MCAT Mindset boils down to: Taking control. Being proactive. Being on top of the testing experience so that you can get as many points as you can as quickly and as easily as possible. Keep this in mind as you read and work through the material in this book and, of course, as you face the challenge on test day.

Now that you have a better idea of what the MCAT is all about, let's take a tour of the individual test sections. Although the underlying skills being tested are similar, each MCAT section requires that you call into play a different domain of knowledge. So, though we encourage you to think of the MCAT as a holistic and unified test, we also recognize that the test is segmented by discipline and that there are characteristics unique to each section. In the overviews, we'll review sample questions and answers and discuss section-specific strategies. For each of the sections—Verbal Reasoning, Physical/Biological Sciences, and the Writing Sample—we'll present you with the following:

- THE BIG PICTURE
  You'll get a clear view of the section and familiarize yourself with what it's really evaluating.

- A CLOSER LOOK
  You'll explore the types of questions that will appear and master the strategies you'll need to deal with them successfully.

- HIGHLIGHTS
  The key approaches to each section are outlined, for reinforcement and quick review.

DON'T GET STUCK

Those perfectionist tendencies that make you a good student, and a good medical school candidate, may work against you in MCAT Land. For example, you're probably used to working through tough questions until you get an answer, or understanding everything in a passage before hitting one question. On the MCAT, you don't have the luxury of indulging your perfectionism. You can't afford to spend twenty minutes on a tough question—the computer won't be impressed and you'll run out of time. And you don't need to understand every word of a passage before you go on to the questions—what's tripping you up may not even be relevant to what you'll be asked.

VERBAL REASONING

THE BIG PICTURE

The Verbal Reasoning section is perhaps the most recognizable section of the MCAT, since it's similar to the reading comprehension sections of other standardized tests. It's 85 minutes long and typically consists of about nine passages, with anywhere from six to 10 questions per passage, for a total of 65 multiple-choice questions. The passages, often complex, are drawn from the social sciences, philosophy, and other humanistic disciplines as well as from the natural sciences.

The Verbal Reasoning section tests your ability to:

- read critically and actively
- "possess" or truly comprehend written material
- capture the essence of a passage by recognizing its main idea
- intuit a writer's tone
- draw inferences/conclusions

The passages you'll confront on test day probably won't be fun to read. Odds are, they'll be boring. If they're too engaging, check the cover. You may be taking the wrong test. As part of the challenge, you must be able to concentrate and glean meaning regardless of the nature of the text. This will involve working through your resistance to dry passages and overcoming any anxiety or frustration. The more control you can muster, the quicker you can move through each passage, through the questions, and to a higher score. Remember, Verbal Reasoning isn't there to entertain you or provide relief from the science, but to put you through a mental obstacle course.

VERBAL REASONING AT A GLANCE

- 85 minutes
- 65 multiple-choice questions
- approximately nine to ten passages with six to ten questions each
- tests for critical reading

DON'T BE FOOLED BY FAMILIARITY

Just because you've dealt with reading comprehension on other standardized tests doesn't mean you can get away with not preparing for the Verbal Reasoning section.

Do You Need to Study for Verbal Reasoning?

Don't make the mistake that so many MCAT participants make in underestimating the challenge of the Verbal Reasoning section. Sometimes it falls under the shadow cast by the looming science sections. Also, students figure that there isn't anything to "study" for this section. Be aware that the scoring gradient for Verbal Reasoning is very steep. It's hard to get a good score, so you can't afford to be cavalier. Some medical schools add all your MCAT scores together for a composite score—if you blow off Verbal Reasoning, you could kill your composite. Practice Verbal Reasoning as you would the other test sections, and challenge yourself to acquire the specialized reading skills required on the MCAT.

How to Read Actively

Usually we read for entertainment or information. Rarely do we read critically, to understand how the writer organizes ideas and uses detail to support themes. MCAT Verbal Reasoning requires that you abandon standard reading habits and take on the role of a critical, or active, reader. This means that you create a mental model of the passage while you're reading, capturing each idea the author constructs and making it part of your vision of the passage.

This can happen only if you resist feeling overwhelmed by the themes in the passage. If you're too awed by the author or bored by the subject matter, you won't be able to take possession of the passage. This notion of "taking possession" is the key to active reading. It means that you keep a distance from the words, and that you remain analytical rather than get emotional.

Your goal from the outset of the passage is to figure out what the author is saying and how the ideas are linked. Every passage contains one main idea. You can usually figure it out in the first few lines of the passage, and redefine your sense of it as you move through the passage. When you're done reading, you should be able to state the main idea in your own words. Being an active reader implies that you constantly ask yourself what the author intends and how that intention is conveyed and supported. Successfully answering the questions depends on your ability to quickly glean the author's point, to map out the passage in your mind, and to assess the inferences.

Pay Attention To Structure

The structure of each passage can help you organize a mental map. You know, for example, that each paragraph will explore a new angle of the main idea or provide detail associated with a key idea. The MCAT Verbal

Reasoning passages are, for the most part, very logical in their construction. They may contain complicated words or ideas, but their structure is very manageable, even predictable. Look for certain keywords (e.g., *consequently*) or phrases (e.g., *on the other hand*) that hold ideas together and can alert you as to what's ahead in the passage.

Some test takers feel more anchored as they read the passage if they've scoped out the questions first. As a rule, it won't save you time or effort to do so. Most of the questions will require that you demonstrate a general understanding of the passage's main idea and overall construction—neither of which can be derived from any particular section of the passage. You need to read for meaning and for organization whether or not you've reviewed the questions.

A Closer Look

Here's a chance to familiarize yourself with Verbal Reasoning passages and questions, to learn how to approach them. You'll have more opportunities to practice this section later; for now we want to open your eyes to structure and strategy.

Sample Passage and Questions

As you read through the MCAT-style passage below, try to articulate the main idea to yourself. Read actively and critically. Consider what the author is trying to say and how the ideas are communicated. You might want to pause between paragraphs to digest what you've read and put the ideas into your own words.

In a real MCAT situation, you'll need to be time-conscious while you read. For now, just go at whatever pace feels comfortable to you. Keep in mind that the passages you'll see on the MCAT can come from history, philosophy, the arts, and other disciplines, and can vary in length and complexity.

KEYWORDS ARE SIGNALS

contrast:
   although, however, but, contrary, on the one hand

comparison:
   likewise, similarly

continuing argument:
   also, further, in addition, moreover

introducing examples:
   for instance, consider the case of, one example of this is

conclusion:
   then, therefore, finally, thus, in conclusion

DON'T SWEAT THE DETAILS

You can always refer to the passage for specifics. The passage isn't going anywhere.

In 1948, *Look* magazine polled America's art critics and major artists, among them Edward Hopper, Stuart Davis, and Charles Burchfield, for a consensus on the creative spirit who could be pronounced the best of the age. It is a fair measure of the art
5 establishment's limited attention span that a generation after John Marin was crowned prince of painters by his peers, his name had begun to fade. New styles raced in to seize the interest of the gallery and museum worlds; fashion embraced Abstract Expressionism, then thrilled to the distancing imagery of Pop Art
10 and later, for about five minutes, went gaga over a frail

phenomenon labeled Op Art. To be sure, Marin's death in 1953 was the occasion for lavish obituary tributes. But mention him today to a reasonably literate American or a cultured, well-traveled European and, likely as not, the response will be a
15 puzzled stare.

That is not only odd but hard to understand. Marin's legacy embraces more than 3,000 works, many of them memorable. There are prime etchings, splendid if demanding oils and, in the main, watercolors—2,500 of them, amazing in color, design,
20 and complexity. He seemed to have set down everything in a transport of excitement, as if he were recording themes for a fevered gavotte. Indeed, he once wrote of the acts of drawing and painting as "a sort of mad wonder dancing."

Everything that came from Marin's loving hand radiated
25 spontaneity. Here, it appeared, was a natural, creative spirit, a lucky man who was freed, rather than constrained, by his magnanimous imagination. In truth, hardly anything Marin turned out was unrehearsed. The paintings which hinted at the impetuosity of an artist struggling to convey the "warring,
30 pushing, pulling forces" of his surroundings were, as often as not, studio works. Even his letters, with their blithe disregard for punctuation, were discovered to be the results of many drafts.

As a husband and father, Marin lived a life of singular regularity. He had one wife and, as far as anyone knows, no
35 extramarital entanglements. When he put away his paints at the end of his working day, Marin became a man of simple, harmless pleasures. Late pictures show a wiry-looking figure with a long, thin Yankee nose, the parched skin of a farmer, and a humorous mouth that often held a cigarette. No one ever saw him down
40 more drink than was good for his speech or balance. His idea of fun was a good game of billiards.

The contrast between the art and the man who made it was extreme, fascinating, and a trifle baffling. Marin's pictures were daring, the work of a sophisticated eye, an unfailing
45 imagination, a virtuoso hand; some of them verge on elegant abstraction, although he looked down on abstract art. He hated efforts to interpret his art—or for that matter anyone else's. The attitude is not uncommon to artists, particularly American artists, but Marin's distrust of the critical and academic
50 establishments verged on the fanatic. "Intellectuals," he once pronounced, "have in their makeup a form of Nazism."

Adapted from Helen Dudar, "The Old Fashioned Modernism of John Marin," *Smithsonian* vol. 20, no. 11 (Feb. 1990), pp. 20, 52–63.

1. The main point of the passage is to:
   A. explain why John Marin's work was virtually forgotten after his death.
   B. consider the contrast between Marin's artistic style and his personal life and habits.
   C. argue that the art establishment was unable to reach a consensus on the "best of the age" because of its limited attention span.
   D. suggest that Marin's vivacious watercolors were a reaction against Nazism in the art world.

2. Of the following, the author of the passage is most likely:
   A. a contemporary painter.
   B. a magazine art critic.
   C. an investigative reporter.
   D. a museum curator.

3. The author refers to Op Art (line 11) in order to:
   A. place Marin's art within a specific category or genre.
   B. identify the origins of Marin's artistic style.
   C. emphasize the fleeting popularity of artistic styles.
   D. compare Marin's stylistic simplicity with later psychedelic trends.

4. The author's attitude toward Marin may be described as one of:
   A. grudging approval.
   B playful irreverence.
   C. flippant disrespect.
   D. reverent appreciation.

5. The passage discusses all of the following aspects of Marin's life EXCEPT his:
   A. political beliefs.
   B. physical appearance.
   C. artistic style.
   D. family life.

6. In saying that intellectuals "have in their makeup a form of Nazism," (line 51), Marin most probably means that:
   A. the academic establishment is clearly fascist in its structure.
   B. intellectuals often have leftist political and social leanings.
   C. critics often misread extremist political messages in the works of artists.
   D. the criticism and interpretation of art represents a sort of tyranny.

7. The author characterizes Marin's work as:
   A. fevered and energetic.
   B. simple and colorful.
   C. constrained and precise.
   D. tortured and impenetrable.

8. The author characterizes Marin's paintings as "studio works" in line 31 in order to make the point that:
   A. Marin's painting exhibit the influences of many studio artists.
   B. despite attempts at objectivity, Marin's works expressed the academic biases of his time.
   C. although Marin's work seemed spontaneous, it was the result of precise crafting.
   D. Marin's paintings never reflected his complexity and vivid imagination.

Did You Catch the Main Idea?

The author's intent was to contrast John Marin's flamboyant artistic style with his subdued personal life. We get the first hint of this theme in the second paragraph, where the author describes the ostensible mechanism by which Marin created his art ("mad wonder dancing"). The idea is further developed in the next paragraph, where we get the sense that the process through which Marin produced art was not as it seemed ("In truth, hardly anything Marin turned out was unrehearsed."). The fourth paragraph describes the subject's personal life, showing it to be as dull as his art was wild. The last paragraph begins with a clear statement of the passage's main idea; the rest of the paragraph solidifies the intent of the passage.

There's more to understanding the passage than just being able to figure out the main idea. You have to construct a mental outline of the structure of the passage so you'll be able to refer back to it while you answer the questions. The questions following a passage test your understanding of the passage, its structure, its implications, and its tone. It's important that you gather information about the passage as you read so you'll be able to answer the questions quickly and confidently.

MAKE A MENTAL MAP

Try labeling each paragraph so you know what's covered in each and how it fits into the overall structure of the passage. This will help you get a fix on the passage as a whole and it will help you locate specific details later on.

Answer Review

1. **B**

   Choice B has the proper scope to reflect the main idea. **Choice A** makes reference to a minor point in the first paragraph, **Choice C** distorts an idea from the passage and magnifies a detail, and **Choice D** connects two ideas presented separately.

2. **B**

   The citation after the passage and the general tone of the writing suggest that "magazine art critic" is most fitting. Were the writer a painter, we would expect more information about the artwork. An investigative reporter would have a confrontational tone. Finally, we might expect that a museum curator would focus more on Marin's artwork and its effect on the public rather than on the relation between his art and his life.

3. **C**

   Go back to the passage to find the reference. We find it in conjunction with the writer's implication that the art world has a short attention span. This is most consistent with **Choice C**. **Choices A** and **B** mistakenly connect Op Art to the work of Marin, a connection the author does not make in the passage. **Choice D** assumes a comparison also not drawn from the passage.

4. **D**

   Only **Choice D** matches the overall tone of the passage. Most tone questions have adjectives and nouns in the answer choices. Remember that both must match the passage for the choice to be correct.

5. **A**

   This type of question requires that you find an exception. **Choice A**—political beliefs—is the only aspect among the answer choices not discussed in the passage. If you misinterpreted Marin's "Nazi" quote as being political instead of philosophical, you might have had a hard time answering this question.

6. **D**

   Here, you must show that you interpreted the quote correctly. Marin used the phrase Nazism to describe a repressive, tyrannical system of criticism—not a political attitude. Only **Choice D** resonates with the metaphorical interpretation of the phrase.

THE PERILS OF KNOWLEDGE

Certainly knowing a little about the topic discussed can be helpful. But remember to answer the questions based on what's in the passage, not based on your own outside knowledge.

7. **A**

The answer can't be found in a particular line from the passage. You must conclude the best answer based on the attitude and tone of the passage. **Choice A** accurately reflects the writer's characterizations of Marin's work. **Choice B** might be tempting because the writer *does* describe Marin as simple, but in his personal life, not in reference to his art. **Choice C** describes Marin's life as depicted by the author but has no connection to his art. Finally, **Choice D** conveys too much negativity to match the tone of the passage.

8. **C**

Refer to the line referenced in the question stem to see how the sentence functions in the passage. We see that the author was trying to suggest that despite their seeming spontaneity, Marin's paintings were actually quite "crafted." **Choice C** is thus consistent with the intent of the passage. **Choice A** is a tricky interpretation of the sentence. **Choice B** sounds erudite, but it has no relation to the passage whatsoever. Lastly, **Choice D** makes an illogical leap to conclude that Marin's paintings showed no imagination, but the passage never suggests this is the case.

Six Question Types

There are six Verbal Reasoning question styles you'll find on the MCAT: Main Idea, Detail, Inference, Application, Tone, and Logic. Familiarity with the question types helps you anticipate the kinds of answers you should be choosing. The ability to anticipate correct answers will speed up your testing time, give you extra confidence, and—ultimately—boost your score!

1. Main Idea

<u>Description</u>: Main Idea questions ask for a restatement of the author's main point, the primary idea, or the overall gist of the passage. Question 1 in the preceding sample is a Main Idea question, because it's asking you for the point of the Marin excerpt.

<u>Strategy</u>: Look for the answer choice that best matches the scope of the main theme. Wrong answers will be either too narrow or too broad in their restatement of the author's main point, or will distort it in some way.

<u>Strategy Applied</u>: If you look for the "big idea" of the preceding sample passage as you read it, you see that your interpretation of the author's purpose matches only one answer choice, that there was a sharp contrast between Marin's artistic style and personal life.

SIX QUESTION TYPES

1. Main Idea
2. Detail
3. Inference
4. Application
5. Tone
6. Logic

MAIN IDEA ALERT

Key phrases in the question stem include:
"The author's main purpose is . . . ."
"The main idea of the passage is . . . ."
"The general theme is . . . ."

2. Detail

<u>Description</u>: Detail questions require you to recall a specific point from the passage or to relocate it using information from the question stem. Correct answer choices will be those that approximate information directly from the passage. One type of Detail question—"Scattered Detail"—will ask you to consider many details from various places in the passage and may ask you to identify a detail as an exception among the answer choices. For example: "The author uses as evidence all the following except . . . ." Question 5 in the preceding sample is a Scattered Detail question, because it requires that you recall or look back to the passage to determine a characteristic of Marin's life that is not mentioned.

<u>Strategy</u>: Refer to any notes you made in the margin or to notes in your mental outline to identify the detail under consideration. If the question is in the "all except" format, you should be looking for the exception, for the choice that fits the stimulus. By all means, look back to the passage. You're not supposed to memorize details!

<u>Strategy Applied</u>: In the case of the sample, you're looking for the exception, so you should ask yourself, "Does this fit the stimulus?" for each answer choice. The answer is "no" for only one—the passage does not discuss Marin's political beliefs.

3. Inference

<u>Description</u>: Inference questions ask you to make a small logical leap from the passage to another idea that would be consistent with the main idea. Correct answers to Inference questions will have the proper degree of "distance" from the passage itself—not so close as to be a detail but not so far as to be illogical.

<u>Strategy</u>: Choose an answer that is consistent with the passage but is not a simple restatement of information already presented.

<u>Strategy Applied</u>: There wasn't an Inference question in the sample, but let's say that you were asked how Marin's work was affected by critical interpretation. Since you're told that Marin did not like interpretation of his or anyone else's art, you can infer that he would not adjust his art to suit the critics, that his work would be unaffected.

4. Application

<u>Description</u>: Application questions ask you to take an essential idea from the passage and relate it to a different context. These questions may set up analogies or metaphors; you'll need to figure out how they relate to

DETAIL ALERT

Phrases that identify a question as a Detail question include:
"According to the passage, ..."
"Based on the information in the passage, ..."

MAJORITY RULE

Most of the questions will be Main Idea, Detail, or Inference question.

INFERENCE ALERT

Inference questions can relate to details or to the general theme of the passage and are indicated by question-stem phrases such as:
"It can be inferred from the passage that . . . ."
"The author suggests that . . . ."

one another and determine which one presents an idea that parallels the passage. Question 2 in the sample is an Application question, because it asks you to use what you know about the passage to guess at the source of the passage.

Strategy: Pick an answer choice that effectively "translates" an idea from the passage into a new context or scenario.

Strategy Applied: Taking what you know about the sample passage (the author's point of view and tone) and applying this to a scenario outside the passage (the source of the piece), you can judge that the author was most likely a magazine art critic.

5. Tone

Description: Questions of Tone require you to identify the author's attitude or opinion about a passage's subject matter. Such questions may be focused on a detail or may refer to the tone of the whole passage. Question 4 from the sample passage is an example of a Tone question, because it asks you to determine the author's attitude.

Strategy: Go with the answer choice that is consistent with your "gut feel" from the passage—positive, neutral, or negative.

Strategy Applied: Based on the first paragraph in the sample passage, you know that the author holds Marin in high esteem, so the correct answer about the author's tone will have to reflect a completely positive attitude. Only one choice does so.

6. Logic

Description: Logic questions require that you analyze the function of certain portions of the passage. You may be asked how a particular detail serves the purpose of the passage, or you may be asked about overall passage structure. A Logic question is derived from the overall plan and layout of the passage—not from the specifics contained within the passage. Question 8 in the sample is a Logic question, because it asks you about the logical structure of the passage.

Strategy: Refer to your mental map and passage outline, the source of all logic questions. Choose an answer that maintains the integrity of your passage blueprint.

Strategy Applied: In the sample, you're asked to determine the meaning of the term *studio works*. To do so, you need to read a few sentences back from the term and figure out its context. You clearly see, then, that "studio works" refers to artistic pieces crafted out of a deliberate process.

APPLICATION ALERT

Here are some phrases to watch for in Application question stems:
"The passage was probably written by a . . . ."
"The example in paragraph 2 would be most similar to . . . ."

TONE ALERT

Key phrases in Tone question stems include:
"The author's attitude can best be described as . . . ."
"The author would likely agree with . . . ."
"The tone of the passage is best described as . . . ."

LOGIC ALERT

Logic stems may include phrases such as:
"The third paragraph serves to . . . ."
"Which of the following would strengthen the author's point?"
"The author raises the point in paragraph 3 in order to . . . ."

Highlights

Getting Off on the Right Foot

- You don't have to do the passages in order. Do the easiest early on, leaving the intimidating or unfamiliar for last. Also, look for the passages with more questions and do those first to maximize points.
- You usually won't save time by scanning the questions before reading the passage, since most of the questions are based on a holistic understanding of the passage. Besides, having the questions in mind can distract you from focusing on the passage.
- Read the opening lines of the passage slowly and carefully to "orient" yourself to the subject matter and the author's style.
- Read for the Main Idea, often but not always expressed in the opening lines.

Reading the Passages

- Read actively!
- Don't get emotional. Read with distance.
- Don't judge the passages. You'll need to overcome the hurdle of reading material that doesn't interest you.
- Create a mental map.
- Feel free to make notes in the margin.
- Don't try to memorize details. Know the purpose of the detail, not the detail itself.
- Look for structural keywords to help you anticipate new ideas in the passage.
- Check the citation at the end of the passage. It may give clues about tone or context.

Facing the Questions

- When you're finished reading, don't rush to the questions. Take a moment to rephrase the main idea to yourself.
- Remember that wrong answer choices will distort or reverse the author's main point, blow a detail out of proportion, confuse or misplace details, or be totally irrational. Use a process of elimination to increase your chances of getting to the right answer.
- You should look back at the passage to find or clarify details while you're answering the questions.

- Answer questions based on the passage—not based on outside knowledge.
- If you don't know an answer, guess! Try to do so while you're still working on the passage, so you won't have to reread it later. There's no penalty for wrong answers.
- If time is running out and there are blank spaces on your grid, by all means, guess.
- Be careful marking your answer grid—especially if you're not answering the questions in numerical order.

PHYSICAL AND BIOLOGICAL SCIENCES

THE BIG PICTURE

The two science sections on the MCAT—Physical and Biological—are similar in their format, though their content obviously differs. In each 100-minute section you'll find about 10–11 passages, each followed by four to eight multiple-choice questions (for a total of 62), and 15 stand-alone multiple-choice questions (also referred to as *discretes*)—not based on any passage. The Physical Sciences section is comprised of physics and general chemistry, approximately evenly divided in content though mixed throughout the section. The Biological Sciences section consists of biology and organic chemistry questions mixed throughout, with greater emphasis on biology (about 65 percent biology, 35 percent organic chemistry).

The passages, each 250–300 words in length, will describe experiments, situations, or ideas from which questions are drawn. The information may be presented in the guise of journal or textbook articles, experimental research, data analysis, or scientific-style editorials. When reading the science passages, you should think about extracting information—not meaning and structure as in Verbal Reasoning. Consider the passages to be data that you must interpret and understand so as to be able to apply it to the specific needs of the questions. The passage-and-question structure allows you to demonstrate many skills, among them:

- understanding the science presented in the passage, no matter how obscure or foreign to you
- confidently connecting elements of your scientific "repertoire" to new situations

PHYSICAL SCIENCES AT A GLANCE

- 100 minutes
- 77 multiple-choice questions
- approximately 10–11 passages with four to eight questions each
- 15 stand-alone questions (not passage based)
- tests basic science concepts, anaytical reasoning, data interpretation

- 100 minutes
- 77 multiple-choice questions
- approximately 10–11 passages with four to eight questions each
- 15 stand-alone questions (not passage based)
- tests basic science concepts, anaytical reasoning, data interpretation

SEEING THE BRAIN AS HALF FULL

Your knowledge of science will get you only so far. To master the MCAT you need to develop the right attitude and thinking skills.

- quickly assessing the kinds of situations feasible given the information in the passage

The stand-alone questions will draw on your knowledge of particular concepts or themes in the respective sciences. They're "wild cards" in the sense that you cannot group them together in any formal way; in fact, they appear scattered throughout the sections. Ranging in scope from a quantitative problem to a conceptual thought experiment, they are the test maker's way of randomly tapping into your knowledge base.

The MCAT Attitude

It's important to approach both science sections with the same mindset: MCAT science is just a window into your mind. The test makers are trying to see how you reason, how you solve problems, and how well you command your knowledge. They are not after a data dump from your core memory. It's crucial that you demonstrate conceptual understanding of scientific material and show proficiency in applying scientific themes in new situations. This is the kind of mental flexibility that will get you a great MCAT score.

Abstract Thinking

Another way to describe flexibility is as a form of abstraction. To think abstractly is to lift ideas out of a specific context and place them in a new context. It's a skill that allows you passage into seemingly unfamiliar territory, and on the MCAT that could mean the question around the corner. In the science sections, this skill is tested repeatedly.

For example, passages may provide hypothetical scenarios or describe experiments you've never seen before. You'll need to take the unfamiliar and make it familiar, and that's where abstract thinking comes in. If you understand the basic framework of experimental design and scientific method, you won't be overwhelmed by a specific unfamiliar context. You'll be able to "rise above" the details rather than get tripped up by them.

What About Formulas And Math?

Contrary to what you may presume, the MCAT is not a math-intensive test. Despite the scientific language on the MCAT, there is nothing more mathematically complex than algebra, exponents, logs, and a little bit of trig. There is no calculus, differential equations, or matrix mechanics. You may need to recall sine and cosine for standard angles, though such values are often provided if necessary. That's it! No higher math.

Similarly, many of the scientific formulas necessary to work through problems and answer questions will be provided on the test. This is just an indicator of how negligible is the value of "straight memorization". You gain little by having every nitty-gritty formula easily accessible unless you also have a broad understanding of what the formulas mean, what they imply, what their units indicate, how they relate to one another, and how to navigate among them.

In light of our discussion of concept-based testing, it makes sense that the MCAT will not reward you merely for the "brute force" of memorization. There will rarely be an opportunity on the MCAT to algebraically crunch away on a formula. The information you're given won't fit neatly into formulas. If it did, the MCAT would be nothing but a memory-and-algebra test. And, as we've discussed, it is much more. Again, you should not be concerned with memorizing formulas. You should be concerned with *understanding* formulas. The key point is that once you understand the scientific concepts behind a formula, you hardly need the formula itself anymore. Though this applies mostly to physics and chemistry, the underlying theme is relevant for both science sections: Think, don't compute!

A CLOSER LOOK

What follows is a review of the content areas you can expect to find in the science sections of the MCAT. This is not to suggest that your MCAT will cover all of these topics; instead, use this list as a guideline of the content that could possibly show up. Therefore, you should make it your business to be thoroughly familiar with the topics below, since you don't know exactly what you'll find on test day.

PHYSICAL SCIENCES

Physics
- Basic Units/Kinematics
- Newtonian Mechanics
- Force and Inertia
- Fluids/Solids
- Electrostatics
- Magnetism
- Circuits

FREE YOUR MIND

Don't let yourself get bogged down in a passage or question. Take a step back to consider the big picture.

- Periodic Motion, Waves, Sound
- Light and Optics
- Atomic Phenomena
- Nuclear Physics

General Chemistry
- Quantum Numbers
- Hund's Rule/Electron Configuration
- Periodic Table
- Reaction Types
- Balancing Equations
- Bonding
- Formal Charge/VSEPR Theory
- Intermolecular Forces
- Chemical Kinetics/Equilibrium
- Thermodynamics/Entropy
- Ideal Gas Law
- Phases of Matter
- Solutions
- Acids and Bases
- Electrochemistry

BIOLOGICAL SCIENCES

Biology
- Eukaryotic and Prokaryotic Cells
- Membrane Traffic
- Cell Division—Mitosis and Meiosis
- Embryogenesis
- Enzymatic Activity
- Cellular Metabolism
- Muscular and Skeletal Systems
- Digestive System
- Respiratory and Circulatory Systems
- Lymphatic System
- Immune System
- Homeostasis
- Endocrine System
- Nervous System

PHEW!

You don't need to memorize as many math and science formulas as you may think. Understanding them is more important than memorizing them.

- Molecular Genetics / Inheritance
- Viruses
- Evolution

Organic Chemistry
- Nomenclature
- Stereochemistry
- Mechanisms
- Carboxylic Acids
- Amines
- Spectroscopy
- Carbohydrates and Lipids
- Hydrolysis and Dehydration
- Amino Acids and Proteins
- Oxygen-containing Compounds
- Hydrocarbons
- Laboratory Techniques
- IR and NMR Spectroscopy

Sample Passage and Questions

This is probably your first chance to see what the passages, passage-based questions, and stand-alone questions will look like in the science sections. An answer key is provided, but try to work through these samples without consulting it. We'll use the following passage and questions to highlight general strategies.

Passage

A physics class is attempting to measure the acceleration due to gravity, g, by throwing balls out of classroom windows. They performed the following two experiments:

Experiment 1

Two class members lean out of different windows at the same height, h = 5.2 m, above the ground and drop two different balls. One ball is made out of lead and has a mass of 5 kg. The other ball is made out of plastic and has a mass of 1 kg. The students measure the velocity of the lead ball just before impact with the ground and find it to be 10 m/s. They also find that when the plastic ball hits the ground it bounces, and its momentum changes by 18 kg × m/s.

Experiment 2

Instead of dropping the plastic ball, a student throws the ball out of a higher window and observes its projectile motion. The ball is thrown from a height of 10 m above the ground with a velocity of 4 m/s directed at an angle of 30° above the horizontal. (Note: Assume that the air resistance is negligible unless otherwise stated.)

Passage-Based Questions

1. The students did not account for air resistance in their measurement of g in Experiment 1. How does the value of g they obtained compare to the actual value of g?

   A. The value of g obtained in Experiment 1 is greater than the actual value of g because air resistance increases the time it takes the balls to fall from the windows to the ground.

   B. The value of g obtained in Experiment 1 is greater than the actual value of g because air resistance decreases the kinetic energy of the balls just before impact.

   C. The value of g obtained in Experiment 1 is less than the actual value of g because air resistance decreases the velocity of the balls just before impact.

   D. The value of g obtained in Experiment 1 is less than the actual value of g because air resistance decreases the time it takes the balls to fall from the windows to the ground.

2. Which of the following would change the measured value of g in Experiment 1?

   I. Increasing the mass of the earth
   II. Using balls having a different mass but the same volume
   III. Throwing the balls horizontally instead of dropping them vertically

   A. I only
   B. III only
   C. I and II only
   D. II and III only

3. In Experiment 1, the change in momentum that the plastic ball experiences when it bounces off the ground does NOT depend on: (Note: Assume that the collision is perfectly elastic.)

A. the velocity of the ball just before impact.
B. the mass of the ball.
C. the mass of Earth.
D. the volume of the ball.

4. In Experiment 2, what was the maximum height above the window reached by the plastic ball? (Note: The acceleration due to gravity is $g = 9.8$ m/s^2, sin 30° = 0.50, and cos 30° = 0.866.)

A. 10.2 cm
B. 20.4 cm
C. 30.6 cm
D. 61.2 cm

5. In a third experiment, a student throws the lead ball out of the same window used in Experiment 1 with a velocity of 3 m/s in the horizontal direction. What is the ratio of the work done by gravity on the lead ball in the first experiment to the work done by gravity on the ball in the third experiment?

A. 1:1
B. 1:3
C. 1:9
D. 3:1

Stand-Alone Questions
6. In the figure below, the velocity vector of a particle is represented at successive times *t*. Which of the following best represents the acceleration vector?

$$\longrightarrow \quad \longrightarrow \quad \longrightarrow \quad \longleftarrow \quad \longleftarrow \quad \longleftarrow$$
$$t = 0 \qquad t = 1 \quad t = 2 \quad t = 3 \quad t = 4 \qquad t = 5$$

A. $\longrightarrow$
B. $\longleftarrow$
C. The acceleration changes direction.
D. The acceleration is zero.

7. All of the following statements are true of most transition elements EXCEPT:

   A. they have partially filled *d* subshells.
   B. they have extremely high ionization energies.
   C. they exhibit metallic character.
   D. they have multiple oxidation states.

8. A patient is taking a drug that has the side effect of being a sympathetic nervous system inhibitor. Which of the following would most likely be seen as a result of this drug?

   A. Decreased bowel motility
   B. Decreased heart rate
   C. Increased pupil diameter
   D. Increased blood supply to skeletal muscles

Were You Able To Think Abstractly?
Did you get bogged down in details, or were you able to rise above them? Were you able to come up with your own answers before looking at the choices? As you review the following answer explanations you'll be able to assess your performance and pick up important strategies.

Answer Review

Passage

The passage describes a series of experiments performed by some students. As you read, you should be making notes in the margins or underlining important information (i.e., the height = 5.2 meters, mass = 5 kg, etcetera). You might make a chart to list out the respective "given" data for each experiment:

Experiment 1
2 balls
masses for each
height
final velocity for lead ball
plastic ball: change in momentum

Experiment 2
height
initial velocity
angle above horizon

SPACE OUT

Use the free space of your margins to make notes or draw charts and diagrams.

Passage-Based Questions

1. **C**

   This is a question you could answer without reference to the passage. It's really asking about how a measurement of *g* would change depending on whether or not air resistance is considered (with all other variables presumed constant). Since air resistance is a force working in the opposite direction from gravity, it's a force of resistance, like friction. Therefore, it slows down the motion of the ball, making it take longer to fall the same distance. Thus the velocity just before impact decreases when air resistance is considered. We know that *g* is proportional to the square of the velocity (from solving for *g* in $v^2 = v_0^2 + 2ad$, where *a* would be *g*, and *d* would be the height). If the velocity is less (because the ball takes more time to travel the same distance if we consider air resistance), then *g* will also be less than the measured value. This line of reasoning rules out **Choices A** and **B**. **Choice D** says that air resistance *decreases* the time it takes for the ball to fall. But we just discussed that resistance *adds* to the time for travel. So, **Choice C** is correct.

DON'T GET DISTRACTED

Some passage-based questions can actually be answered without referring to the passage. Don't let unnecessary information confuse you.

Key strategy: A chart helps you organize what you know from the passage, so you can access the information quickly while answering the questions. Remember, you're reading for data—not for meaning or structure. Be sure, however, that you understand the context of every piece of data you collect.

Key Strategy: Don't read more complexity into a question than is there. In some cases, passage-based questions will actually be testing in a stand-alone style, with little or no reference back to the passage.

2. A

This roman numeral–style question asks about what factors would change the measured value of g in the first experiment. Be careful to consider only the information from Experiment 1 when answering this question.

Let's consider the first statement. If it's wrong, then you can eliminate any answer choice that has it listed. If you decide it is true, then you must choose an answer that includes it in its list of numerals. In the first experiment, the students neglected air resistance, so we have only gravity to consider. The first statement requires that we think about how g is related to the mass of the earth. You should recall that the gravitational force between an object and the earth is $G = mM/R_2$, where G is the universal gravitational constant, m is the mass of the object, M is the mass of the earth, and R is the distance between. But remember also that the weight of an object = mg. We can equate these two forces ($mM/R_2 = mg$) to solve for $g = GM/R_2$. Therefore, changing the mass of the earth would indeed change the value of g. So, Statement I is true, and you can eliminate **Choices B** and **D**. Now we need only consider Statement II to decide between **A** and **C**. Let's look at Statement II. It says that using balls with different mass but the same volume would change g. We know that in Experiment 1, the students ignored air resistance, so the volume of the balls is not relevant. What about the mass? Well, we saw above that g is independent of the object's mass. So, Statement II is not true and **Choice A** is correct.

If you were unsure about Statement I, though, you'd have to work through Statement III to decide which answer choice is correct. The key to the third statement is realizing that vertical trajectory will be unchanged by any initial horizontal velocity. The same vertical force—gravity—will be at work. So, Statement III is untrue, confirming **A** as the correct answer choice.

Key Strategy: Use the structure of a Roman numeral question to your advantage! Eliminate choices as soon as you find them to be inconsistent with the truth or falsehood of a statement in the stimulus. Similarly, consider only those choices that include a statement that you've already determined to be true.

LEAD YOURSELF TO THE ANSWER

Eliminate answer choices you know are wrong, and you'll be left with the correct answer (or at the very least you'll increase your chances of getting to the correct answer).

Key Strategy: You don't have to consider the statements in order. Knowing about any one of them will get you off to a great start answering the question, so if you're unsure about the first statement, go on to the second or third.

3. **D**

    This question asks about which variable is *not* a factor in determining the change in momentum for the plastic ball in Experiment 1. You'll be looking for the answer choice that does not play a role in the momentum shift. One of the first things to note is that you're given a hint about the collision between the ball and the ground—it is elastic, implying that both kinetic energy and momentum are conserved during the collision. The question stimulus tells you, then, that at the time of impact, the two surfaces act like solid, hard surfaces (like billiard balls) with no energy lost to the collision.

    Since the mass of the ball doesn't change, its change in momentum is dependent on its change in velocity. So change in momentum = mv_{final} - mv initial. In considering the answer choices, however, there is no need to painstakingly step through calculations. There is one choice that jumps out as inconsistent. **Choice D** mentions a variable—the volume of the ball—which has no bearing on the ball's change in momentum. All the other choices mention variables which are relevant in considering the change in momentum of the ball as it hits the earth.

Key Strategy: Don't do more work than you have to on the test. Work smart. The MCAT rewards test takers who can save time by seeing a creative strategy (i.e., looking for a variable that's not relevant rather than plodding though every choice, solving equations, and wasting time).

4. **B**

    Be careful to read the question. It asks for the maximum height above the window reached by the plastic ball in Experiment 2. Since we're looking for maximum height, we know the vertical velocity will be 0 (that's when the ball stops and turns around to fall back to the ground). From the passage, we know that the ball's initial velocity is 4 meters per second at an angle of 30°. The initial vertical velocity component is $4 \times \sin 30$, or $4 \times 1/2$, which is 2 meters per second. Using kinematics, we know that $v^2 - v_0^2 = 2ay$, where a is acceleration and y is distance. We know $v_0 = 2$ meters per second; we can esti-

WHEN IT'S NOT AN EXACT SCIENCE

You won't always be dealing with exact numerical factors or solutions. You may be working with ratios, or be required to estimate.

mate g to be 10 meters per second squared. Solving the equation, we see that y maximum = .2 meters or 20 centimeters. This is closest to **Choice B**, the correct answer. The height of the window doesn't even come into play. Notice that **Choice D** derives from using the cosine rather than sine of 30° to find the vertical component of velocity. **Choice A** results from a simple calculation error. **Choice C** is incorrect as well.

<u>Key Strategy</u>: Estimate whenever you can to save time.

<u>Key Strategy</u>: Don't get flustered by unnecessary information. In this case, you had more information than you needed to solve the problem. Don't just plug in numbers and hope for a match. Think before you calculate!

5. **A**

You're asked for a ratio. The implication is that some component of the problem is not solvable, so don't expect to work with actual numbers. In this case, you need to compare the work done in two different scenarios. We need to know that work is force through a distance, or $F \times d$. Since gravity works only along the vertical axis, we need to know the vertical distance traveled by both balls to compare the work done. In both cases, the ball drops 5.2 meters. The ball mentioned in the question has some horizontal velocity, but this has no bearing on the vertical dynamics. So, the distance traveled by the balls in the two different experiments is the same. Furthermore, because the mass is identical, the work done is the same. So, the ratio is 1:1—or **Choice A**.

<u>Key Strategy</u>: In many cases with ratio questions, you will not be able to solve for actual numbers. You may have to work with relationships, fractions, and formulas to arrive at the solution.

<u>Key Strategy</u>: We reviewed these questions in order, but you don't have to do the questions order. Start with the ones that seem most feasible and leave the ones that seem difficult or time-intensive for last.

Stand-Alone Questions

6. B

This question is a great example of how the MCAT rewards the careful thinker. You're told that the vectors represent successive measurements of velocity for a particle. You're then asked which answer choice best represents the acceleration vector. Without having actual numbers to work with, you have to be able to construct a relationship between velocity and acceleration and "visualize" that relationship using vectors. The way to approach this question is to ask yourself, "What is the connection between velocity and acceleration?" Once you answer that, you can begin to home in on an appropriate answer choice. So, what *is* the relationship? Recall that, dimensionally, acceleration is velocity per unit time or displacement per time squared. Theoretically speaking, acceleration is the *rate of change of velocity through a period of time.*

So, the answer choice will be a vector that matches the general rate of change amongst the given velocity vectors. At $t = 0$, the velocity is positive and at a maximum. At $t = 1$, it is still positive but the magnitude has decreased, indicating a *deceleration*). At $t = 2$, the velocity is still positive but is diminished in magnitude even more. What the vectors are describing is a particle, mass, car, thing, object, whatever slowing down. At $t = 3$, something that looks a little tricky happens: the velocity becomes negative but with the same magnitude as $t = 2$. The object we're tracking has changed direction from "forward" to "reverse." The trend continues through $t = 4$ and $t = 5$; we see that the particle is going faster (greater magnitude) but in the opposite direction from its original orientation. Let's get a picture of what we've just figured out. A particle—suppose it's a car—is moving forward at some velocity. It slows down, stops at some point, and then reverses direction and speeds up.

OK, now that we understand the stimulus, we're ready to tackle the answer choices. Remember, we're looking for acceleration. We said earlier that acceleration is the rate of change in velocity. Even though the velocity vectors change direction, the acceleration vector maintains its negative direction throughout the time sampled. So, even though the car speeds up in the "negative" direction, its acceleration remains negative. It continually *decelerates* throughout its movement. The implication is that the force acting on the car is in a direction *opposing* the original direction of movement. Once this clicks, the correct answer choice—**Choice B**—leaps out as correct.

THE RIGHT ANSWER TO THE WRONG QUESTION?

Before you go to the answer choices, make certain you understand the question.

Let's step through the others. **Choice A** suggests that the particle keeps accelerating, but the velocity vectors get *smaller* in magnitude at first, not larger. So, even if you forgot that the "negative acceleration" for time markers 3, 4, and 5 has a negative direction, there's no way **Choice A** makes sense. **Choice C** replicates the behavior of the velocity vectors, and if you're not thinking carefully, you might fall for this choice because it *seems* to be consistent with the information you're given. **Choice D** presumes that you might visually "add up" all the vectors in the stimulus rather than apply them. If you do try to add them, you'll get a sum of 0. However, that sum is *not* the acceleration. In fact, it's the total *displacement*. The car essentially moves forward, slowing down to a stop, and then reverses, speeding up back to its original position.

Key Strategy: Understand the question clearly before you move to the answer choices. Otherwise, you'll be vulnerable to persuasive but incorrect choices.

Key Strategy: Use reason. Don't compute.

7. **B**
    This question has the "all except" format, which means you're looking for the answer choice that is the *exception* (i.e., it's *not* true). The stimulus asks about transition elements. Before you rush to the answer choices, think about what you know of transition elements. They're in the middle of the periodic table and have partially filled *d* subshells. You might also recall that their electrons are loosely held by the nucleus and they are sometimes called *transition metals*.

    Choice B—they have high ionization energies—is the correct choice because its statement about transition elements is false. Transition elements are easy to ionize because their electrons are not strongly bound. **Choice A** can't be the correct choice because it says something *true* about transition elements. **Choice C** is also true—they do exhibit metallic properties because their electrons are mobile. **Choice D** is also true about transition elements; they can lose electrons from both s and d orbitals, resulting in multiple oxidation states.

Key Strategy: When answering a question in the "all/except" format, remember that you're looking for the choice that is not true.

Key Strategy: When answer questions in the "all/except" format, be sure to consider all the answer choices to be confident you've picked the most appropriate one.

8. **B**

This question is based on various functions of the different branches of the nervous system. Specifically, it requires knowledge of the pathways innervated by the sympathetic division of the autonomic nervous system. The autonomic nervous system is divided into two branches—the sympathetic and the parasympathetic. The sympathetic system mediates the "fight or flight" responses that ready the body for action. The parasympathetic system innervates those pathways that return the body to its normal state following fight or flight. The sympathetic system prepares the body by increasing heart rate, inhibiting digestion, causing vasoconstriction of blood vessels in the skin, causing vasodilation of blood vessels in skeletal muscle, and promoting pupil dilation.

From this list of functions, you can eliminate **Choices A**, **C**, and **D** since they're all functions of the sympathetic nervous system and would therefore not be likely responses to a drug that inhibits the activity of the sympathetic system. So by the process of elimination you see that **Choice B** is the correct answer. Since sympathetic innervation normally increases heart rate, of the four choices, an inhibitor of the system would most likely result in a *decrease* in heart rate.

Key Strategy: If you approach a stand-alone question that tests specific knowledge you do not possess, skim the choices carefully to see if you can glean any clues or information from them. If not, guess quickly, don't look back, and move on. You don't have time to waste.

HIGHLIGHTS

Reading the Passages
- Passages may sound difficult or unfamiliar. Don't be daunted!
- Feel free to skip around within each section. Tackle the easiest passages first, leaving the harder ones for later, and check for passages with the most questions. Maximize your opportunity for points.
- Make notes in the margin or draw diagrams to help you summarize the information presented.

DON'T PULL YOUR HAIR OUT

If a question is completely out of reach, guess and move on.

Facing the Questions

- Again, you can skip around. Tackle the easiest questions first, leaving the harder ones for later. The difficult questions are worth the same as the easy ones.
- Use numerical approximations when you can. Don't do any long calculations.
- Base your answers on the passage, not on your own knowledge.
- Use a process of elimination to get to the right answer, or to increase your chances of guessing the right answer.
- If you don't know an answer, guess! Try to do so while you're still working on the passage, so you won't have to reread it later. There's no penalty for wrong answers.

Using the Grid

- If time is running out and there are blank spaces on your grid, guess.
- Be careful marking your answer grid—especially if you're not answering the questions in numerical order.

WRITING SAMPLE

THE BIG PICTURE

Medical schools want an assessment of your written communication skills, since this is a reflection of your ability to effectively convey information to your future patients, healthcare colleagues, and the public. This is where the Writing Sample section of the MCAT comes in.

You'll be writing two essays during the MCAT, each in response to a stimulus and each within a half-hour allotment. The Writing Sample is the only section that is not comprised of multiple-choice questions. Like the Verbal Reasoning section, this one tends to be underestimated by MCAT test takers. Most think they can just apply their everyday writing skills to the MCAT and do OK on the essays. This is a dangerous presumption. In every facet, the MCAT is a test of analytical reasoning—even in the Writing Sample.

The Stimulus

The statement you're to respond to will be in a format along the lines of: *True leadership leads by example rather than by command.* It may be an opinion, a widely shared belief, a philosophical dictum, or an assertion regarding general policy concerns in such areas as history, political science, business, ethics, or art. You can be sure that the statement will not concern scientific or technical subjects, your reasons for entering the medical profession, emotionally charged religious or social issues, or obscure social or political issues that might require specialized knowledge. In fact, you will not need any specialized knowledge to do well on this part of the MCAT.

Most test takers make the mistake of using the essay stimulus as a platform from which to emote, lecture, convince, or just babble. Instead, your goal should be to analyze the statement, present it from two perspectives, and explain how and when you might apply the statement. Your essays need to be written with a critical mind, not an emotional one. This theme is in keeping with the overall goals and intentions of the MCAT—the test makers want to see how you think.

The Three-Task Essay

Though worded slightly differently each time, the instructions that follow the statement will ask you to perform three tasks. When completed properly, the following tasks create a balanced essay.

Task One

Provide your interpretation or explanation of the statement. The degree to which you develop the statement in this first task dictates the depth and sophistication of your entire essay.

Task Two

Offer a concrete example that illustrates a point of view *directly opposite* to the one expressed in or implied by the statement. You must give an explicit counter example; it can be factual or hypothetical.

Task Three

Explain how the conflict between the viewpoint expressed in the statement and the viewpoint you described in the second task might be resolved. You'll be coming up with a kind of "test" or rule that you could apply in situations to see whether or not the statement holds true.

A CLOSER LOOK

Here's an opportunity to familiarize yourself with the essay subjects and an actual essay. You should try your hand at addressing the three tasks (observing the 30-minute time limit, of course), compare your essay with the sample that's provided below, and review the strategies that follow. By assessing your writing skills, learning key strategies, and reinforcing the lessons in later practice essays, you'll confidently face the Writing Sample on the day of the test.

BECOME A TASK MASTER

It's essential that you keep the three tasks in mind as you write. The graders will look carefully to see if you fulfilled them.

Sample Stimulus and Essay

Stimulus
Consider this statement:

Heroes are people who place the needs of others above their own needs.

Write a unified essay in which you perform the following tasks:
- Explain what you think the above statement means.
- Describe a specific situation in which a person could be heroic while placing his or her own needs above the needs of others.
- Discuss what you think determines whether or not people who put their own needs above the needs of others can be heroes.

Essay
  The statement suggests that being heroic means subjugating one's own needs to external forces of need, relinquishing one's inner compass to be directed by the power of others in need. The classic hero, of course, is the firefighter who runs back into a burning building to save a child. The urgency of momentary crisis can compel people to forget their own safety, their own need for security, in order to guarantee the safety or security of others. In that a hero, by definition, is someone who is emulated and respected, the statement above carries with it the assumption that we respect people who sacrifice themselves to the needs of others.

  In a more sophisticated sense, however, many of our historical and fictional heroes have been men and women who stood strong against a tide of negative judgment—people who did not indulge the needs of others but rather played out their own needs. Shakespeare's famous line is often quoted: "This above all: To thine own self be true and good will follow thee as night the day." We make heroes out of individualists who implement unique and personal vision. Ayn Rand is famous and well-read in part because her characters—such as Howard Roark in The Fountainhead— refuse to place the needs of others above their own. Indeed, the more lyrical classic hero is the one who stands alone without the title of "hero" until long after the true heroism has passed—the heroism of maintaining a course consistent with one's principles regardless of outside pressure or persuasion. It is in the fuller circle of time that the person comes to be seen as heroic. These are the kinds of heroes who last through history—not just through tomorrow's news.

There are indeed times when sacrifice is heroic. No one would deny a soldier a Purple Heart earned in battle. However, we also see that there are circumstances in which self-actualization rather than self-denial is the heroic choice. Being a hero, then, seems to be more about courage and choice-making than about any particular outcome or event. Heroes of all kind—those who put their own needs first (i.e., the "compassionate hero") and those who don't (i.e., the "principled hero")—are people who act according to a standard of "what is right." So, the thing that determines whether or not a sacrificial person can be a hero seems to be the gradient of courage he or she must climb on the way to action.

Did You Address All Three Tasks?
Don't be intimidated by this ideal essay. It's there for you to learn from, not for you to hold up as a standard that may be unrealistic considering the time limit. The sample completes all three tasks and does so with vivid examples and a strong organization. The statement is handled confidently, leading to an essay with interpretive depth, and the writing is crisp, focused, and easy to follow. On the whole the essay is well-balanced, with strong counter examples and a strong resolution.

It begins by immediately defining the "classic hero" and developing an understanding of what is meant by the word *hero*. This gives the reader a context for the essay. When we get to the next paragraph—where we see a discussion of heroes who don't place others' needs above their own—the polarity emerges immediately. Through a series of examples, the essay becomes balanced in its discussion of heroism in relation to self-sacrifice. The stage is set for the resolution in the last paragraph.

As you familiarize yourself with the following seven-step approach to the Writing Sample, you'll see exactly how this particular essay follows each step.

Seven-Step Approach to the Writing Sample
Your writing skills are directly linked to your ability to think analytically and logically. You might have a wonderful command of the English language, but if you can't get your thoughts organized and your ideas clear in your mind, your essay will be a jumbled mess.

Step 1: Read and Annotate

<u>Purpose:</u> Clarify for yourself what the statement says and what the instructions require.

<u>Process:</u>
- Read the statement and instructions carefully.
- Annotate the statement, marking any words or phrases that are easy to miss but crucial to a good understanding, are ambiguous or confusing, or refer to vague or abstract concepts.
- Annotate the instructions, numbering the tasks and marking any words that will help you remember exactly what it is you're supposed to do.

<u>Application:</u> Key words from the preceding sample statement, *heroes are people who place the needs of others above their own needs*, would be *hero*, *needs*, and *above*. These words form the seed of thought from which grows a personal interpretation of the statement.

Step 2: Prewrite the First Task

<u>Purpose:</u> Develop a clear interpretation of the statement.

<u>Process:</u>
- Think of one or more supporting examples.
- Clarify/define/interpret abstract, ambiguous, or confusing words.
- Ask yourself questions to get beyond the superficial meaning of the statement.

<u>Application:</u> For the preceding sample, you would want to expand the ideas in the statement by asking, "What is a hero? What are examples of self-sacrificial heroism and what makes those situations heroic?" Try to distill the implications of the statement. This is where the idea of the classic hero comes in as a context for understanding the statement.

Step 3: Prewrite the Second Task

<u>Purpose:</u> Further explore the meaning of the statement by examining a situation that represents an opposing point of view.

<u>Process:</u>
- Think up one or more specific situations that demonstrate a way in which the statement is not true (even if you agree with the statement).

SEVEN-STEP APPROACH

1. Read and annotate.
2. Prewrite the first task.
3. Prewrite the second task.
4. Prewrite the third task.
5. Clarify the main idea and plan.
6. Write.
7. Proofread.

PACE YOURSELF

5 minutes—Steps 1–5
23 minutes—Step 6
2 minutes—Step 7

- It's OK to discuss more than one example, but don't spread yourself too thin.

Application: Here's where, for the sample essay, you would consider opposing situations along the lines of, "When is a hero not sacrificial?" and "What are instances in which heroism has been defined by lack of self-sacrifice?" These extremes help balance and deepen the essay. Shakespeare's quote and Ayn Rand's characters help set up the duality of the essay by opposing the fireman example introduced earlier.

Step 4: Prewrite the Third Task
Purpose: Find a way to resolve the conflict between the statement given in the essay topic and the opposing situation(s) you conceived for the second task.

Process:
- Read the instructions for the third task carefully.
- Look back at the ideas you generated for the first and second tasks.
- Develop your response based on these ideas.
- You don't have to resolve the conflict in support of, or in opposition to, the statement. It's your reasoning that counts, not your stance on the conflict.

Application: Once the seeming dichotomy is set up, as in the hero essay, you need to find a way to resolve it. Sometimes a hero must act to save another. Sometimes saving oneself from moral inconsistency is the heroic act. Both must exist in the context of heroism, so there must be some "deciding" factor. Perhaps it's the difficulty of the act—the amount of courage it requires—or the degree of risk taken in order to achieve one's goal, selfless or otherwise.

Step 5: Clarify the Main Idea and Plan
Purpose: Do final organization and clarification of ideas; take a mental "breath" before beginning to write.

Process:
- Take a quick moment to look back over your notes in light of the ideas you have reached in prewriting the third task.
- Check to make sure your ideas are consistent with each other.
- Decide in what order your essay will address the three tasks.

NO RIGHT OR WRONG ANSWERS

Essays won't be judged on whether or not the readers agree with your position or think your points are valid. The instructions won't even ask you to take a position. If you feel that offering your position will make a better essay, that's fine, but don't feel pressured to agree or disagree with the statement.

Application: Take note of how solid organization provides a sense of unity in the sample essay.

Step 6: Write

Purpose: Write a straightforward essay that thoroughly presents your response to each of the three tasks.

Process:
- Write on every other line so you have room for corrections.
- Use your prewriting notes for guidance.
- Stick to the tasks.
- Think about the quality of the essay, not the length.
- Try not to use clichés, slang expressions, redundant words or phrases (e.g., "refer back" instead of "refer"), and water-treading sentences (sentences that get you nowhere or serve only to restate the essay directions).
- Vary sentence length and structure, to give your essay a rhythm.
- Avoid making repeated references to yourself (e.g., "I feel").

Application: You can see in the hero essay what a difference writing in a strong, confident voice makes.

Step 7: Proofread

Purpose: Quickly review your essay for blatant errors or significant omissions.

Process:
- You don't have time to revise your essay substantially.
- Look for problems in meaning (missing words, sentence fragments, illegible words, confusing punctuation, etcetera) and problems in mechanics (misspelled words, capitalization, etcetera).
- Learn the types of mistakes you tend to make and look for them.

Application: The sample essay would have made quite a different impression if words had been misspelled throughout. Reading through the essay carefully to see how it sounds is an important step.

BEGINNING, MIDDLE, END

Although there's no specific format required, your essay must have a sense of unity—a beginning, middle, and end. Use the three tasks to keep you on track.

CROSS-OUTS

Your graders know that these are first-draft essays. You don't have time (and shouldn't try to make time) to recopy your essay. Legibility is important, but it's perfectly all right to cross out or make corrections. If you write your essay on every other line, it's easier to make these corrections.

Your Essay Score

Your essays will be graded on a six-tier scale, with Level 6 being the highest. Graders will be looking for an overall sense of your essay; they won't be assigning separate scores for specific elements like grammar or substance. They realize you're writing under time pressure and expect you to make a certain number of mistakes of this kind. A series of mistakes can mar your essay's overall impression, though, so work on any areas you're particularly weak in.

Two readers read each essay and score them independently. If the two graders differ by more than a point, a third grader is called in as a final judge. The four scores are added together, and this combined score will then be converted into an alphabetical rating (ranging from J to T). Statistically speaking, there will be few Level 6 essays. An essay of 4 or 5 would place you at the upper range of those taking the exam.

Here's a quick look at what determines your score:

Score Level 6
- Fulfills all three tasks
- Develops the statement in depth
- Demonstrates careful thought
- Presents an organized structure
- Uses language in sophisticated manner

Score Level 5
- Fulfills all three tasks
- Interprets statement in some depth
- Demonstrates some in-depth thought
- Presents a fairly organized essay
- Shows good command of word choice and structure

Score Level 4
- Addresses all three tasks
- Considers the statement somewhat but not in depth
- Shows logical thought but nothing very complex
- Shows overall organization but may have digressions
- Demonstrates strong skills in word use

Score Level 3
- Overlooks or misses one or more of the tasks
- Offers a barely adequate consideration of the statement
- Contains ideas that lack depth
- Shows basic control of word choice and essay structure
- May have problems with clarity of meaning

Score Level 2
- Glaringly omits or misinterprets one or more task
- Offers an unacceptable consideration of the statement
- Shows lack of unity or is incoherent
- Exhibits errors in basic grammar, punctuation, or word use
- May be hard to follow or understand

Score Level 1
- Shows significant problems in basic writing construction
- Presents confusing or disjointed ideas
- May disregard or ignore the given assignment

You can see by this scoring outline that in order to receive higher than a Level 3 score you must successfully address all three tasks. Also note that to receive a top-level score you must develop the statement in depth and show sophisticated thought. Furthermore, for a great writing score, you must demonstrate a strong and logical style, a confident tone, and an eloquent use of language.

HIGHLIGHTS

Getting Off on the Right Foot
- Spend about five minutes prewriting, outlining your thoughts before you start writing.
- If you can't come up with real-life examples, use literary examples or your imagination!

Writing the Essay
- Write on every other line. This way it's easy to make corrections later.
- Write neatly. If you don't think your poor handwriting will work against you, guess again. Readers will be prejudiced against your Writing Sample if it's hard to decipher.

- Use a paragraph structure that matches the tasks, so your essay will be easy for readers to follow.
- Avoid clichés, slang expressions, junk phrases, redundant words or phrases, and water-treading sentences.
- Don't get emotional—admissions officers don't care *what* you think, they care *how* you think.

Reviewing Your Essay

- Be strict with yourself so you have at least a few minutes left at the end to read over what you've written. Don't let yourself get cut off.
- Go ahead and make corrections on your essay—these are timed first drafts, not term papers.
- Be sure you've addressed all three tasks. Your essay must be balanced.

TEST EXPERTISE

The first year of medical school is a frenzied experience for most students. In order to meet the requirements of a rigorous work schedule, they either learn to prioritize and budget their time or else fall hopelessly behind. It's no surprise, then, that the MCAT, the test specifically designed to predict success in the first year of medical school, is a high-speed, time-intensive test. It demands excellent time-management skills as well as that sine qua non of the successful physician—grace under pressure.

It's one thing to answer a Verbal Reasoning question correctly; it's quite another to answer 65 of them correctly in 85 minutes. And the same goes for Physical and Biological Sciences—it's a whole new ball game once you move from doing an individual passage at your leisure to handling a full section under actual timed conditions. You also need to budget your time for the Writing Sample, but this section isn't as time sensitive. But when it comes to the multiple-choice sections, time pressure is a factor that affects virtually every test taker.

So when you're comfortable with the content of the test, namely, the type of material discussed in the previous chapter, your next challenge will be to take it to the next level—test expertise—which will enable you to manage the all-important time element of the test.

THE FIVE BASIC PRINCIPLES OF TEST EXPERTISE

On some tests, if a question seems particularly difficult you spend significantly more time on it, since you'll probably be given more points for correctly answering a hard question. Not so on the MCAT. Remember, every

A MATTER OF TIME

For complete MCAT success, you've got to get as many correct answers as possible *in the time you're allotted.* Knowing the strategies is not enough. You have to perfect your time management skills so that you get a chance to use those strategies on as many questions as possible.

MCAT question, no matter how hard, is worth a single point. There's no partial credit or "A" for effort. And since there are so many questions to do in so little time, you'd be a fool to spend ten minutes getting a point for a hard question and then not have time to get a couple of quick points from three easy questions later in the section.

Given this combination—limited time, all questions equal in weight—you've got to develop a way of handling the test sections to make sure you get as many points as you can as quickly and easily as you can. Here are the principles that will help you do that:

1. Feel Free to Skip Around

One of the most valuable strategies to help you finish the sections in time is to learn to recognize and deal first with the questions and passages that are easier and more familiar to you. That means temporarily skipping those that promise to be difficult and time-consuming, if you feel comfortable doing so. You can always come back to these at the end, and if you run out of time, you're much better off not getting to questions you may have had difficulty with, rather than to potentially feasible material. Of course, since there's no guessing penalty, always fill in an answer to every question on the test, whether you get to it or not. Remember, too, to work on those passages with the most questions, so you maximize your points.

This strategy is difficult for most test takers; we're conditioned to do things in order. But give it a try when you practice. Remember, if you do the test in the exact order given, you're letting the test makers control you. But you control how you take this test. On the other hand, if skipping around goes against your moral fiber and makes you a nervous wreck—don't do it. Just be mindful of the clock and don't get bogged down with the tough questions.

2. Recognize and Seek Out Questions You Can Do

Another thing to remember about managing the test sections is that MCAT questions and passages, unlike items on the SAT and other standardized tests, are not presented in order of difficulty. There's no rule that says you have to work through the sections in any particular order; in fact, the test makers scatter the easy and difficult questions throughout the section, in effect rewarding those who actually get to the end. Don't lose sight of what you're being tested for along with your reading and thinking skills: efficiency and cleverness. If organic chemistry questions are your thing, head straight for them when you first turn to the Biological Sciences section.

BE A TEST EXPERT

In order to meet the stringent time requirements of the MCAT, you have to cultivate the following elements of test expertise:
• feel free to skip around
• learn to recognize and seek out questions you can do
• out questions you can do
• use a process if answer elimination
• remain calm
• keep track of time

GUESS!

We've said it before and we'll say it again: If you can't do a question or can't get to it, guess! Fill in an answer—any answer—on the answer grid. There's no penalty if you're wrong, but there's a big fat point if you're right.

Don't waste time on questions you can't do. We know that skipping a possibly tough question is easier said than done; we all have the natural instinct to plow through test sections in their given order. But it just doesn't pay off on the MCAT. The computer won't be impressed if you get the toughest question right. If you dig in your heels on a tough question, refusing to move on until you've cracked it, well, you're letting your ego get in the way of your test score. A test section (not to mention life itself) is too short to waste on lost causes.

3. Use a Process of Answer Elimination

Using a process of elimination is another way to answer questions both quickly and effectively. There are two ways to get all the answers right on the MCAT. You either know all the right answers, or you know all the wrong answers. Since there are three times as many wrong answers, you should be able to eliminate some if not all of them. By doing so you either get to the correct response or increase your chances of guessing the correct response. You start out with a 25 percent chance of picking the right answer, and with each eliminated answer your odds go up. Eliminate one, and you'll have a 33 1/3 percent chance of picking the right one, eliminate two, and you'll have a 50 percent chance, and, of course, eliminate three, and you'll have a 100 percent chance. Increase your efficiency by actually crossing out the wrong choices.

Remember to look for wrong-answer traps when you're eliminating. Some answers are designed to seduce you by distorting the correct answer.

4. Remain Calm

It's imperative that you remain calm and composed while working through a section. You can't allow yourself to become so rattled by one hard reading passage that it throws off your performance on the rest of the section. Expect to find at least one killer passage in every section, but remember, you won't be the only one to have trouble with it. The test is curved to take the tough material into account. Having trouble with a difficult question isn't going to ruin your score—but getting upset about it and letting it throw you off track will. When you understand that part of the test maker's goal is to reward those who keep their composure, you'll recognize the importance of not panicking when you run into challenging material.

5. Keep Track of Time

Of course, the last thing you want to happen is to have time called on a par-

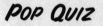

Every question is worth exactly one point. But questions vary dramatically in difficulty level. Given a shortage of time, which questions should you work on—easy or hard?

LEGGO YOUR EGO

Don't let your ego sabotage your score. It isn't easy for some of us to give up on a tough, time-consuming question, but sometimes it's better to say "uncle." Remember, there's no point of honor at stake here, but there are MCAT points at stake.

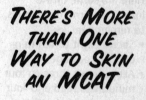

If you don't know the right answer, eliminate as many wrong answers as you can. This way you'll either get to, or increase your chances of getting to, the right one.

ticular section before you've gotten to half the questions. Therefore, t's essential that you pace yourself, keeping in mind the general guidelines for how long to spend on any individual question or passage. Have a sense of how long you have to do each question, so you know when you're exceeding the limit and should start to move faster.

So, when working on a section, always remember to keep track of time. Don't spend a wildly disproportionate amount of time on any one question or group of questions. Also, give yourself 30 seconds or so at the end of each section to fill in answers for any questions you haven't gotten to.

SECTION-SPECIFIC PACING

Let's now look at the section-specific timing requirements and some tips for meeting them. Keep in mind that the times per question or passage are only averages; there are bound to be some that take less time and some that take more. Try to stay balanced. Remember, too, that every question is of equal worth, so don't get hung up on any one. Think about it—if a question is so hard that it takes you a long time to answer it, chances are you may get it wrong anyway. In that case, you'd have nothing to show for your extra time but a lower score.

Verbal Reasoning

Allow yourself approximately eight or ten minutes per passage and respective questions. It may sound like a lot of time, but it goes quickly. Do the easiest passages first. Within a section, if you're deciding which passage to do based on time alone, do the one with the most questions. That way you maximize your reading efficiency. However, keep in mind that some passages are longer than others. On average, give yourself about three or four minutes to read and then four to six minutes for the questions.

Physical and Biological Sciences

Averaging over each section, you'll have about one minute and 20 seconds per question. Some questions, of course, will take more time, some less. A science passage plus accompanying questions should take about eight to nine minutes, depending on how many questions there are. Stand-alone questions can take anywhere from a few seconds to a minute or more. Again, the rule is to do your best work first. Also, don't feel that you have to understand everything in a passage before you go on to the questions. You may not need that deep an understanding to answer questions, since a lot of information may be extraneous. You should overcome your perfectionism and use your time wisely.

VERBAL REASONING EXPERTISE

Here are some of the important time techniques to remember:
- Spend eight to ten minutes per passage
- Allow about three to four minutes to read and four to six minutes for the questions
- Deal with passages you're most comfortable with first, or those passages with the most questions

Writing Sample

You have exactly 30 minutes for each essay. As mentioned in discussion of the seven-step approach to this section, you should allow approximately five minutes to prewrite the essay, 23 minutes to write the essay, and two minutes to proofread. It's important that you budget your time, so you don't get cut off.

ANSWER GRID EXPERTISE

An important part of MCAT test expertise is knowing how to handle the answer grid. After all, you not only have to get right answers; you also have to transfer those right answers onto the answer grid in an efficient and accurate way. It sounds simple but it's extremely important: **Don't make mistakes filling out your answer grid!** When time is short, it's easy to get confused going back and forth between your test book and your grid. If you know the answer, but misgrid, you won't get the point. Here are a few methods of avoiding mistakes on the answer grid.

Always Circle the Questions You Skip

Put a big circle in your test book around the number of any question you skip (you may even want to circle the whole question itself). When you go back, such questions will then be easy to locate. Also, if you accidentally skip an oval on the grid, you can easily check your grid against your book to see where you went wrong.

Always Circle the Answers You Choose

Circle the correct answers in your test booklet, but don't transfer the answer to the grid right away. Circling your answers in the test book will also make it easier to check your grid against your book.

Grid Five or More Answers at Once

As we said, don't transfer your answers to the grid after every question. Transfer your answers after every five questions, or at the end of each passage (find the method that works best for you). That way, you won't keep breaking your concentration to mark the grid. You'll save time and improve accuracy. Just make sure you're not left at the end of the section with ungridded answers!

PHYSICAL AND BIOLOGICAL SCIENCES EXPERTISE

Some suggestions for maximizing your time on the science sections:
- Spend about eight to nine minutes per passage
- Maximize points by doing the questions you can do first
- Don't waste valuable time trying to understand extraneous material

AVOID GRIDLOCK

Yes, it's purely bookkeeping, but you won't get the points if you put your answers in the wrong place, or if you waste time searching for the right place to put your answers. Take the time now to develop some good answer grid habits.

Save Time at the End for a Final Grid Check

Make sure you have enough time at the end of every section to make a quick check of your grid, to make sure you've got an oval filled in for each question in the section. Remember, a blank grid has no chance of earning a point, but a guess does.

TEST MENTALITY

In this MCAT section, we first looked at the content that makes up each specific section of the MCAT, focusing on the strategies and techniques you'll need to tackle individual questions and passages. Then we discussed the test expertise involved in moving from individual items to working through full-length sections. Now we're ready to turn our attention to the often overlooked attitudinal aspects of the test, to put the finishing touches on your comprehensive MCAT approach.

THE FOUR BASIC PRINCIPLES OF GOOD TEST MENTALITY

We've already armed you with the weapons you need to do well on the MCAT. But you must wield those weapons with the right frame of mind and in the right spirit. Otherwise, you could end up shooting yourself in the foot. This involves taking a certain stance toward the entire test. Here's what's involved:

1. Test Awareness

To do your best on the MCAT, you must always keep in mind that the test is like no other test you've taken before, both in terms of content and in terms of the scoring system. If you took a test in high school or college and got a number of the questions wrong, you wouldn't receive a perfect grade. But on the MCAT, you can get a handful of questions wrong and still get a "perfect" score. The test is geared so that only the very best test takers are able to finish every section. But even these people rarely get every question right.

WHAT MAKES FOR GOOD TEST MENTALITY?

We're glad you asked. The important elements are:
- Test awareness
- Stamina
- Confidence
- The right attitude

BE COOL

Losing a few extra points here and there won't do serious damage to your score, but losing your head will. Keeping your composure is an important test-taking skill.

What does this mean for you? Well, just as you shouldn't let one bad passage ruin an entire section, you shouldn't let what you consider to be a subpar performance on one section ruin your performance on the entire test. If you allow that subpar performance to rattle you, it can have a cumulative negative effect, setting in motion a downward spiral. It's that kind of thing that could potentially do serious damage to your score. Losing a few extra points won't do you in, but losing your cool will.

Remember, if you feel you've done poorly on a section, don't sweat it. Chances are it's just a difficult section, and that factor will already be figured into the scoring curve. The point is, remain calm and collected. Simply do your best on each section, and once a section is over, forget about it and move on.

2. Stamina

You must work on your test-taking stamina. Overall, the MCAT is a fairly grueling experience, and some test takers simply run out of gas on the last section. To avoid this, you must prepare by taking a few full-length practice tests in the weeks before the test, so that on test day, three sections plus a writing sample will seem like a breeze. (Well, maybe not a breeze, but at least not a hurricane.)

Take the full-length practice test included in this book. You'll be able to review answer explanations and assess your performance. For additional practice material, contact the Association of American Medical Colleges to receive the MCAT Practice Tests it publishes:

HOW DO I GET TO MED SCHOOL?

Practice, practice, practice the MCAT.

AAMC
Membership and Publication Orders
2450 N Street, NW
Washington, DC 20037
(202) 828–0416
http://www.aamc.org

The AAMC sells three full-length practice tests: Practice Test I, Practice Test II, and Practice Test III. You can't get a scaled score by taking Practice Test I, but there's a table to help you translate your raw score to an estimated percentile, and you'll certainly get a good feel for MCAT format and pacing. Practice Test II is the actual MCAT from April 1991. It is accompanied by a score conversion chart, so you'll be able to estimate a test score for yourself. You should, of course, keep in mind that every MCAT administration differs and Practice Test II is now five years old. You can't be assured that your actual score will be predicted by your score on a practice test. The score you'll get on Practice Test II is less important than the practice itself. Nineteen ninety-five saw the advent of Practice Test III, which includes supplementary material to help you analyze your strengths and weaknesses. The AAMC also publishes Practice Items. These are two booklets of MCAT-style passages and sample essay topics.

Your best option, if you have some time, would be to take the full Kaplan course. We'll give you access to all the released material plus loads of additional material (more than 500 MCAT-style passages in total), so you can really build up your MCAT stamina. You'll also have the benefit of our expert live instruction on every aspect of the MCAT. To go this route, call 1–800–KAP–TEST for a Kaplan center location near you.

Reading this chapter is a great start in your preparation for the test, but it won't get you your best score. That can only happen after lots of practice and skill-building. You've got to train your brain to be test smart! Kaplan has been helping people do that for over 50 years, so giving us a call would be a great way to move your test prep into high gear!

3. Confidence

Confidence feeds on itself, and unfortunately, so does the opposite of confidence—self-doubt. Confidence in your ability leads to quick, sure answers and a sense of well-being that translates into more points. If you lack confidence, you end up reading the sentences and answer choices two, three, or four times, until you confuse yourself and get off track. This leads to timing difficulties, which only perpetuate the downward spiral, causing anxiety and a tendency to rush in order to finish sections.

If you subscribe to the MCAT Mindset we've described, however, you'll gear all of your practice toward the major goal of taking control of the test. When you've achieved that goal—armed with the principles, techniques, strategies, and approaches set forth in this book—you'll be ready to face the MCAT with supreme confidence. And that's the one sure way to score your best on test day.

4. The Right Attitude

Those who approach the MCAT as an obstacle, who rail against the necessity of taking it, who make light of its importance, who spend more time making fun of the AAMC than studying for the test, usually don't fare as well as those who see the MCAT as an opportunity to show off the reading and reasoning skills that the medical schools are looking for. Don't waste time making value judgments about the MCAT. It's not going to go

GET TOUGH

You wouldn't run a marathon without working on your stamina well in advance of the race, would you? The same goes for taking the MCAT.

DEVELOP AN MCATTITUDE

It sounds touchy-feely, we know. But your attitude toward the test really does affect your performance. We're not asking you to "think nice thoughts about the MCAT," but we are recommending that you change your mental stance toward the test.

away. Deal with it. Those who look forward to doing battle with the MCAT—or, at least, who enjoy the opportunity to distinguish themselves from the rest of the applicant pack—tend to score better than do those who resent or dread it.

It may sound a little dubious, but take our word for it: Attitude adjustment is a proven test-taking technique. Here are a few steps you can take to make sure you develop the right MCAT attitude:

- Look at the MCAT as a challenge, but try not to obsess over it; you certainly don't want to psyche yourself out of the game.
- Remember that, yes, the MCAT is obviously important, but, contrary to what some premeds think, this one test will not single-handedly determine the outcome of your life.
- Try to have fun with the test. Learning how to match your wits against the test makers can be a very satisfying experience, and the reading and thinking skills you'll acquire will benefit you in medical school as well as in your future medical career.
- Remember that you're more prepared than most people. You've trained with Kaplan. You have the tools you need, plus the know-how to use those tools.

KAPLAN'S TOP TEN MCAT TIPS

1. **Relax!**

2. **Remember: It's primarily a thinking test.**
   Never forget the purpose of the MCAT: It's designed to test your powers of analytical reasoning. You need to know the content, as each section has its own particular "language," but the underlying MCAT intention is consistent throughout the test.

3. **Feel free to skip around within each section.**
   Attack each section confidently. You're in charge. Move around if you feel comfortable doing so. Work your best areas first to maximize your opportunity for MCAT points. Choose the order in which to complete passages. Don't be a passive victim of the test structure!

4. **For passage-based questions, answer based on the information given.**

   Be careful not to be "too smart for your own good." Passages—especially those that describe experimental findings (an MCAT favorite, by the way)—often generate their own data. Your answer choices must be consistent with the information in the passage, even if that means an answer choice is inconsistent with the science of ideal theoretical situations.

5. **Avoid wrong-answer traps.**

   Try to anticipate answers before you read the answer choices. This helps boost your confidence and protects you from persuasive or tricky incorrect choices. Most wrong answer choices are logical twists on the correct choice.

6. **Think, think, think!**

   We said it before, but it's important enough to say again: Think. Don't Compute.

7. **Don't look back.**

   Don't spend time worrying about questions you had to guess on. Keep moving forward. Don't let your spirit start to flag, or your attitude will slow you down. You can recheck answers within a section if you have time left, but don't worry about a section after time has been called.

8. **Be careful transferring answers to your grid.**

   Be sure that you are very careful transcribing answers to your grid, especially if you do skip around within the test sections.

9. **Don't leave any blanks on your answer grid.**

   There are no points taken off for wrong answers, so if you're not sure of an answer, **guess**. And guess quickly, so you'll have more time to work through other questions.

10. **Call us! We're here to help! 1-800-KAP-TEST.**

THE KAPLAN ADVANTAGE™

THE KAPLAN ADVANTAGE™ STRESS MANAGEMENT SYSTEM

The countdown has begun. Your date with THE TEST is looming on the horizon. Anxiety is on the rise. The butterflies in your stomach have gone ballistic. Perhaps you feel as if the last thing you ate has turned into a lead ball in your stomach. Your thinking is getting cloudy. Maybe you think you won't be ready. Maybe you already know your stuff, but you're going into panic mode anyway. Worst of all, you're not sure of what to do about it.

Don't freak! It is possible to tame that anxiety and stress—before and during the test. We'll show you how. You won't believe how quickly and easily you can deal with that killer anxiety.

MAKING THE MOST OF YOUR PREP TIME

Lack of control is one of the prime causes of stress. A ton of research shows that if you don't have a sense of control over what's happening in your life you can easily end up feeling helpless and hopeless. So, just having concrete things to do and to think about—taking control—will help reduce your stress. This section shows you how to take control during the days leading up to taking the MCAT—or any other test.

IDENTIFY THE SOURCES OF STRESS

The first step in gaining control is identifying the sources of your test-related stress. The idea is to pin down that free-floating anxiety so that you can take control of it. Here are some examples:

- I always freeze up on tests.

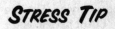

STRESS TIP

Don't forget that your school probably has counseling available. If you can't conquer test stress on your own, make an appointment at the counseling center. That's what counselors are there for.

- I'm nervous about the organic chem (or the physics or general chem, etcetera).
- I need a good/great score to go to Acme School of Medicine.
- My older brother/sister/best friend/girl- or boyfriend did really well. I must match their scores or do better.
- My parents, who are paying for school, will be really disappointed if I don't test well.
- I'm afraid of losing my focus and concentration.
- I'm afraid I'm not spending enough time preparing.
- I study like crazy but nothing seems to stick in my mind.
- I always run out of time and get panicky.
- I feel as though thinking is becoming like wading through thick mud.

Take a few minutes to think about your own particular sources of test related stress. Then write them down in some sort of order. List the statements you most associate with your stress and anxiety first, and put the least disturbing items last. As you write the list, you're forming a hierarchy of items so you can deal first with the anxiety-provokers that bug you most. Very often, taking care of the major items from the top of the list goes a long way toward relieving overall testing anxiety. You probably won't have to bother with the stuff you placed last.

TAKE STOCK OF YOUR STRENGTHS AND WEAKNESSES

Take one minute to list the areas of the test that you are good at. They can be general ("biology") or specific ("molecular genetics"). Put down as many as you can think of, and if possible, time yourself. Write for the entire time; don't stop writing until you've reached the one-minute stopping point.

Next, take one minute to list areas of the test you're not so good at, just plain bad at, have failed at, or keep failing at. Again, keep it to one minute, and continue writing until you reach the cutoff. Don't be afraid to identify and write down your weak spots! In all probability, as you do both lists you'll find you are strong in some areas and not so strong in others. Taking stock of your assets *and* liabilities lets you know the areas you don't have to worry about, and the ones that will demand extra attention and effort.

VERY SUPERSTITIOUS

Stress expert Stephen Sideroff, Ph.D., tells of a client who always stressed out before, during, and even after taking tests. Yet she always got outstanding scores. It became obvious that she was thinking superstitiously—subconsciously believing that the great scores were a result of her worrying. She also didn't trust herself, and believed that if she didn't worry she wouldn't study hard enough. Sideroff convinced her to take a risk and work on relaxing before her next test. She did, and her test results were still as good as ever—which broke her cycle of superstitious thinking.

Now, go back to the "good" list, and expand it for two minutes. Take the general items on that first list and make them more specific; take the specific items and expand them into more general conclusions. Naturally, if anything new comes to mind, jot it down. Focus all of your attention and effort on your strengths. Don't underestimate yourself or your abilities. Give yourself full credit. At the same time, don't list strengths you don't really have; you'll only be fooling yourself.

Every area of strength and confidence you can identify is much like having a reserve of solid gold at Fort Knox. You'll be able to draw on your reserves as you need them. You can use your reserves to solve difficult questions, maintain confidence, and keep test stress and anxiety at a distance. The encouraging thing is that every time you recognize another area of strength, succeed at coming up with a plan to strengthen a weak area, or get a good score on a practice test, you increase your reserves. And, there is absolutely no limit to how much self-confidence you can have or how good you can feel about yourself.

WHAT DO YOU WANT TO ACCOMPLISH IN THE TIME REMAINING?

The whole point of this next exercise is sort of like checking out a used car you might want to buy. You'd want to know up front what the car's weak points are, right? Knowing that influences your whole shopping-for-a-used-car campaign. So it is with your conquering-test-stress campaign: Knowing your weak points ahead of time helps you prepare.

So let's get back to the list of your weak points. Take two minutes to expand it just as you did with your "good" list. Be honest with yourself without going overboard. It's an accurate appraisal of the test areas that give you troubles.

Facing your weak spots gives you some distinct advantages. It helps a lot to find out where you need to spend extra effort. Increased exposure to tough material makes it more familiar and less intimidating. (After all, we mostly fear what we don't know and are probably afraid to face.) You'll feel better about yourself because you're dealing directly with areas of the test that bring on your anxiety. You can't help feeling more confident when you know you're actively strengthening your chances of earning a higher overall test score.

STRESS TIP

Don't work in a messy or cramped area. Before you sit down to study, clear yourself a nice, open space. And make sure you have books, paper, pencils—whatever tools you will need—within easy reach before you sit down to study.

LINK YOUR THOUGHTS

When you're committing new information to memory, link one fact to another, much as elephants are linked trunk to tail in a circus parade. Visualize an image (preferably a bizarre one) that connects the thoughts. You'll remember them in the same linked way, with one thought easily bringing the next to your mind.

IMAGINE YOURSELF SUCCEEDING

This next little group of exercises is both physical and mental. It's a natural followup to what you've just accomplished with your lists.

First, get yourself into a comfortable sitting position in a quiet setting. Wear loose clothes. If you wear glasses, take them off. Then, close your eyes and breathe in a deep, satisfying breath of air. Really fill your lungs until your rib cage is fully expanded and you can't take in any more. Then, exhale the air completely. Imagine you're blowing out a candle with your last little puff of air. Do this two or three more times, filling your lungs to their maximum and emptying them totally. Keep your eyes closed, comfortably but not tightly. Let your body sink deeper into the chair as you become even more comfortable.

With your eyes shut you can notice something very interesting. You're no longer dealing with the worrisome stuff going on in the world outside of you. Now you can concentrate on what happens inside you. The more you recognize your own physical reactions to stress and anxiety, the more you can do about them. You may not realize it, but you've begun to regain a sense of being in control.

Let images begin to form on the "viewing screens" on the back of your eyelids. You're experiencing visualizations from the place in your mind that makes pictures. Allow the images to come easily and naturally; don't force them. Imagine yourself in a relaxing situation. It might be in a special place you've visited before or one you've read about. It can be a fictional location that you create in your imagination, but a real-life memory of a place or situation you know is usually better. Make it as detailed as possible and notice as much as you can.

If you don't see this relaxing place sharply or in living color, it doesn't mean the exercise won't work for you. Some people can visualize in great detail, while others get only a sense of an image. What's important is not how sharp the details or colors, but how well you're able to manipulate the images. If you can conjure up finely detailed images, great. If you only have a faint sense of the images, that's okay—you'll still experience all the benefits of the exercise.

Think about the sights, the sounds, the smells, even the tastes and textures associated with your relaxing situation. See and feel yourself in this special place. Say you're special place is the beach, for example. Feel how warm the sand is. Are you lying on a blanket, or sitting up and looking out at the water? Hear the waves hitting the shore, and the occasional seagull. Feel a comfortable breeze. If your special place is a garden or park, look up

STRESS TIP

If you want to play music, keep it low and in the background. Music with a regular, mathematical rhythm—reggae, for example—aids the learning process. A recording of ocean waves is also soothing.

and see the way sunlight filters through the trees. Smell your favorite flowers. Hear some chimes gently playing and birds chirping.

Stay focused on the images as you sink farther back into your chair. Breathe easily and naturally. You might have the sensations of any stress or tension draining from your muscles and flowing downward, out your feet and away from you.

Take a moment to check how you're feeling. Notice how comfortable you've become. Imagine how much easier it would be if you could take the test feeling this relaxed and in this state of ease. You've coupled the images of your special place with sensations of comfort and relaxation. You've also found a way to become relaxed simply by visualizing your own safe, special place.

Now, close your eyes and start remembering a real-life situation in which you did well on a test. If you can't come up with one, remember a situation in which you did something (academic or otherwise) that you were really proud of—a genuine accomplishment. Make the memory as detailed as possible. Think about the sights, the sounds, the smells, even the tastes associated with this remembered experience. Remember how confident you felt as you accomplished your goal. Now start thinking about the upcoming test. Keep your thoughts and feelings in line with that successful experience. Don't make comparisons between them. Just imagine taking the upcoming test with the same feelings of confidence and relaxed control.

This exercise is a great way to bring the test down to earth. You should practice this exercise often, especially when the prospect of taking the exam starts to bum you out. The more you practice it, the more effective the exercise will be for you.

EXERCISE YOUR FRUSTRATIONS AWAY

Whether it is jogging, walking, biking, mild aerobics, pushups, or a pick-up basketball game, physical exercise is a very effective way to stimulate both your mind and body and to improve your ability to think and concentrate. A surprising number of students get out of the habit of regular exercise, ironically because they're spending so much time prepping for exams. Also, sedentary people—this is medical fact—get less oxygen to the blood and hence to the head than active people. You can live fine with a little less oxygen; you just can't think as well.

Any big test is a bit like a race. Thinking clearly at the end is just as

OCEAN DUMPING

Visualize a beautiful beach, with white sand, blue skies, sparkling water, a warm sun, and seagulls. See yourself walking on the beach, carrying a small plastic pail. Stop at a good spot and put your worries and whatever may be bugging you into the pail. Drop it at the water's edge and watch it drift out to sea. When the pail is out of sight, walk on.

TAKE A HIKE, PAL

When you're in the middle of studying and hit a wall, take a short, brisk walk. Breathe deeply and swing your arms as you walk. Clear your mind. (And don't forget to look for flowers that grow in the cracks of the sidewalk.)

CYBERSTRESS

If you spend a lot of time in cyberspace anyway, do a search for the phrase *stress management*. There's a ton of stress advice on the Net, including material specifically for students.

NUTRITION AND STRESS: THE DOS AND DON'TS

Do eat:

- Fruits and vegetables (raw is best, or just lightly steamed or nuked)
- Low-fat protein such as fish, skinless poultry, beans, and legumes (like lentils)
- Whole grains such as brown rice, whole wheat bread, and pastas

Don't eat:

- Refined sugar; sweet, high-fat snacks (simple carbohydrates like sugar make stress worse and fatty foods lower your immunity)
- Salty foods (they can deplete potassium, which you need for nerve functions)

important as having a quick mind early on. If you can't sustain your energy level in the last sections of the exam, there's too good a chance you could blow it. You need a fit body that can weather the demands any big exam puts on you. Along with a good diet and adequate sleep, exercise is an important part of keeping yourself in fighting shape and thinking clearly for the long haul.

There's another thing that happens when students don't make exercise an integral part of their test preparation. Like any organism in nature, you operate best if all your "energy systems" are in balance. Studying uses a lot of energy, but it's all mental. When you take a study break, do something active instead of raiding the fridge or vegging out in front of the TV. Take a five- to ten-minute activity break for every fifty or sixty minutes that you study. The physical exertion gets your body into the act which helps to keep your mind and body in sync. Then, when you finish studying for the night and hit the sack you won't lie there, tense and unable to sleep, because your head is overtired and your body wants to pump iron or run a marathon.

One warning about exercise, however: It's not a good idea to exercise vigorously right before you go to bed. This could easily cause sleep-onset problems. For the same reason, it's also not a good idea to study right up to bedtime. Make time for a "buffer period" before you go to bed: For thirty to sixty minutes, just take a hot shower, meditate, simply veg out.

GET HIGH . . . NATURALLY

Exercise can give you a natural high, which is the only kind of high you can afford right now. Using drugs (prescription or recreational) specifically to prepare for and take a big test is definitely self-defeating. Except for the drugs that occur naturally in your brain, every drug has major drawbacks—and a false sense of security is only one of them.

You may have heard that popping uppers helps you study by keeping you alert. If they're illegal, definitely forget about it. You're just wasting your time. Amphetamines make it hard to retain information. So you'll stay awake, but you probably won't remember much of what you read. And, taking an upper before you take the test could really mess things up. You're already going to be a little anxious and hyper; adding a strong stimulant could easily push you over the edge into panic. Remember, a little anxiety is a good thing. The adrenaline that gets pumped into your bloodstream helps you stay alert and think more clearly. But, too much anxiety and you can't think straight at all.

Mild stimulants, such as coffee, cola, or over-the-counter caffeine pills can sometimes help as you study, since they keep you alert. On the down side, they can also lead to agitation, restlessness, and insomnia. Some people can drink a pot of high-octane coffee and sleep like a baby. Others have one cup and start to vibrate. It all depends on your tolerance for caffeine.

Alcohol and other depressants are out, too. Again, if they're illegal, forget about it. Depressants wouldn't work, anyway, since they lead to the inevitable hangover/crash, the fuzzy thinking, and lousy sense of judgment. These are not going to help you ace the test.

Instead, go for endorphins—the "natural morphine." Endorphins have no side effects and they're free—you've already got them in your brain. It just takes some exercise to release them. Running around on the basketball court, bicycling, swimming, aerobics, power walking—these activities cause endorphins to occupy certain spots in your brain's neural synapses. In addition, exercise develops staying power and increases the oxygen transfer to your brain. Go into the test naturally.

TAKE A DEEP BREATH . . .

Here's another natural route to relaxation and invigoration. It's a classic isometric exercise that you can do whenever you get stressed out—just before the test begins, even *during* the test. It's very simple and takes just a few minutes.

Close your eyes. Starting with your eyes and—*without holding your breath*—gradually tighten every muscle in your body (but not to the point of pain) in the following sequence:

1. Close your eyes tightly.
2. Squeeze your nose and mouth together so that your whole face is scrunched up. (If it makes you self-conscious to do this in the test room, skip the face-scrunching part.)
3. Pull your chin into your chest, and pull your shoulders together.
4. Tighten your arms to your body, then clench your hands into tight fists.
5. Pull in your stomach.
6. Squeeze your thighs and buttocks together, and tighten your calves.
7. Stretch your feet, then curl your toes (watch out for cramping in this part).

STRESS TIP

Don't study on your bed, especially if you have problems with insomnia. Your mind may start to associate the bed with work, and make it even harder for you to fall asleep.

THE RELAXATION PARADOX

Forcing relaxation is like asking yourself to flap your arms and fly. You can't do it, and every push and prod only gets you more frustrated. Relaxation is something you don't work at. You simply let it happen. Think about it. When was the last time you tried to force yourself to go to sleep, and it worked?

At this point, every muscle should be tightened. Now, relax your body, one part at a time, in reverse order, starting with your toes. Let the tension drop out of each muscle. The entire process might take five minutes from start to finish (maybe a couple of minutes during the test). This clenching and unclenching exercise should help you to feel very relaxed.

AND KEEP BREATHING

Conscious attention to breathing is an excellent way of managing test stress (or any stress, for that matter). The majority of people who get into trouble during tests take shallow breaths. They breathe using only their upper chests and shoulder muscles, and may even hold their breath for long periods of time. Conversely, the test taker who by accident or design keeps breathing normally and rhythmically is likely to be more relaxed and in better control during the entire test experience.

So, now is the time to get into the habit of relaxed breathing. Do the next exercise to learn to breathe in a natural, easy rhythm. By the way, this is another technique you can use during the test to collect your thoughts and ward off excess stress. The entire exercise should take no more than three to five minutes.

With your eyes still closed, breathe in slowly and deeply through your nose. Hold the breath for a bit, and then release it through your mouth. The key is to breathe slowly and deeply by using your diaphragm to draw air in and out naturally and effortlessly. Breathing with your diaphragm encourages relaxation and helps minimize tension.

As you breathe, imagine that colored air is flowing into your lungs. Pick any color you like, from a single color to a rainbow. With each breath, the air fills your body from the top of your head to the tips of your toes. Continue inhaling the colored air until it occupies every part of you, bones and muscles included. Once you've completely filled yourself with the colored air, picture an opening somewhere on your body, either natural or imagined. Now, with each breath you exhale, some of the colored air will pass out the opening and leave your body. The level of the air (much like the water in a glass as it is emptied) will begin to drop. It will descend progressively lower, from your head down to your feet. As you continue to exhale the colored air, watch the level go lower and lower, farther and farther down your body. As the last of the colored air passes out of the opening, the level will drop down to your toes and disappear. Stay quiet for just a moment. Then notice how relaxed and comfortable you feel.

BREATHE LIKE A BABY

A baby or young child is the best model for demonstrating how to breathe most efficiently and comfortably. Only its stomach moves as it inhales and exhales. The action is virtually effortless.

STRESS TIP

A lamp with a 75-watt bulb is optimal for studying. But don't put it so close to your study material that you create a glare.

THUMBS UP FOR MEDITATION

Once relegated to the fringes of the medical world, meditation, biofeedback, and hypnosis are increasingly recommended by medical researchers to reduce pain from headaches, back problems—even cancer. Think of what these powerful techniques could do for your test-related stress and anxiety.

Effective meditation is based primarily on two relaxation methods you've already learned: body awareness and breathing. A couple of different meditation techniques follow. Experience them both, and choose the one that works best for you.

Breath Meditation

Make yourself comfortable, either sitting or lying down. For this meditation you can keep your eyes open or close them. Concentrate on your breathing. The goal of the meditation is to notice everything you can about your breath as it enters and leaves your body. Take three to five breaths each time you practice the meditation, which should take about a minute for the entire procedure.

Take a deep breath and hold it for five to ten seconds. When you exhale, let the breath out very slowly. Feel the tension flowing out of you along with the breath that leaves your body. Pay close attention to the air as it flows in and out of your nostrils. Observe how cool it is as you inhale and how warm your breath is when you exhale. As you expel the air, say a cue word such as *calm* or *relax* to yourself. Once you've exhaled all the air from your lungs, start the next long, slow inhale. Notice how relaxed feelings increase as you slowly exhale and again hear your cue words.

Mantra Meditation

For this type of meditation experience you'll need a mental device (a mantra), a passive attitude (don't try to do anything), and a position in which you can be comfortable. You're going to focus your total attention on a mantra you create. It should be emotionally neutral, repetitive, and monotonous, and your aim is to fully occupy your mind with it. Furthermore, you want to do the meditation passively, with no goal in your head of how relaxed you're supposed to be. This is a great way to prepare for studying or taking the test. It clears your head of extraneous thoughts and gets you focused and at ease.

Sit comfortably and close your eyes. Begin to relax by letting your body go limp. Create a relaxed mental attitude and know there's no

THINK GOOD THOUGHTS

Create a set of positive, but brief affirmations and mentally repeat them to yourself just before you fall asleep at night. (That's when your mind is very open to suggestion.) You'll find yourself feeling a lot more positive in the morning. Periodically repeating your affirmations during the day makes them even more effective.

need for you to force anything. You're simply going to let something happen. Breathe through your nose. Take calm, easy breaths and as you exhale, say your mantra (*one, ohhm, aah, soup*—whatever is emotionally neutral for you) to yourself. Repeat the mantra each time you breathe out. Let feelings of relaxation grow as you focus on the mantra and your slow breathing. Don't worry if your mind wanders. Simply return to the mantra and continue letting go. Experience this meditation for ten to fifteen minutes.

QUICK TIPS FOR THE DAYS JUST BEFORE THE EXAM

- The best test takers do less and less as Test Day approaches. Taper off your study schedule and take it easy on yourself. You want to be relaxed and ready on the day of the test. Give yourself time off, especially the evening before the exam. By that time, if you've studied well, everything you need to know is firmly stored in your memory banks.

- Positive self-talk can be extremely liberating and invigorating, especially as the test looms closer. Tell yourself things such as, "I choose to take this test" rather than "I have to"; "I will do well" rather than "I hope things go well"; "I can" rather than "I cannot." Be aware of negative, self-defeating thoughts and images and immediately counter any you become aware of. Replace them with affirming statements that encourage your self-esteem and confidence. Create and practice doing visualizations that build on your positive statements.

- Get your act together sooner rather than later. Have everything (including choice of clothing) laid out days in advance. Most important, know where the test will be held and the easiest, quickest way to get there. You will gain great peace of mind if you know that all the little details—gas in the car, directions—are firmly in your control before Test Day.

- Experience the test site a few days in advance. This is very helpful if you are especially anxious. If at all possible, find out what room your part of the alphabet is assigned to, and try to sit there (by yourself) for a while. Better yet, bring some practice material and do at least a section or two, if not an entire practice test, in that room. In this case, familiarity doesn't breed contempt; it generates comfort and confidence.

- Forego any practice on the day before the test. It's in your best interest to marshal your physical and psychological resources for twenty-four hours or so. Even race horses are kept in the paddock and treated like princes the day before a race. Keep the upcoming test out of your consciousness; go to a movie, take a pleasant hike, or just relax. Don't eat junk food or tons of sugar. And—of course—get plenty of rest the night before. Just don't go to bed too early. It's hard to fall asleep earlier than you're used to, and you don't want to lie there thinking about the test.

HANDLING STRESS DURING THE TEST

The biggest stress monster will be Test Day itself. Fear not; there are methods of quelling your stress during the test.

- Keep moving forward instead of getting bogged down in a difficult question or passage. You don't have to get everything right to achieve a fine score. So, don't linger out of desperation on a question that is going nowhere even after you've spent considerable time on it. The best test takers skip (temporarily) difficult material in search of the easier stuff. They mark the ones that require extra time and thought. This strategy buys time and builds confidence so you can handle the tough stuff later.

- Don't be thrown if other test takers seem to be working more busily and furiously than you are. Continue to spend your time patiently but doggedly thinking through your answers; it's going to lead to higher-quality test taking and better results. Don't mistake the other people's sheer activity as signs of progress and higher scores.

- *Keep breathing!* Weak test takers tend to share one major trait: they forget to breathe properly as the test proceeds. They start holding their breath without realizing it, or they breathe erratically or arrhythmically. Improper breathing hurts confidence and accuracy. Just as important, it interferes with clear thinking.

- Some quick isometrics during the test—especially if concentration is wandering or energy is waning—can help. Try this: Put your palms together and press intensely for a few seconds. Concentrate on the tension you feel through your palms, wrists, forearms, and up into your

WHAT ARE "SIGNS OF A WINNER," ALEX?

Here's some advice from a Kaplan instructor who won big on *Jeopardy!*™ In the green room before the show, he noticed that the contestants who were quiet and "within themselves" were the ones who did great on the show. The contestants who did not perform as well were the ones who were fact-cramming, talking a lot, and generally being manic before the show. Lesson: Spend the final hours leading up to the test getting sleep, meditating, and generally relaxing.

DON'T FORCE IT

Never try to force relaxation. You'll only get frustrated and find yourself even more uptight. Be passive.

AVOID MUST-Y THINKING

Let go of "must-y" thoughts, those notions that you must do something a certain way—for example, "I must get a great score or else!" or "I must meet my parents' expectations."

biceps and shoulders. Then, quickly release the pressure. Feel the difference as you let go. Focus on the warm relaxation that floods through the muscles. Now you're ready to return to the task.

• Here's another isometric that will relieve tension in both your neck and eye muscles. Slowly rotate your head from side to side, turning your head and eyes to look as far back over each shoulder as you can. Feel the muscles stretch on one side of your neck as they contract on the other. Repeat five times in each direction.

With what you've just learned here, you're armed and ready to do battle with the test. This book and your studies will give you the information you'll need to answer the questions. It's all firmly planted in your mind. You also know how to deal with any excess tension that might come along, both when you're studying for and taking the exam. You've experienced everything you need to tame your test anxiety and stress. You are going to get a great score.

PRACTICE MCAT

Instructions for Taking the Practice Test

Before taking the practice test, find a quiet place where you can work uninterrupted. Make sure you have a comfortable desk and several No. 2 pencils.

Use the answer grid on the following page to record your answers. You'll find the answer key and score converter following the test.

Good luck.

MARK ONE AND ONLY ONE ANSWER TO EACH QUESTION. BE SURE TO FILL IN COMPLETELY THE SPACE FOR YOUR INTENDED ANSWER CHOICE. IF YOU ERASE, DO SO COMPLETELY. MAKE NO STRAY MARKS.

RIGHT MARK: ●   WRONG MARKS: ✓ ✗ ⊙

1   Ⓐ Ⓑ Ⓒ Ⓓ
2   Ⓐ Ⓑ Ⓒ Ⓓ
3   Ⓐ Ⓑ Ⓒ Ⓓ
4   Ⓐ Ⓑ Ⓒ Ⓓ
5   Ⓐ Ⓑ Ⓒ Ⓓ
6   Ⓐ Ⓑ Ⓒ Ⓓ
7   Ⓐ Ⓑ Ⓒ Ⓓ
8   Ⓐ Ⓑ Ⓒ Ⓓ
9   Ⓐ Ⓑ Ⓒ Ⓓ
10 Ⓐ Ⓑ Ⓒ Ⓓ
11 Ⓐ Ⓑ Ⓒ Ⓓ
12 Ⓐ Ⓑ Ⓒ Ⓓ
13 Ⓐ Ⓑ Ⓒ Ⓓ
14 Ⓐ Ⓑ Ⓒ Ⓓ
15 Ⓐ Ⓑ Ⓒ Ⓓ
16 Ⓐ Ⓑ Ⓒ Ⓓ
17 Ⓐ Ⓑ Ⓒ Ⓓ
18 Ⓐ Ⓑ Ⓒ Ⓓ
19 Ⓐ Ⓑ Ⓒ Ⓓ
20 Ⓐ Ⓑ Ⓒ Ⓓ
21 Ⓐ Ⓑ Ⓒ Ⓓ
22 Ⓐ Ⓑ Ⓒ Ⓓ
23 Ⓐ Ⓑ Ⓒ Ⓓ
24 Ⓐ Ⓑ Ⓒ Ⓓ
25 Ⓐ Ⓑ Ⓒ Ⓓ
26 Ⓐ Ⓑ Ⓒ Ⓓ
27 Ⓐ Ⓑ Ⓒ Ⓓ
28 Ⓐ Ⓑ Ⓒ Ⓓ
29 Ⓐ Ⓑ Ⓒ Ⓓ
30 Ⓐ Ⓑ Ⓒ Ⓓ
31 Ⓐ Ⓑ Ⓒ Ⓓ
32 Ⓐ Ⓑ Ⓒ Ⓓ
33 Ⓐ Ⓑ Ⓒ Ⓓ
34 Ⓐ Ⓑ Ⓒ Ⓓ
35 Ⓐ Ⓑ Ⓒ Ⓓ
36 Ⓐ Ⓑ Ⓒ Ⓓ
37 Ⓐ Ⓑ Ⓒ Ⓓ
38 Ⓐ Ⓑ Ⓒ Ⓓ
39 Ⓐ Ⓑ Ⓒ Ⓓ
40 Ⓐ Ⓑ Ⓒ Ⓓ

41 Ⓐ Ⓑ Ⓒ Ⓓ
42 Ⓐ Ⓑ Ⓒ Ⓓ
43 Ⓐ Ⓑ Ⓒ Ⓓ
44 Ⓐ Ⓑ Ⓒ Ⓓ
45 Ⓐ Ⓑ Ⓒ Ⓓ
46 Ⓐ Ⓑ Ⓒ Ⓓ
47 Ⓐ Ⓑ Ⓒ Ⓓ
48 Ⓐ Ⓑ Ⓒ Ⓓ
49 Ⓐ Ⓑ Ⓒ Ⓓ
50 Ⓐ Ⓑ Ⓒ Ⓓ
51 Ⓐ Ⓑ Ⓒ Ⓓ
52 Ⓐ Ⓑ Ⓒ Ⓓ
53 Ⓐ Ⓑ Ⓒ Ⓓ
54 Ⓐ Ⓑ Ⓒ Ⓓ
55 Ⓐ Ⓑ Ⓒ Ⓓ
56 Ⓐ Ⓑ Ⓒ Ⓓ
57 Ⓐ Ⓑ Ⓒ Ⓓ
58 Ⓐ Ⓑ Ⓒ Ⓓ
59 Ⓐ Ⓑ Ⓒ Ⓓ
60 Ⓐ Ⓑ Ⓒ Ⓓ
61 Ⓐ Ⓑ Ⓒ Ⓓ
62 Ⓐ Ⓑ Ⓒ Ⓓ
63 Ⓐ Ⓑ Ⓒ Ⓓ
64 Ⓐ Ⓑ Ⓒ Ⓓ
65 Ⓐ Ⓑ Ⓒ Ⓓ
66 Ⓐ Ⓑ Ⓒ Ⓓ
67 Ⓐ Ⓑ Ⓒ Ⓓ
68 Ⓐ Ⓑ Ⓒ Ⓓ
69 Ⓐ Ⓑ Ⓒ Ⓓ
70 Ⓐ Ⓑ Ⓒ Ⓓ
71 Ⓐ Ⓑ Ⓒ Ⓓ
72 Ⓐ Ⓑ Ⓒ Ⓓ
73 Ⓐ Ⓑ Ⓒ Ⓓ
74 Ⓐ Ⓑ Ⓒ Ⓓ
75 Ⓐ Ⓑ Ⓒ Ⓓ
76 Ⓐ Ⓑ Ⓒ Ⓓ
77 Ⓐ Ⓑ Ⓒ Ⓓ
78 Ⓐ Ⓑ Ⓒ Ⓓ
79 Ⓐ Ⓑ Ⓒ Ⓓ
80 Ⓐ Ⓑ Ⓒ Ⓓ

81 Ⓐ Ⓑ Ⓒ Ⓓ
82 Ⓐ Ⓑ Ⓒ Ⓓ
83 Ⓐ Ⓑ Ⓒ Ⓓ
84 Ⓐ Ⓑ Ⓒ Ⓓ
85 Ⓐ Ⓑ Ⓒ Ⓓ
86 Ⓐ Ⓑ Ⓒ Ⓓ
87 Ⓐ Ⓑ Ⓒ Ⓓ
88 Ⓐ Ⓑ Ⓒ Ⓓ
89 Ⓐ Ⓑ Ⓒ Ⓓ
90 Ⓐ Ⓑ Ⓒ Ⓓ
91 Ⓐ Ⓑ Ⓒ Ⓓ
92 Ⓐ Ⓑ Ⓒ Ⓓ
93 Ⓐ Ⓑ Ⓒ Ⓓ
94 Ⓐ Ⓑ Ⓒ Ⓓ
95 Ⓐ Ⓑ Ⓒ Ⓓ
96 Ⓐ Ⓑ Ⓒ Ⓓ
97 Ⓐ Ⓑ Ⓒ Ⓓ
98 Ⓐ Ⓑ Ⓒ Ⓓ
99 Ⓐ Ⓑ Ⓒ Ⓓ
100 Ⓐ Ⓑ Ⓒ Ⓓ
101 Ⓐ Ⓑ Ⓒ Ⓓ
102 Ⓐ Ⓑ Ⓒ Ⓓ
103 Ⓐ Ⓑ Ⓒ Ⓓ
104 Ⓐ Ⓑ Ⓒ Ⓓ
105 Ⓐ Ⓑ Ⓒ Ⓓ
106 Ⓐ Ⓑ Ⓒ Ⓓ
107 Ⓐ Ⓑ Ⓒ Ⓓ
108 Ⓐ Ⓑ Ⓒ Ⓓ
109 Ⓐ Ⓑ Ⓒ Ⓓ
110 Ⓐ Ⓑ Ⓒ Ⓓ
111 Ⓐ Ⓑ Ⓒ Ⓓ
112 Ⓐ Ⓑ Ⓒ Ⓓ
113 Ⓐ Ⓑ Ⓒ Ⓓ
114 Ⓐ Ⓑ Ⓒ Ⓓ
115 Ⓐ Ⓑ Ⓒ Ⓓ
116 Ⓐ Ⓑ Ⓒ Ⓓ
117 Ⓐ Ⓑ Ⓒ Ⓓ
118 Ⓐ Ⓑ Ⓒ Ⓓ
119 Ⓐ Ⓑ Ⓒ Ⓓ
120 Ⓐ Ⓑ Ⓒ Ⓓ

121 Ⓐ Ⓑ Ⓒ Ⓓ
122 Ⓐ Ⓑ Ⓒ Ⓓ
123 Ⓐ Ⓑ Ⓒ Ⓓ
124 Ⓐ Ⓑ Ⓒ Ⓓ
125 Ⓐ Ⓑ Ⓒ Ⓓ
126 Ⓐ Ⓑ Ⓒ Ⓓ
127 Ⓐ Ⓑ Ⓒ Ⓓ
128 Ⓐ Ⓑ Ⓒ Ⓓ
129 Ⓐ Ⓑ Ⓒ Ⓓ
130 Ⓐ Ⓑ Ⓒ Ⓓ
131 Ⓐ Ⓑ Ⓒ Ⓓ
132 Ⓐ Ⓑ Ⓒ Ⓓ
133 Ⓐ Ⓑ Ⓒ Ⓓ
134 Ⓐ Ⓑ Ⓒ Ⓓ
135 Ⓐ Ⓑ Ⓒ Ⓓ
136 Ⓐ Ⓑ Ⓒ Ⓓ
137 Ⓐ Ⓑ Ⓒ Ⓓ
138 Ⓐ Ⓑ Ⓒ Ⓓ
139 Ⓐ Ⓑ Ⓒ Ⓓ
140 Ⓐ Ⓑ Ⓒ Ⓓ
141 Ⓐ Ⓑ Ⓒ Ⓓ
142 Ⓐ Ⓑ Ⓒ Ⓓ
143 Ⓐ Ⓑ Ⓒ Ⓓ
144 Ⓐ Ⓑ Ⓒ Ⓓ
145 Ⓐ Ⓑ Ⓒ Ⓓ
146 Ⓐ Ⓑ Ⓒ Ⓓ
147 Ⓐ Ⓑ Ⓒ Ⓓ
148 Ⓐ Ⓑ Ⓒ Ⓓ
149 Ⓐ Ⓑ Ⓒ Ⓓ
150 Ⓐ Ⓑ Ⓒ Ⓓ
151 Ⓐ Ⓑ Ⓒ Ⓓ
152 Ⓐ Ⓑ Ⓒ Ⓓ
153 Ⓐ Ⓑ Ⓒ Ⓓ
154 Ⓐ Ⓑ Ⓒ Ⓓ
155 Ⓐ Ⓑ Ⓒ Ⓓ
156 Ⓐ Ⓑ Ⓒ Ⓓ
157 Ⓐ Ⓑ Ⓒ Ⓓ
158 Ⓐ Ⓑ Ⓒ Ⓓ
159 Ⓐ Ⓑ Ⓒ Ⓓ
160 Ⓐ Ⓑ Ⓒ Ⓓ

161 Ⓐ Ⓑ Ⓒ Ⓓ
162 Ⓐ Ⓑ Ⓒ Ⓓ
163 Ⓐ Ⓑ Ⓒ Ⓓ
164 Ⓐ Ⓑ Ⓒ Ⓓ
165 Ⓐ Ⓑ Ⓒ Ⓓ
166 Ⓐ Ⓑ Ⓒ Ⓓ
167 Ⓐ Ⓑ Ⓒ Ⓓ
168 Ⓐ Ⓑ Ⓒ Ⓓ
169 Ⓐ Ⓑ Ⓒ Ⓓ
170 Ⓐ Ⓑ Ⓒ Ⓓ
171 Ⓐ Ⓑ Ⓒ Ⓓ
172 Ⓐ Ⓑ Ⓒ Ⓓ
173 Ⓐ Ⓑ Ⓒ Ⓓ
174 Ⓐ Ⓑ Ⓒ Ⓓ
175 Ⓐ Ⓑ Ⓒ Ⓓ
176 Ⓐ Ⓑ Ⓒ Ⓓ
177 Ⓐ Ⓑ Ⓒ Ⓓ
178 Ⓐ Ⓑ Ⓒ Ⓓ
179 Ⓐ Ⓑ Ⓒ Ⓓ
180 Ⓐ Ⓑ Ⓒ Ⓓ
181 Ⓐ Ⓑ Ⓒ Ⓓ
182 Ⓐ Ⓑ Ⓒ Ⓓ
183 Ⓐ Ⓑ Ⓒ Ⓓ
184 Ⓐ Ⓑ Ⓒ Ⓓ
185 Ⓐ Ⓑ Ⓒ Ⓓ
186 Ⓐ Ⓑ Ⓒ Ⓓ
187 Ⓐ Ⓑ Ⓒ Ⓓ
188 Ⓐ Ⓑ Ⓒ Ⓓ
189 Ⓐ Ⓑ Ⓒ Ⓓ
190 Ⓐ Ⓑ Ⓒ Ⓓ
191 Ⓐ Ⓑ Ⓒ Ⓓ
192 Ⓐ Ⓑ Ⓒ Ⓓ
193 Ⓐ Ⓑ Ⓒ Ⓓ
194 Ⓐ Ⓑ Ⓒ Ⓓ
195 Ⓐ Ⓑ Ⓒ Ⓓ
196 Ⓐ Ⓑ Ⓒ Ⓓ
197 Ⓐ Ⓑ Ⓒ Ⓓ
198 Ⓐ Ⓑ Ⓒ Ⓓ
199 Ⓐ Ⓑ Ⓒ Ⓓ
200 Ⓐ Ⓑ Ⓒ Ⓓ

201 Ⓐ Ⓑ Ⓒ Ⓓ
202 Ⓐ Ⓑ Ⓒ Ⓓ
203 Ⓐ Ⓑ Ⓒ Ⓓ
204 Ⓐ Ⓑ Ⓒ Ⓓ
205 Ⓐ Ⓑ Ⓒ Ⓓ
206 Ⓐ Ⓑ Ⓒ Ⓓ
207 Ⓐ Ⓑ Ⓒ Ⓓ
208 Ⓐ Ⓑ Ⓒ Ⓓ
209 Ⓐ Ⓑ Ⓒ Ⓓ
210 Ⓐ Ⓑ Ⓒ Ⓓ
211 Ⓐ Ⓑ Ⓒ Ⓓ
212 Ⓐ Ⓑ Ⓒ Ⓓ
213 Ⓐ Ⓑ Ⓒ Ⓓ
214 Ⓐ Ⓑ Ⓒ Ⓓ
215 Ⓐ Ⓑ Ⓒ Ⓓ
216 Ⓐ Ⓑ Ⓒ Ⓓ
217 Ⓐ Ⓑ Ⓒ Ⓓ
218 Ⓐ Ⓑ Ⓒ Ⓓ
219 Ⓐ Ⓑ Ⓒ Ⓓ

Verbal Reasoning

Time: 85 Minutes

Questions: 1–65

DIRECTIONS:

You are allotted 85 minutes to work on this part of the exam. You may work only on the Verbal Reasoning part during that time. Should you finish early, you are permitted to check your work in this part of the exam only.

Verbal Reasoning

DIRECTIONS: This Verbal Reasoning test is composed of nine passages. Several questions follow each passage. After reading a passage, select the best answer choice for each question. If you are uncertain of a correct answer, eliminate the answer choices known to be incorrect and select an answer from the remaining alternatives. Indicate your answer selection by blackening the corresponding oval on your answer sheet.

Passage I (Questions 1–8)

Although nihilism is commonly defined as a form of extremist political thought, the term has a broader meaning. Nihilism is in fact a complex intellectual stance with venerable roots in the
[5] history of ideas, which forms the theoretical basis for many positive assertions of modern thought. Its essence is the systematic negation of all perceptual orders and assumptions. A complete view must account for the influence of two
[10] historical crosscurrents: philosophical skepticism about the ultimacy of any truth, and the mystical quest for that same pure truth. These are united by their categorical rejection of the "known."

The outstanding representative of the former
[15] current, David Hume (1711–1776), maintained that external reality is unknowable, since sense perceptions give no information whatsoever about what really exists. Hume points out that sense impressions are actually part of the contents
[20] of the mind. Their presumed correspondence to external "things" cannot be verified, since it can be checked only by other sense impressions. Hume further asserts that all abstract conceptions turn out, on examination, to be generalizations
[25] from sense impressions. He concludes that even such an apparently objective phenomenon as a cause-and-effect relationship between events may be no more than a subjective fabrication of the observer. Stanley Rosen notes: "Hume terminates
[30] in skepticism because he finds nothing within the subject but individual impressions and ideas."

For mystics of every faith, the "experience of nothingness" is the goal of spiritual practice. Buddhist meditation techniques involve the
[35] systematic negation of all spiritual and intellectual constructs to make way for the apprehension of pure truth. St. John of the Cross similarly rejected every physical and mental symbolization of God as illusory. St. John's spiritual legacy is, as Michael
[40] Novak puts it, "the constant return to inner solitude, an unbroken awareness of the emptiness at the heart of consciousness. It is a harsh refusal to allow idols to be placed in the sanctuary. It requires also a scorching gaze upon all the
[45] bureaucracies, institutions, manipulators, and hucksters who employ technology and its supposed realities to bewitch and bedazzle the psyche."

Novak's interpretation points to the way these philosophical and mystical traditions prepared
[50] the ground for the political nihilism of the nineteenth and twentieth centuries. The rejection of existing social institutions and their claims to authority is in the most basic sense made possible by Humean skepticism. The political nihilism of the
[55] Russian intelligentsia combined this radical skepticism with a near-mystical faith in the power of a new beginning. Hence, their desire to destroy becomes a revolutionary affirmation; in the words of Stanley Rosen, "Nihilism is an attempt to overcome
[60] or repudiate the past on behalf of an unknown and unknowable, yet hoped-for, future." This fusion of skepticism and mystical recreation can be traced in contemporary thought, for example as an element in the counterculture of the 1960s.

1. The author's working definition of nihilism, as it functions in the passage, is:

   A. systematic doubt of that which one takes for granted.

   B. a mystical quest for nothingness.

   C. a form of extremist political thought.

   D. rejection of all presently established institutions.

GO ON TO THE NEXT PAGE.

2. The passage implies that the two strands of nihilist thought:

A. are combined in nineteenth and twentieth century political nihilism.

B. remained essentially separate after the eighteenth century.

C. are necessary prerequisites for any positive modern social thought.

D. are derived from distinct Eastern and Western philosophical traditions.

3. In the passage, quotations from writers about nihilism are used in order to:

I. summarize specific points made in the course of the passage.

II. contrast points of view on the subject under discussion.

III. make transitions between points in the discussion.

A. I only

B. I and II only

C. I and III only

D. II and III only

4. Which is a necessary assumption underlying Hume's conclusion that external reality is unknowable, as discussed in the passage?

A. Nothing outside the mind exists.

B. The contents of the mind consist exclusively of sense impressions.

C. Causality is a subjective projection of the mind.

D. Sense impressions provide our only information about external reality.

5. Novak's interpretation of St. John's spiritual legacy (lines 40–47) is important to the author's argument primarily because it:

A. characterizes the essence of St. John's mystical doctrine.

B. gives insight into the historical antecedents of political nihilism.

C. draws a parallel between Christian mysticism and the Humean tradition of philosophical skepticism.

D. suggests that St. John's teachings are influential mainly because of their sociopolitical implications.

6. The author uses all of the following techniques in developing the topic EXCEPT:

A. discussion of individuals as representative of intellectual trends.

B. a contrast between a common definition and his own.

C. identification of the common elements in distinct intellectual traditions.

D. examination of the practical consequences of a social doctrine.

7. In the last paragraph, the author quotes Stanley Rosen in order to make the point that modern nihilism is:

A. impractical because of its faith in an unknowable future.

B. more than just a movement to do away with existing institutions.

C. a living doctrine rather than merely a part of the history of political theory.

D. based more on the tradition of philosophical skepticism than on that of mystical affirmation.

8. Which of the following provides the best continuation for the final paragraph of the passage?

A. Thus, the negative effects of nihilism are still being felt.

B. Classical nihilism has thus been superseded by a new and unrelated type.

C. The revolutionaries of that time did, after all, reject society and hope for something better.

D. The study of nihilism, then, belongs to the past rather than to the present.

GO ON TO THE NEXT PAGE.

Passage II (Questions 9–15)

Agonistic behavior, or aggression, is exhibited by most of the more than three million species of animals on this planet. Animal behaviorists still disagree on a comprehensive definition of the term, but aggressive behavior can be loosely described as any action that harms an adversary or compels it to retreat. Aggression may serve many purposes, such as food gathering, establishing territory, and enforcing social hierarchy. In a general Darwinian sense, however, the purpose of aggressive behavior is to increase the individual animal's—and thus, the species'—chance of survival.

Aggressive behavior may be directed at animals of other species, or it may be conspecific—that is, directed at members of an animal's own species. One of the most common examples of conspecific aggression occurs in the establishment and maintenance of social hierarchies. In a hierarchy, social dominance is usually established according to physical superiority; the classic example is that of a pecking order among domestic fowl. The dominance hierarchy may be viewed as a means of social control that reduces the incidence of attack within a group. Once established, the hierarchy is rarely threatened by disputes because the inferior animal immediately submits when confronted by a superior.

Two basic types of aggressive behavior are common to most species: attack and defensive threat. Each type involves a particular pattern of physiological and behavioral responses, which tends not to vary regardless of the stimulus that provokes it. For example, the pattern of attack behavior in cats involves a series of movements, such as stalking, biting, seizing with the forepaws and scratching with the hind legs, that changes very little regardless of the stimulus—that is, regardless of who or what the cat is attacking.

The cat's defensive threat response offers another set of closely linked physiological and behavioral patterns. The cardiovascular system begins to pump blood at a faster rate, in preparation for sudden physical activity. The eyes narrow and the ears flatten against the side of the cat's head for protection, and other vulnerable areas of the body such as the stomach and throat are similarly contracted. Growling or hissing noises and erect fur also signal defensive threat. As with the attack response, this pattern of responses is generated with little variation regardless of the nature of the stimulus.

Are these aggressive patterns of attack and defensive threat innate, genetically programmed, or are they learned? The answer seems to be a combination of both. A mouse is helpless at birth, but by its 12th day of life can assume a defensive threat position by backing up on its hind legs. By the time it is one month old, the mouse begins to exhibit the attack response. Nonetheless, copious evidence suggests that animals learn and practice aggressive behavior; one need look no further than the sight of a kitten playing with a ball of string. All the elements of attack—stalking, pouncing, biting, and shaking—are part of the game that prepares the kitten for more serious situations later in life.

9. The passage asserts that animal social hierarchies are generally stable because:

   A. the behavior responses of the group are known by all its members.
   B. the defensive threat posture quickly stops most conflicts.
   C. inferior animals usually defer to their physical superiors.
   D. the need for mutual protection from other species inhibits conspecific aggression.

10. According to the author, what is the most significant physiological change undergone by a cat assuming the defensive threat position?

   A. An increase in cardiovascular activity
   B. A sudden narrowing of the eyes
   C. A contraction of the abdominal muscles
   D. The author does not say which change is most significant

11. Based on the information in the passage about agonistic behavior, it is reasonable to conclude that:

   I. the purpose of agonistic behavior is to help ensure the survival of the species.
   II. agonistic behavior is both innate and learned.
   III. conspecific aggression is more frequent than interspecies aggression.

   A. I only
   B. II only
   C. I and II only
   D. I, II, and III

GO ON TO THE NEXT PAGE.

12. The author suggests that the question of whether agonistic behavior is genetically programmed or learned:

- **A.** still generates considerable controversy among animal behaviorists.
- **B.** was first investigated through experiments on mice.
- **C.** is outdated since most scientists now believe the genetic element to be most important.
- **D.** has been the subject of extensive clinical study.

13. Which of the following topics related to agonistic behavior is NOT explicitly addressed in the passage?

- **A.** The physiological changes that accompany attack behavior in cats
- **B.** The evolutionary purpose of aggression
- **C.** Conspecific aggression that occurs in dominance hierarchies
- **D.** The relationship between play and aggression

14. Which of the following would be most in accord with the information presented in the passage?

- **A.** The aggressive behavior of sharks is closely linked to their need to remain in constant motion.
- **B.** The inability of newborn mice to exhibit the attack response proves that aggressive behavior must be learned.
- **C.** Most animal species that do not exhibit aggressive behavior are prevented from doing so by environmental factors.
- **D.** Members of a certain species of hawk use the same method to prey on both squirrels and gophers.

15. The author of this passage is primarily concerned with:

- **A.** analyzing the differences between attack behavior and defensive threat behavior.
- **B.** introducing a subject currently debated among animal behaviorists.
- **C.** providing a general overview of aggressive behavior in animals.
- **D.** illustrating various manifestations of agonistic behavior among mammals.

GO ON TO THE NEXT PAGE.

At a recent meeting of the American Public Transit Association, the Environmental Protection Agency unveiled stringent new standards for pollution control. The transit authorities were particularly concerned about the implementation of a proposed "Clean Air Act." They believed the provisions of the Clean Air Act could severely affect basic services to their local communities. Many transit agencies were concerned that it would be difficult to comply with the pollution and emissions control standards while continuing to operate within realistic budgets.

The aim of the Clean Air Act is to assure that by the year 2000, there will be a reduction of at least 10 million tons of sulfur dioxide from 1980 levels. The bill also calls for a reduction in pollutants that contribute to the depletion of ozone. Strict regulations of toxic air emissions would have to be established and enforced. Additionally, the Clean Air Act would establish specific acid-rain reduction quotas and enforce severe penalties for transgressors of any of the new clean air regulations.

There is little doubt that mass-transit suppliers will be considerably affected by this new legislation, just as the chemical and petroleum industries have already been affected by similar legislation. Transit authorities are challenged to strike a difficult balance between complying with the government's new standards and developing an official concern for the environment, while continuing to fulfill the transportation needs of the general population.

Among the areas addressed by the Clean Air Act, the topic of mobile resources is of particular interest to mass transit authorities. Provisions contained in the Act under this title are aimed at encouraging the development and practical use of alternative fuel sources, like solar energy and methane fuel. The goal of this section of the Act is to eradicate toxic fuel emissions in order to provide cleaner air and a more favorable environment. The Act even goes so far as to declare that in cities like New York, Los Angeles, and Houston—where air quality is particularly noxious and toxins exceed the limits of federal regulations—forms of mass transit should run on so-called "clean-burning fuels" by the year 2000. Such fuels include reformulated gasoline, propane, electricity, natural gas, ethanol, methanol, or any similar type of low emission fuel. In addition, the Act proposes that, by 1994, all new urban buses in cities with populations exceeding one million must operate solely on clean-burning fuels.

The topics of alternative fuels and alternative fuel vehicles represent, by far, the most controversial issue in the Clean Air Act. Former President Bush has called alternative fuels "bold and innovative" means to control pollution, but according to many transportation experts, the Act's proposals on alternative fuel usage are unrealistic. The transit authorities recognize that concern for the environment and health hazards like pollution are global issues. However, most transit officials concur that inventing and developing new ways to fuel mass transit will take at least 50 years to realize. They point out that the Act does not mention the political and social ramifications of usurping the role of the petroleum industries. The Act does not mention if or how the thousands of people employed by the oil industry will get retrained to produce and implement the use of "clean" fuel.

No one disputes the fact that people need some form of transportation to get from place to place. Preserving the environment should be a priority, yet we need to remember that even if toxic emissions are completely eliminated sometime in the future, the challenge of moving mass numbers of people where they want to go will still exist and must remain a priority. Transit authorities contend that unless the Clean Air Act also acknowledges this, and develops a way to encourage mass transit over personal transportation, the problems of pollution might not be significantly altered. They suggest that there are many areas in this country that have little or no mass transit and that, if the Clean Air Act's goal is to reduce pollution, perhaps the most practical and realistic means to achieve that goal is to encourage the development and maintenance of mass transit systems.

16. In general, transit authorities feel that complying with the provisions in the Clean Air Act will:

   A. be fairly easy as long as strict compliance is followed by all agencies of mass transit.
   B. prove difficult because only wealthy private corporations can afford to drastically change their methods of business.
   C. demand an increase in government funding for mass transit.
   D. be challenging because transit authorities must meet the public's transportation needs while adhering to the new provisions.

GO ON TO THE NEXT PAGE.

17. According to transit authorities, unless the Clean Air Act acknowledges the necessity for mass transit, and encourages its use over that of personal transportation:

   A. the cost of mass transit will rise to a prohibitive level.
   B. private automobile manufacturers will take advantage of the loopholes in the Clean Air Act.
   C. pollution may continue unabated.
   D. the use of public transportation in rural areas will decrease.

18. The majority of transit officials seem to agree that developing new ways to power mass transit:

   A. is an unrealistic goal, at least for the short term.
   B. must be preceded by governmental restrictions on petroleum products.
   C. should be subsidized at the state and federal levels.
   D. will increase the cost of transportation to consumers.

19. The main goal of the Clean Air Act is to:

   A. make sure that pollution is completely eradicated by the year 2000.
   B. reduce the amount of sulfur dioxide levels in the air by at least 10 million tons.
   C. eliminate toxic air emissions.
   D. enforce harsh penalties for transgressors of any of the new clean air regulations.

20. The Clean Air Act proposes:

   A. emphasizing the use of mass-transit over private transportation.
   B. a method to increase public awareness of the effects that pollution has on the atmosphere.
   C. total eradication of pollutants, including acid rain and toxic air emissions.
   D. encouraging oil companies and mass-transportation systems to convert to clean-burning fuel.

21. The major fear that transportation officials have about the effects of the Clean Air Act is:

   A. that it may discourage the use of mass transit.
   B. the difficulty they will encounter in attempting to conform to the Clean Air Act's stringent pollution-control requirements.
   C. the high cost of switching to new sources of energy.
   D. the political and social ramifications of usurping the role of the petroleum industries.

22. Which of the following statements about transit officials' reactions to the Clean Air Act is false?

   A. Transit officials feel that they will have a great deal of difficulty complying with the stringent pollution and emission standards while continuing to operate on a financially practical level.
   B. Transit authorities believe that the Act's proposals on alternative fuel usage are unrealistic.
   C. Transit officials argue that unless the Clean Air Act recognizes the importance of mass transit, pollution may not be fundamentally modified.
   D. Mass transit authorities feel incapable of meeting the Clean Air Act's demand that all new buses in cities with populations exceeding one million must run solely on clean burning fuel such as ethanol or propane.

23. The main goal of the "Mobile Resources" section of the Clean Air Act is to:

   A. reduce toxic vehicle emissions for cleaner air and a better environment.
   B. encourage the development and practical use of different forms of mass transportation.
   C. convince the general public of the environmental benefits of mass transit over private transportation.
   D. force private oil industries to redevelop their methods of production so there is less pollution.

GO ON TO THE NEXT PAGE.

24. Transit authorities feel that the Act does NOT:

    A. sufficiently discuss the problems of lead emissions in the atmosphere.

    B. adequately acknowledge the fact that people need some form of transportation.

    C. offer financial incentives to induce private automobile owners to use mass transit instead.

    D. adequately emphasize the role and responsibility of private industry in the current global warming crisis.

GO ON TO THE NEXT PAGE.

Passage IV (Questions 25–33)

The rich analyses of Fernand Braudel and his fellow *Annales* historians have made significant contributions to historical theory and research. In a departure from traditional historical approaches, the *Annales* historians assume (as do Marxists) that history cannot be limited to a simple recounting of conscious human actions, but must be understood in the context of forces and material conditions that underlie human behavior. Braudel was the first *Annales* historian to gain widespread support for the idea that history should synthesize data from various social sciences, especially economics, in order to provide a broader view of human societies over time (although Febvre and Bloch, founders of the *Annales* school, had originated this approach).

Braudel conceived of history as the dynamic interaction of three temporalities. The first of these, the *evenementielle*, involved short-lived dramatic "events," such as battles, revolutions, and the actions of great men, which had preoccupied traditional historians like Carlyle. *Conjonctures* was Braudel's term for larger cyclical processes that might last up to half a century. The *longue duree*, a historical wave of great length, was for Braudel the most fascinating of the three temporalities. Here he focused on those aspects of everyday life that might remain relatively unchanged for centuries. What people ate, what they wore, their means and routes of travel—for Braudel these things create "structures" that define the limits of potential social change for hundreds of years at a time.

Braudel's concept of the *longue duree* extended the perspective of historical space as well as time. Until the *Annales* school, historians had taken the juridical political unit—the nation-state, duchy, or whatever—as their starting point. Yet, when such enormous timespans are considered, geographical features may well have more significance for human populations than national borders. In his doctoral thesis, a seminal work on the Mediterranean during the reign of Philip II, Braudel treated the geohistory of the entire region as a "structure" that had exerted myriad influences on human lifeways since the first settlements on the shores of the Mediterranean Sea. And so the reader is given such arcane information as the list of products that came to Spanish shores from North Africa, the seasonal routes followed by Mediterranean sheep and their shepherds, and the cities where the best ship timber could be bought.

Braudel has been faulted for the imprecision of his approach. With his Rabelaisian delight in concrete detail, Braudel vastly extended the realm of relevant phenomena; but this very achievement made it difficult to delimit the boundaries of observation, a task necessary to beginning any social investigation. Further, Braudel and other *Annales* historians minimize the differences among the social sciences. Nevertheless, the many similarly designed studies aimed at both professional and popular audiences indicate that Braudel asked significant questions that traditional historians had overlooked.

25. The primary purpose of the passage is to:

   A. show how Braudel's work changed the conception of Mediterranean life held by previous historians.
   B. evaluate Braudel's criticisms of traditional and Marxist historiography.
   C. contrast the perspective of the *longue duree* with the actions of major historical figures.
   D. outline some of Braudel's influential conceptions and distinguish them from conventional approaches.

26. The author refers to the work of Febvre and Bloch in order to:

   A. illustrate the limitations of the *Annales* tradition of historical interpretation.
   B. suggest the relevance of economics to historical investigation.
   C. debate the need for combining various sociological approaches.
   D. show that previous *Annales* historians anticipated Braudel's focus on economics.

27. According to the passage, all of the following are aspects of Braudel's approach to history EXCEPT that he:

   A. attempted to draw on various social sciences.
   B. studied social and economic activities that occurred across national boundaries.
   C. pointed out the link between increased economic activity and the rise of nationalism.
   D. examined seemingly unexciting aspects of everyday life.

GO ON TO THE NEXT PAGE.

28. In the third paragraph, the author is primarily concerned with discussing:

   A. Braudel's fascination with obscure facts.
   B. Braudel's depiction of the role of geography in human history.
   C. the geography of the Mediterranean region.
   D. the irrelevance of national borders.

29. The passage suggests that, compared with traditional historians, *Annales* historians are:

   A. more interested in other social sciences than in history.
   B. critical of the achievements of famous historical figures.
   C. skeptical of the validity of most economic research.
   D. more interested in the underlying context of human behavior.

30. Which of the following statements would be most likely to follow the last sentence of the passage?

   A. Few such studies, however, have been written by trained economists.
   B. It is time, perhaps, for a revival of the Carlylean emphasis on personalities.
   C. Many historians believe that Braudel's conception of three distinct "temporalities" is an oversimplification.
   D. Such diverse works as Gascon's study of Lyon and Barbara Tuchman's *A Distant Mirror* testify to his relevance.

31. The author is critical of Braudel's perspective for which of the following reasons?

   A. It seeks structures that underlie all forms of social activity.
   B. It assumes a greater similarity among the social sciences than actually exists.
   C. It fails to consider the relationship between short-term events and long-term social activity.
   D. It rigidly defines boundaries for social analysis.

32. The passage implies the Braudel would consider which of the following as exemplifying the *longue duree*?

   I. The prominence of certain crops in the diet of a region
   II. The annexation of a province by the victor in a war
   III. A reduction in the population of an area following a disease epidemic

   A. I only
   B. III only
   C. I and II only
   D. II and III only

33. Which of the following statements is most in keeping with the principles of Braudel's work as described in the passage?

   A. All written history is the history of social elites.
   B. The most important task of historians is to define the limits of potential social change.
   C. Those who ignore history are doomed to repeat it.
   D. People's historical actions are influenced by many factors that they may be unaware of.

GO ON TO THE NEXT PAGE.

Passage V (Questions 34–39)

Although we know more about so-called Neanderthal men than about any other early population, their exact relation to present-day human beings remains unclear. Long considered subhuman, Neanderthals are now known to have been fully human. They walked erect, used fire, and made a variety of tools. They lived partly in the open and partly in caves. The Neanderthals are even thought to have been the first humans to bury their dead, a practice that has been interpreted as demonstrating the capacity for religious and abstract thought.

The first monograph on Neanderthal anatomy, published by Marcellin Boule in 1913, presented a somewhat misleading picture. Boule took the Neanderthals' low-vaulted cranium and prominent brow ridges, their heavy musculature, and the apparent overdevelopment of certain joints as evidence of a prehuman physical appearance. In postulating for the Neanderthal such "primitive" characteristics as a stooping, bent-kneed posture, a rolling gait, and a forward-hanging head, Boule was a victim of the rudimentary state of anatomical science. Modern anthropologists recognize the Neanderthal bone structure as that of a creature whose bodily orientation and capacities were very similar to those of present-day human beings. The differences in the size and shape of the limbs, shoulder blades, and other parts are simply adaptations that were necessary to handle the Neanderthal's far more massive musculature. Current taxonomy considers the Neanderthals to have been fully human and thus designates them not as a separate species, *Homo neanderthalensis*, but as a subspecies of *Homo sapiens*: *Homo sapiens neanderthalensis*.

The rise of the Neanderthals occurred over some 100,000 years—a sufficient period to account for evolution of the specifically Neanderthal characteristics through free interbreeding over a broad geographical range. Fossil evidence suggests that the Neanderthals inhabited a vast area from Europe through the Middle East and into Central Asia from approximately 100,000 years ago until 35,000 years ago. Then, within a brief period of five to ten thousand years, they disappeared. Modern humans, not found in Europe prior to about 33,000 years ago, thenceforth became the sole inhabitants of the region. Anthropologists do not believe that the Neanderthals evolved into modern human beings. Despite the similarities between Neanderthal and modern human anatomy, the differences are major enough that, among a population as broad-ranging as the Neanderthals, such an evolution could not have taken place in a period of only ten thousand years. Furthermore, no fossils of types intermediate between Neanderthals and moderns have been found.

A major alternative hypothesis, advanced by E. Trinkaus and W.W. Howells, is that of localized evolution. Within a geographically concentrated population, free interbreeding could have produced far more pronounced genetic effects within a shorter time. Thus modern humans could have evolved relatively quickly, either from Neanderthals or from some other ancestral type, in isolation from the main Neanderthal population. These humans may have migrated throughout the Neanderthal areas, where they displaced or absorbed the original inhabitants. One hypothesis suggests that these "modern" humans immigrated to Europe from the Middle East.

No satisfactory explanation of why modern human beings replaced the Neanderthals has yet been found. Some have speculated that the modern humans wiped out the Neanderthals in warfare; however, there exists no archeological evidence of a hostile encounter. It has also been suggested that the Neanderthals failed to adapt to the onset of the last Ice Age; yet their thick bodies should have been heat-conserving and thus well-adapted to extreme cold. Finally, it is possible that the improved tools and hunting implements of the late Neanderthal period made the powerful Neanderthal physique less of an advantage than it had been previously. At the same time, the Neanderthals' need for a heavy diet to sustain this physique put them at a disadvantage compared to the less massive moderns. If this was the case, then it was improvements in human culture—including some introduced by the Neanderthals themselves—that made the Neanderthal obsolete.

34. Boule considered all of the following as evidence that Neanderthals were subhuman EXCEPT:

   A. posture.
   B. bone structure.
   C. cranial structure.
   D. ability to use tools.

GO ON TO THE NEXT PAGE.

35. The passage *best* supports which of the following conclusions?

   A. Neanderthals were less intelligent than early modern humans.

   B. Neanderthals were poorly adapted for survival.

   C. There was probably no contact between Neanderthals and early modern humans.

   D. Neanderthals may have had a capacity for religious and abstract thought.

36. According to the passage, the latest that any Neanderthal might have existed was:

   A. 100,000 years ago.

   B. 35,000 years ago.

   C. 33,000 years ago.

   D. 25,000 years ago.

37. By inference from the passage, the most important evidence that Neanderthals did NOT evolve into modern humans is the:

   A. major anatomical differences between Neanderthals and modern humans.

   B. brief time in which Neanderthals disappeared.

   C. difference in the geographical ranges of Neanderthals and modern humans.

   D. gap of many thousands of years between the latest Neanderthal fossils and the earliest modern human fossils.

38. All of the following are hypotheses about the disappearance of the Neanderthals EXCEPT:

   A. the Neanderthal physique became a handicap instead of an advantage.

   B. the Neanderthals failed to adapt to climatic changes.

   C. the Neanderthals evolved into modern humans.

   D. modern humans exterminated the Neanderthals.

39. It can be inferred from the passage that the rate of evolution is directly related to the:

   A. concentration of the species population.

   B. anatomical features of the species.

   C. rate of environmental change.

   D. adaptive capabilities of the species.

GO ON TO THE NEXT PAGE.

Passage VI (Questions 40–45)

The Russia that emerged from the terrible civil war after the 1917 Revolution was far from the Bolsheviks' original ideal of a nonexploitative society governed by workers and peasants. By 1921, the regime was weakened by widespread famine, persistent peasant revolts, a collapse of industrial production stemming from the civil war, and the consequent dispersal of the industrial working class—the Bolsheviks' original base of support. To buy time for recovery, the government in 1921 introduced the New Economic Policy, which allowed private trade in farm products (previously banned) and relied on a fixed grain tax instead of forced requisitions to provide food for the cities. The value of the ruble was stabilized. Trade unions were again allowed to seek higher wages and benefits, and even to strike. However, the Bolsheviks maintained a strict monopoly of power by refusing to legalize other parties.

After the death of the Revolution's undisputed leader, Lenin, in January 1924, disputes over the long-range direction of policy led to an open struggle among the main Bolshevik leaders. Since open debate was still possible within the Bolshevik Party in this period, several groups with differing programs emerged in the course of this struggle.

The program supported by Nikolai Bukharin—a major ideological leader of the Bolsheviks with no power base of his own—called for developing agriculture through good relations with wealthy peasants, or "kulaks." Bukharin favored gradual industrial development, or "advancing towards Socialism at a snail's pace." In foreign affairs, Bukharin's policy was to ally with non-Socialist regimes and movements that were favorable to Russia.

A faction led by Leon Trotsky, head of the Red Army and the most respected revolutionary leader after Lenin, called for rapid industrialization and greater central planning of the economy, financed by a heavy tax on the kulaks. Trotsky rejected the idea that a prosperous, humane Socialist society could be built in Russia alone (Stalin's slogan of "Socialism in One Country"), and therefore called for continued efforts to promote working-class revolutions abroad. As time went on, he became bitterly critical of the new privileged elite emerging within both the Bolshevik Party and the Russian state.

Joseph Stalin, General Secretary of the party, was initially considered a "center," conciliating figure, not clearly part of a faction. Stalin's eventual supremacy was ensured by three successive struggles within the party, and only during the last did his own program become clear.

First, in 1924–25, Stalin isolated Trotsky, allying for this purpose with Grigori Zinoviev and Lev Kamenev, Bolshevik leaders better known than Stalin himself whom Trotsky mistakenly considered his main rivals. Stalin maneuvered Trotsky out of leadership of the Red Army, his main potential power base. Next, Stalin turned on Zinoviev and Kamenev, using his powers as head of the Party organization to remove them from Party leadership in Leningrad and Moscow, their respective power bases. Trotsky, Zinoviev, and Kamenev then belatedly formed the "Joint Opposition" (1926–27). With Bukharin's help, Stalin easily outmaneuvered the Opposition: Bukharin polemicized against Trotsky, while Stalin prevented the newspapers from printing Trotsky's replies, organized gangs of toughs to beat up his followers, and transferred his supporters to administrative posts in remote regions. At the end of 1927, Stalin expelled Trotsky from the Bolshevik Party and exiled him. (Later, in 1940, he had him murdered.) Zinoviev and Kamenev, meanwhile, recanted their views in order to remain within the Party.

The final act now began. A move by kulaks to gain higher prices by holding grain off the market touched off a campaign against them by Stalin. Bukharin protested, but with the tradition of Party democracy now all but dead, Stalin had little trouble silencing Bukharin. Meanwhile, he began a campaign to force all peasants—not just kulaks—onto state-controlled "collective farms," and a crash industrialization program during which he deprived the trade unions of all rights and cut real wages by 50 percent. Out of the factional struggle in which he emerged by 1933 as sole dictator of Russia, Stalin's political program of building up heavy industry on the backs of both worker and peasant emerged with full clarity.

40. All of the following were among the factors contributing to the weakness of the Bolshevik regime in 1921 EXCEPT:

   A. the aftereffects of the civil war.
   B. low production.
   C. opposition by peasants.
   D. lack of democracy within the Party.

GO ON TO THE NEXT PAGE.

41. The main feature of the New Economic Policy of 1921 was:

    A. a strict economic centralization.
    B. stimulation of the economy through deliberate inflation.
    C. a limitation of trade union activity.
    D. a relaxation of economic controls.

42. An important feature of Bukharin's program was:

    A. a tax on the peasants.
    B. avoiding confrontations with the trade unions.
    C. forming alliances with friendly foreign regimes.
    D. maintaining open debate within the Party.

43. According to the passage, a similarity between Stalin and Trotsky was their attitude and policy toward:

    A. the elite of the Bolshevik Party.
    B. the importance of industrialization.
    C. democracy within the party.
    D. trade unions.

44. In his struggle with rival factions of the Party, Stalin was apparently MOST helped by:

    A. his control of the party organization.
    B. his control of the army.
    C. Trotsky's misjudgment of threats to his position.
    D. the appearance of standing above factional politics.

45. The passage supports the idea that struggles within the Bolshevik Party were primarily:

    A. reflections of struggles among important groups in the general population.
    B. the result of differences over economic policy.
    C. the result of differences over foreign policy.
    D. caused by Russian social elites outside the Party.

GO ON TO THE NEXT PAGE.

Passage VII (Questions 46–53)

One of the basic principles of ecology is that population size is to some extent a function of available food resources. Recent field experiments demonstrate that the interrelationship may be far
5 more complex than hitherto imagined. Specifically, the browsing of certain rodents appears to trigger biochemical reactions in the plants they feed on that help regulate the size of the rodent populations. Two such examples of
10 phytochemical regulation (regulation involving plant chemistry) have been reported so far.

Patricia Berger and her colleagues at the University of Utah have demonstrated the instrumentality of 6-methoxybenzoxazolinone (6-
15 MBOA) in triggering reproductive behavior in the mountain vole (*Microtus montanus*), a small rodent resembling the field mouse. 6-MBOA forms in young mountain grasses in response to browsing by predators such as voles. The
20 experimenters fed rolled oats coated with 6-MBOA to nonbreeding winter populations of *Microtus*. After three weeks, the sample populations revealed a high incidence of pregnancy among the females and pronounced
25 swelling of the testicles among the males. Control populations receiving no 6-MBOA revealed no such signs. Since the timing of reproductive effort is crucial to the short-lived vole in an environment in which the onset of vegetative growth can vary by as
30 much as two months, the phytochemical triggering of copulatory behavior in *Microtus* represents a significant biological adaptation.

A distinct example is reported by John Bryant of the University of Alaska. In this case, plants
35 seem to have adopted a form of phytochemical self-defense against the depredations of the snowshoe hare (*Lepus americanus*) of Canada and Alaska. Every ten years or so, for reasons that are not entirely understood, the *Lepus* population swells
40 dramatically. The result is intense overbrowsing of early and midsuccessional deciduous trees and shrubs. Bryant has shown that, as if in response, four common boreal forest trees favored by *Lepus* produce adventitious shoots high in terpene and
45 phenolic resins that effectively discourage hare browsing. He treated mature non-resinous willow twigs with resinous extracts from the adventitious shoots of other plants and placed treated and untreated bundles at hare feeding stations, weighing

50 them at the end of each day. Bryant found that bundles containing only half the resin concentration of natural twigs were left untouched. The avoidance of these unpalatable resins, he concludes, may play a significant role in the subsequent decline in the
55 *Lepus* population to its normal level.

These results suggest obvious areas for further research. For example, observational data should be reviewed to see whether the periodic population explosions among the prolific lemming (like the
60 vole and the snowshoe hare, a small rodent in a marginal northern environment) occur during years in which there is an early onset of vegetative growth; if so, a triggering mechanism similar to that found in the vole may be involved.

46. The author of the passage is primarily concerned to:
   A. review some findings suggesting biochemical regulation of predator populations by their food sources.
   B. outline the role of 6-MBOA in regulating the population of browsing animals.
   C. summarize available data on the relationship between food resources and population size.
   D. argue that earlier researchers have misunderstood the relationship between food supply and population size.

47. The passage describes the effect of 6-MBOA on voles as a "significant biological adaptation" (line 32) because it:
   A. limits reproductive behavior in times of food scarcity.
   B. leads the vole population to seek available food resources.
   C. tends to ensure the survival of the species in a situation of fluctuating food supply.
   D. maximizes the survival prospects of individual voles.

GO ON TO THE NEXT PAGE.

48. It can be inferred that the study of lemmings proposed by the author would probably:

A. fully explain the interrelationship between food supply and reproductive behavior in northern rodent populations.

B. disprove the conclusions of Berger and her colleagues.

C. be irrelevant to the findings of Berger and her colleagues.

D. provide evidence indicating whether the conclusions of Berger and her colleagues can be generalized.

49. The statement: "The interrelationship may be far more complex than hitherto imagined" (lines 4–5) suggests that scientists previously believed that:

A. the amount of food available is the only food factor that affects population size.

B. reproductive behavior is independent of environmental factors.

C. food resources biochemically affect reproduction and the lifespan of some species.

D. population size is not influenced by available food resources.

50. The experiments described in the passage involved all of the following EXCEPT:

A. measuring alterations in reproductive organs after a specific compound was ingested.

B. testing whether breeding behavior could be induced in normally nonbreeding animals by a change in diet.

C. measuring animals' consumption of treated and untreated foods.

D. measuring changes in the birth rate of test animals as opposed to control animals.

51. Bryant's interpretation of the results of his experiment (lines 52–55) depends on which of the following assumptions?

A. The response of *Lepus* to resinous substances in nature may be different from its response under experimental conditions.

B. The decennial rise in the *Lepus* population is triggered by an unknown phytochemical response.

C. Many *Lepus* will starve to death rather than eat resinous shoots or change their diet.

D. *Lepus* learns to search for alternative food sources once resinous shoots are encountered.

52. The experiments performed by Berger and Bryant BOTH study:

I. the effect of diet on reproduction in rodents.

II. a relationship between food source and population size.

III. phytochemical phenomena in northern environments.

A. II only

B. III only

C. I and II only

D. II and III only

53. The author provides specific information to answer which of the following questions?

A. Why does 6-MBOA form in response to browsing?

B. Why is the timing of the voles' reproductive effort important?

C. Are phytochemical reactions found only in northern environments?

D. How does 6-MBOA trigger reproductive activity in the montane vole?

GO ON TO THE NEXT PAGE.

Passage VIII (Questions 54–58)

In examining "myths of women" in literature, Simone de Beauvoir found the images put forward by Stendhal romantic, yet feministic. Stendhal's ideal woman was the one best able to reveal him to himself. For Stendhal, such a task required an equal. Women's emancipation was required, then, not simply in the name of liberty, but—more importantly—for the sake of individual happiness and fulfillment.

De Beauvoir wrote: "Stendhal wants his mistress intelligent, cultivated, free in spirit and behavior: an equal." Love, in Stendhal's scheme, will be more true if woman, being man's equal, is able to understand him more completely.

De Beauvoir found it rather refreshing—a kind of relief—that in Stendhal, at least, we can find a man who lived among women of flesh and blood. He rejected the mystification of women: his women were "not fury, nymph, morning star, nor siren, but human." Humanity sufficed for Stendhal, and no dream or myth could have been more entrancing.

Stendhal believes that the human, living souls of women, having rejected "the heavy sleep in which humanity is mired," may rise through passion to heroism, if they can find an objective worthy of them—an objective worthy of their spiritual and creative powers, their energies, and the ferocity and purity of total dedication. Certainly Stendhal believes such an objective exists for woman, and it is man. It is in this belief that Stendhal becomes ultimately unsatisfying to de Beauvoir. While Stendhal does grant women emotions, aspirations, and some sense of self, the only way he believes they can fully realize and fulfill their own selves is through man. It is in loving a man that the ennui of these truly living souls is driven away. Any boredom—any lack of focus, in essence, the lack of men—represents also a lack of any reason for living or dying, absolute stagnation. Meanwhile, passion—the love of a man—has an aim and that is enough justification for woman's life.

Yet de Beauvoir is still compelled by Stendhal. She finds him unique—or, at least, distinct—in going to the point of projecting himself into a female character. He does not "hover over" Lamiel, but assumes her destiny. On account of that, de Beauvoir notes, "Lamiel's outline remains somewhat speculative," but also singularly significant.

Lamiel is typical of Stendhal's women. Her creator has raised every imaginable obstacle before her: she is a poor peasant, raised by coarse, ignorant people imbued with all sorts of common prejudices. But, as de Beauvoir notes, "she clears from her path all moral barriers once she understands the full meaning of the little words: 'that's silly.' It is her freedom of mind that allows her to see through the meaninglessness and superficiality of so much social ritual, so that she may act in the world in her own fashion, responding fully to the impulses of her own curiosity and ambition, and shaping a destiny worthy of herself in a mediocre world."

In this, Lamiel conveys Stendhal's ultimate message to his readers: There is no comfortable place for great souls in society as it exists. It is in this sense that his men and women are the same: equals. Together, two who may have the chance to know each other in love, man and woman, defy time and universe—and come into absolute harmony with it. Such a couple is sufficient unto itself and realizes the absolute.

54. According to the passage, Stendhal believed that in order to experience self-realization, an individual requires the presence of:

A. a muse.
B. God.
C. an equal.
D. family.

55. The author suggests de Beauvoir considers Stendhal's portrait of Lamiel "somewhat speculative" (lines 47–48) because Stendhal:

A. bases his story upon myths.
B. sensationalizes his plot.
C. takes on the identity of a woman.
D. exaggerates the aspirations of his female characters.

56. The passage mentions that de Beauvoir saw the mystification of women in all of the following forms EXCEPT:

A. nymph.
B. morning star.
C. fury.
D. mistress.

GO ON TO THE NEXT PAGE.

57. It can be inferred from the passage that Stendhal's notion of love between a man and woman both includes and requires:

A. faithfulness in the relationship.
B. the mystification of woman.
C. understanding of each other.
D. the blessing of the union before God.

58. The author states that de Beauvoir finds Stendhal "ultimately unsatisfying" (line 31) in that Stendhal:

A. stifles the lively spirits of women.
B. reduces women to mere flesh and blood.
C. defines the fulfillment of women by way of men.
D. refuses to acknowledge the aspirations of women.

GO ON TO THE NEXT PAGE.

Passage IX (Questions 59–65)

The population of the United States is growing older and will continue to do so until well into the next century. For the first time in American history, elders outnumber teenagers. The U.S. Census Bureau projects that 39 million Americans will be 65 or older by the year 2010, 51 million by 2020, and 65 million by 2030. This demographic trend is due mainly to two factors: increased life expectancy, and the occurrence of a "baby boom" in the generation born immediately after World War II. People are living well beyond the average life expectancy in greater numbers than ever before, too. In fact, the number of U.S. citizens 85 years old and older is growing six times as fast as the rest of the population.

The "graying" of the United States is also due in large measure to the aging of the generation born after World War II, the "baby boomers." The baby boom peaked in 1957, with over 4.3 million births that year. More than 75 million Americans were born between 1946 and 1964, the largest generation in U.S. history. Today, millions of "boomers" are already moving into middle age; in less than two decades, they will join the ranks of America's elderly.

What will be the social, economic, and political consequences of the aging of America? One likely development will involve a gradual restructuring of the family unit, moving away from the traditional nuclear family and towards an extended, multigenerational family dominated by elders, not by their adult children.

The aging of the U.S. population is also likely to have far-reaching effects on the nation's workforce. In 1989 there were approximately 3.5 workers for every person 65 and older; by the year 2030, there'll be only 2 workers for every person 65 and older. As the number of available younger workers shrinks, elderly people will become more attractive as prospective employees. Many will simply retain their existing jobs beyond the now-mandatory retirement age of 65. In fact, the phenomenon of early retirement, which has transformed the U.S. workforce over the past four decades, will probably become a thing of the past. In 1950, about 50 percent of all 65-year-old men still worked; today, only 15 percent of them do. The median retirement age is currently 61. Yet recent surveys show that almost half of today's retirees would prefer to be working, and in decades to come, their counterparts will be doing just that.

Finally, the great proportional increase in the number of older Americans will have significant effects on the nation's economy in the areas of Social Security and health care. A recent government survey showed that 77 percent of elderly Americans have annual incomes of less than $20,000; only 3 percent earn more than $50,000. As their earning power declines and their need for health care increases, most elderly Americans come to depend heavily on federal and state subsidies. With the advent of Social Security in 1935, and Medicaid/Medicare in 1965, the size of those subsidies has grown steadily until by 1990, spending on the elderly accounted for 30 percent of the annual federal budget.

Considering these figures, and the fact that the elderly population will double within the next forty years, it's clear that major government policy decisions lie ahead. In the first 50 years of its existence, for example, the Social Security fund has received $55 billion more in employee/employer contributions than it has paid out in benefits to the elderly. Yet time and again the federal government has "borrowed" this surplus without repaying it in order to pay interest on the national debt.

Similarly, the Medicaid/Medicare system is threatened by the continuous upward spiral of medical costs. The cost of caring for disabled elderly Americans is expected to double in the next decade alone. And millions of Americans of all ages are currently unable to afford private health insurance. In fact, the United States is practically unique among developed nations in lacking a national health care system. Its advocates say such a system would be far less expensive than the present state of affairs, but the medical establishment and various special-interest groups have so far blocked legislation aimed at creating it. Nonetheless, within the next few decades, an aging U.S. population may well demand that such a program be implemented.

59. Based on the information contained in the passage, which of the following statements about the U.S. elderly population is true?

   A. It is largely responsible for the nation's current housing shortage.
   B. It is expected to double within the next forty years.
   C. It is the wealthiest segment of the U.S. population.
   D. It represents almost 30 percent of the U.S. population.

GO ON TO THE NEXT PAGE.

60. According to the passage, the majority of elderly people in the United States:

A. currently earn less than $20,000 per year.
B. will suffer some sort of disability between the ages of 65 and 75.
C. have been unable to purchase their own homes.
D. continue to work at least 20 hours per week.

61. The fact that health care costs for disabled elderly Americans are expected to double in the next ten years indicates that:

A. the federal government will be unable to finance a national health care system.
B. the Medicaid/Medicare system will probably become even more expensive in the future.
C. money will have to be borrowed from the Social Security fund in order to finance the Medicaid/Medicare system.
D. "baby boomers" will be unable to receive federal health benefits as they grow older.

62. According to the U.S. Census Bureau, today's elderly population is:

A. larger than the current population of teenagers.
B. larger than the current population of "boomers."
C. smaller than the number of elderly people in 1950.
D. smaller than the number of elderly people in 1970.

63. The author speculates that, in future decades, the typical U.S. family will probably be:

A. youth oriented.
B. subsidized by Social Security.
C. multigenerational.
D. wealthier than today's family.

64. The author suggests that, over the past three decades, many of today's elderly people:

A. supplemented their incomes by working past the age of retirement.
B. lost their Social Security benefits.
C. have experienced a doubling in their cost of living.
D. have come to depend heavily on government subsidies.

65. According to the author, the federal government has not yet instituted a program mandating health care for all U.S. citizens because:

A. the federal deficit must first be eliminated.
B. such a program would be too expensive.
C. legislative lobbies have prevented it.
D. Medicaid and Medicare have made it unnecessary.

STOP. IF YOU FINISH BEFORE TIME HAS EXPIRED, CHECK YOUR WORK. YOU MAY GO BACK TO ANY QUESTION IN THIS PART ONLY.

Physical Sciences

Time: 100 Minutes

Questions: 66–142

DIRECTIONS:

You are allotted 100 minutes to work on this part of the exam. You may work only on the Physical Sciences part during that time. Should you finish early, you are permitted to check your work in this part of the exam only.

PHYSICAL SCIENCES

DIRECTIONS: The majority of the questions in the following Physical Sciences test are arranged in groups addressing a preceding descriptive passage. Select the single best answer to each question in the group after thorough analysis of the passage. Some discrete questions are not based on a descriptive passage. Similarly, select the best answer to these questions. If you are not certain of an answer, eliminate the answer choices known to be incorrect and select an answer from the remaining alternatives. Indicate your answer selection by blackening the corresponding oval on your answer sheet. A periodic table is provided below for your assistance with the passages and questions.

Periodic Table of the Elements

1 H 1.0																	2 He 4.0
3 Li 6.9	4 Be 9.0											5 B 10.8	6 C 12.0	7 N 14.0	8 O 16.0	9 F 19.0	10 Ne 20.2
11 Na 23.0	12 Mg 24.3											13 Al 27.0	14 Si 28.1	15 P 31.0	16 S 32.1	17 Cl 35.5	18 Ar 39.9
19 K 39.1	20 Ca 40.1	21 Sc 45.0	22 Ti 47.9	23 V 50.9	24 Cr 52.0	25 Mn 54.9	26 Fe 55.8	27 Co 58.9	28 Ni 58.7	29 Cu 63.5	30 Zn 65.4	31 Ga 69.7	32 Ge 72.6	33 As 74.9	34 Se 79.0	35 Br 79.9	36 Kr 83.8
37 Rb 85.5	38 Sr 87.6	39 Y 88.9	40 Zr 91.2	41 Nb 92.9	42 Mo 95.9	43 Tc (98)	44 Ru 101.1	45 Rh 102.9	46 Pd 106.4	47 Ag 107.9	48 Cd 112.4	49 In 114.8	50 Sn 118.7	51 Sb 121.8	52 Te 127.6	53 I 126.9	54 Xe 131.3
55 Cs 132.9	56 Ba 137.3	57 La* 138.9	72 Hf 178.5	73 Ta 180.9	74 W 183.9	75 Re 186.2	76 Os 190.2	77 Ir 192.2	78 Pt 195.1	79 Au 197.0	80 Hg 200.6	81 Tl 204.4	82 Pb 207.2	83 Bi 209.0	84 Po (209)	85 At (210)	86 Rn (222)
87 Fr (223)	88 Ra 226.0	89 Ac† 227.0	104 Unq (261)	105 Unp (262)	106 Unh (263)	107 Uns (262)	108 Uno (265)	109 Une (267)									

*	58 Ce 140.1	59 Pr 140.9	60 Nd 144.2	61 Pm (145)	62 Sm 150.4	63 Eu 152.0	64 Gd 157.3	65 Tb 158.9	66 Dy 162.5	67 Ho 164.9	68 Er 167.3	69 Tm 168.9	70 Yb 173.0	71 Lu 175.0
†	90 Th 232.0	91 Pa (231)	92 U 238.0	93 Np (237)	94 Pu (244)	95 Am (243)	96 Cm (247)	97 Bk (247)	98 Cf (251)	99 Es (252)	100 Fm (257)	101 Md (258)	102 No (259)	103 Lr (260)

Passage I (Questions 66–70)

A continuous spectrum of light, sometimes called blackbody radiation, is emitted from a region of the Sun called the photosphere. Although the continuous spectrum contains light of all wavelengths, the intensity of the emitted light is much greater at some wavelengths than at others. The relationship between the most intense wavelength of blackbody radiation and the temperature of the emitting body is given by Wien's law, $\lambda = 2.9 \times 10^6/T$, where λ is the wavelength in nanometers and T is the temperature in kelvins.

As the blackbody radiation from the Sun passes through the cooler gases in the Sun's atmosphere, some of the photons are absorbed by the atoms in these gases. A photon will be absorbed if it has just enough energy to excite an electron from a lower energy state to a higher one. The absorbed photon will have an energy equal to the energy difference between these two states. The energy of a photon is given by $E = hf = hc/\lambda$, where $h = 6.63 \times 10^{-34}$ J $\cdot$ s is Planck's constant and $c = 3 \times 10^8$ m/s is the speed of light in a vacuum.

The Sun is composed primarily of hydrogen. Electron transitions in the hydrogen atom from energy state $n = 2$ to higher energy states are listed below along with the energy of the absorbed photon.

Final Energy State	Energy ($\times 10^{-19}$ J)
$n = 3$	3.02
$n = 4$	4.08
$n = 5$	4.57
$n = 6$	4.84
$n = \infty$	5.44

66. If the temperature of the Sun's photosphere is 5,800 K, what wavelength of radiation does the Sun emit with the greatest intensity?

A.   2 nm
B.   50 nm
C.   500 nm
D. 4,500 nm

67. From the data in the table, what is the approximate wavelength of a photon emitted in the electron transition from energy state $n = 4$ to energy state $n = 3$?

A.   5 nm
B.   30 nm
C.   100 nm
D. 2,000 nm

68. The energy absorbed by a hydrogen atom as its electron undergoes a transition from the $n = 1$ energy state to the $n = \infty$ state is: (Note: The $n = 1$ energy state is the ground state of hydrogen.)

A. infinite.
B. equal to the binding energy of the electron.
C. equal to the energy of a zero frequency photon.
D. smaller than the energy absorbed in the $n = 2$ to $n = \infty$ transition.

69. At the center of the visible spectrum is light with a wavelength of $\lambda = 550$ nm. What is the frequency of this light?

A. 9.0×10^8 Hz
B. 1.8×10^{12} Hz
C. 5.4×10^{14} Hz
D. 1.8×10^{16} Hz

70. If a star suddenly doubles in size but remains at the same temperature, how does its continuous spectrum change?

A. The peak intensity occurs at the same wavelength.
B. The peak intensity occurs at a longer wavelength.
C. The peak intensity occurs at a shorter wavelength.
D. The intensity peak narrows.

GO ON TO THE NEXT PAGE.

Passage II (Questions 71–77)

The lead-acid battery, also called a lead storage battery, is the battery of choice for starting automobiles. It contains 6 cells connected in series, each composed of a lead oxide cathode "sandwiched" between 2 lead anodes. Insulating separators are placed between the electrodes to prevent internal short-circuits. Aqueous sulfuric acid is the electrolyte.

When the battery is being discharged, the following reaction takes place.

$$Pb(s) + PbO_2(s) + 2 H_2SO_4(aq) \rightarrow 2 PbSO_4(s) + 2 H_2O$$

Reaction 1

The electrode reactions, both written as reductions, are shown in Table 1.

Table 1

Half-reaction	$E°$ (V)
$PbO_2(s) + SO_4^{2-} (aq) + 4H^+ (aq) + 2e^- \rightarrow$ $PbSO_4 (s) + 2H_2O$	1.69
$PbSO_4 (s) + 2e^- \rightarrow Pb (s) + SO_4^{2-} (aq)$	–0.36

As a car operates, the battery is recharged by electricity produced by the car's alternator, an AC generator whose ultimate power source is the car's internal combustion engine. In spite of this, batteries eventually lose their power. The battery is said to be "dead" when Reaction 1 has proceeded completely to the right.

71. How many cells would be required to produce a 20-volt lead-acid battery of the type described in the passage?

   A. 5
   B. 10
   C. 15
   D. 20

72. Which reaction takes place at the anode as the battery is discharging?

   A. The first half-reaction, proceeding to the left
   B. The first half-reaction, proceeding to the right
   C. The second half-reaction, proceeding to the left
   D. The second half-reaction, proceeding to the right

73. Where does oxidation occur in the lead storage battery?

   A. At the lead oxide cathodes
   B. At the lead oxide anodes
   C. At the lead cathodes
   D. At the lead anodes

74. Which of the following occurs as the battery is being recharged?

   A. An increase in the concentration of H^+ ions
   B. An increase in the amount of $PbSO_4$ and lead
   C. An increase in the concentration of H_2O
   D. A decrease in the amount of PbO_2

75. The graph below shows the change in potential versus time of a 12 V lead storage battery during discharge.

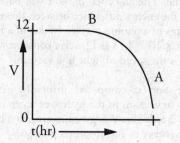

Which of the following is true?

   A. The electrolyte density at point A is greater than it is at point B.
   B. The electrolyte density at point A is less than it is at point B.
   C. The electrolyte density at point A is the same as that at point B.
   D. The electrolyte density at points A and B cannot be compared without more information.

76. Currents as small as 0.1 A can be fatal to humans. If the typical resistance of the human body is 10 kW, what is the minimum voltage that could be fatal?

   A.   0.1 V
   B.   1 V
   C.   100 V
   D. 1,000 V

GO ON TO THE NEXT PAGE.

77. Often in cold weather the battery goes "dead." Thermodynamic data confirms that the voltage of most electrochemical cells decrease with decreasing temperature. If the battery is warmed to room temperature, it often recovers its ability to deliver normal power. The battery appeared "dead" because:

  I. the resistance of the electrolyte had decreased.
  II. the viscosity of the electrolyte had increased.
  III. the viscosity of the electrolyte had decreased.

  A. I only
  B. II only
  C. I and II only
  D. I and III only

GO ON TO THE NEXT PAGE.

Passage III (Questions 78–82)

The resistance of a resistor is defined as the ratio of the voltage drop across it to the current passing through it. The resistance of a resistor can be measured using the circuit illustrated in Figure 1.

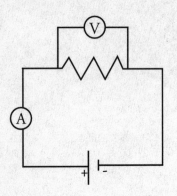

Figure 1

In the above circuit, a variable voltage source with negligible internal resistance is connected to a resistor. The voltage across the resistor is measured by a voltmeter and the current through the resistor is measured by an ammeter.

Additional resistors may be added to the circuit. The total resistance can be calculated as follows: If R_1 and R_2 are two resistances of two resistors, then the total resistance is given by $R_{total} = R_1 + R_2$ when the resistors are connected in series, and by $1/R_{total} = 1/R_1 + 1/R_2$ when the resistors are connected in parallel.

Circuits similar to the one above are used in the common household appliance known as the toaster. The rate by which energy in the form of heat is dissipated by the resistor equals I^2R, where I is the current that passes through the resistor and R is the resistance of the resistor. Energy is dissipated in a resistor because moving electrons collide with atoms in the resistor, causing the atoms to vibrate.

78. The variable voltage supply in the circuit in Figure 1 is replaced by a battery connected in series with the resistor and ammeter. The battery has a small internal resistance. How will the circuit be affected?

- **A.** The current measured by the ammeter at a specific voltage will be larger in the circuit with the battery.
- **B.** The current measured by the ammeter at a specific voltage will be smaller in the circuit with the battery.
- **C.** The resistance of the resistor at a specific voltage will be larger in the circuit with the battery.
- **D.** The resistance of the resistor at a specific voltage will be smaller in the circuit with the battery.

79. In which direction do the electrons travel and in which direction does the current flow in the circuit in Figure 1?

- **A.** The electrons travel clockwise, and the current flows counterclockwise.
- **B.** The electrons travel clockwise, and the current flows clockwise.
- **C.** The electrons travel counterclockwise, and the current flows clockwise.
- **D.** The electrons travel counterclockwise, and the current flows counterclockwise.

80. In order for the ammeter to have a very small effect on the current flowing through the resistor, the ammeter should:

- **A.** be connected to the resistor with insulated wire.
- **B.** be connected nearest to the positive terminal of the voltage source.
- **C.** have a very low resistance.
- **D.** be sensitive to currents flowing either way around the circuit.

GO ON TO THE NEXT PAGE.

81. As current passes through a resistor, the temperature of the resistor will increase. Which of the following is a reason the temperature increases?

   A. The average kinetic energy of the atoms in the resistor increases as a result of the collisions with the electrons in the current.
   B. The average potential energy of the atoms in the resistor increases as a result of the collisions with the electrons in the current.
   C. The average kinetic energy of the electrons in the current increases as a result of the collisions with the atoms in the resistor.
   D. The average potential energy of the electrons in the current increases as a result of the collisions with the atoms in the resistor.

82. What is the energy delivered to a piece of toast in one second when it is inside a toaster in which a 4×10^{-3}-A current passes through a 10-kΩ resistor?

   A. 0.04 J
   B. 0.16 J
   C. 2.5 J
   D. 40 J

GO ON TO THE NEXT PAGE.

Passage IV (Questions 83–88)

It is critical that human blood be kept at a pH of approximately 7.4. Decreased or increased blood pH are called acidosis and alkalosis respectively; both are serious metabolic problems that can cause death. The table below lists the major buffers found in the blood and/or kidneys.

Table 1

Buffer	pK_a of a typical conjugate acid:[1]
$HCO_3^- \rightleftharpoons CO_2 + H_2O$	6.1
Histidine side chains	6.3
$HPO_4^{2-} \rightleftharpoons H_2PO_4^-$	6.8
Organic phosphates	7.0
N-terminal amino groups	8.0
$NH_3 \rightleftharpoons NH_4^+$	9.2

[1] For buffers in many of these categories, there is a range of actual pK_a values.

The relationship between blood pH and the pK_a of any buffer can be described by the Henderson-Hasselbach equation:

$$pH = pK_a + \log([\text{conjugate base}]/[\text{conjugate acid}])$$

Equation 1

Bicarbonate, the most important buffer in the plasma, enters the blood in the form of carbon dioxide, a byproduct of metabolism, and leaves in two forms: exhaled CO_2 and excreted bicarbonate. Blood pH can be adjusted rapidly by changes in the rate of CO_2 exhalation. The reaction given below, which is catalyzed by carbonic anhydrase in the erythrocytes, describes how bicarbonate and CO_2 interact in the blood.

$$CO_2 + H_2O \rightleftharpoons H^+ + HCO_3^-$$

Reaction 1

83. If the pH of blood were to increase to 7.6, what would be the likely outcome?

   A. An increase in carbonic anhydrase activity
   B. A decrease in carbonic anhydrase activity
   C. An increase in the rate of CO_2 exhalation
   D. A decrease in the rate of CO_2 exhalation

84. The equilibrium as shown in Reaction 1 is most likely to proceed through which of the following intermediates?

   A. H_2CO_3
   B. $2H^+$ and CO_3^{2-}
   C. CO_2 and H_3O^+
   D. CO_2 and H_2

85. What would be the order of conjugate acid strength in the following buffers?

   A. Histidine side chains=organic phosphates > NH_4^+
   B. NH_4^+ > organic phosphates > histidine side chains
   C. Histidine side chains > organic phosphates > NH_4^+
   D. NH_4^+ > organic phosphates=histidine side chains

86. The following graph shows the titration of 0.01 M H_3PO_4 with 10 M NaOH. Within which area of the titration curve will the concentration of $H_2PO_4^-$ become equal to that of HPO_4^{2-}?

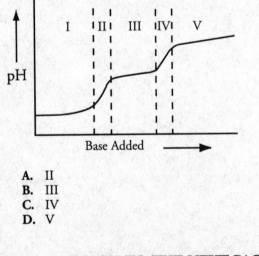

   A. II
   B. III
   C. IV
   D. V

GO ON TO THE NEXT PAGE.

87. How does the titration of a weak monoprotic acid with a strong base differ from the titration of a strong monoprotic acid with a strong base?

- **A.** The equivalence point will occur at a higher pH.
- **B.** The equivalence point will occur at a lower pH.
- **C.** The equivalence point will occur at the same pH.
- **D.** Whether the equivalence point is higher or lower depends on the particular acids used.

88. What would be the nature of the compensatory change that would take place in response to acidosis caused by organic acids?

- **A.** Breathing rate would increase and total blood CO_2/HCO_3^- concentration would increase
- **B.** Breathing rate would increase and total blood CO_2/HCO_3^- concentration would decrease
- **C.** Breathing rate would decrease and total blood CO_2/HCO_3^- concentration would increase
- **D.** Breathing rate would decrease and total blood CO_2/HCO_3^- concentration would decrease

GO ON TO THE NEXT PAGE.

Questions 89 through 93 are **NOT** based on a descriptive passage.

89. The mouthpiece of a telephone handset has a mass of 100 g, and the earpiece has a mass of 150 g. To balance the handset on one finger, that finger must be: (Note: Assume the bridge connecting the mouthpiece and the earpiece has a negligible mass.)

   A. one and one half times farther from the earpiece than from the mouthpiece.
   B. two times farther from the earpiece than from the mouthpiece.
   C. one and one half times farther from the mouthpiece than from the earpiece.
   D. two times farther from the mouthpiece than from the earpiece.

90. The reaction below is not spontaneous at any temperature.

$$2ICl(g) \rightarrow I_2(g) + Cl_2(g)$$

   Which of the following is TRUE?

   A. $\Delta H > 0, \Delta S > 0$
   B. $\Delta H > 0, \Delta S < 0$
   C. $\Delta H < 0, \Delta S > 0$
   D. $\Delta H < 0, \Delta S < 0$

91. Which of the following is the reason that water boils at a much higher temperature than hydrogen sulfide?

   A. The intramolecular O–H bonds are stronger than the intramolecular S–H bonds.
   B. The enthalpy of vaporization of water is less than that of hydrogen sulfide.
   C. The relative molecular mass of water is less than that of hydrogen sulfide.
   D. The intermolecular O–H bonds are stronger than the intermolecular S–H bonds.

92. In the figure below, aqueous solutions A and B are separated by a semipermeable membrane. Which of the following will occur?

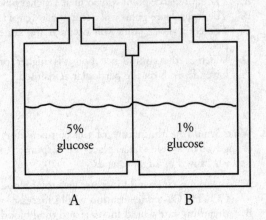

   A. Glucose molecules will move from side B to side A.
   B. Glucose molecules will move from side A to side B.
   C. Both water and glucose molecules will move from side A to side B.
   D. Water molecules will move from side B to side A.

93. What is the normality of a solution containing 49 g of H_3PO_4 (MW 98) in 2,000 mL of solution?

   A. 0.25
   B. 0.50
   C. 0.75
   D. 1.50

GO ON TO THE NEXT PAGE.

Passage V (Questions 94–98)

Band theory explains the conductivity of certain solids by stating that the atomic orbitals of the individual atoms in the solid merge to produce a series of atomic orbitals comprising the entire solid. The closely spaced energy levels of the orbitals form bands. The band corresponding to the outermost occupied subshell of the original atoms is called the valence band. If partially full, as in metals, it serves as a conduction band through which electrons can move freely. If the valence band is full, then electrons must be raised to a higher band for conduction to occur. The greater the band gap between the separate valence and conduction bands, the poorer the material's conductivity. Figure 1 shows the valence and conduction bands of a semiconductor, which is intermediate in conductivity between conductors and insulators.

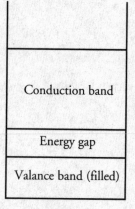

Figure 1

When silicon, a semiconductor with tetrahedral covalent bonds, is heated, a few electrons escape into the conduction band. Doping the silicon with a few phosphorus atoms provides unbonded electrons that escape more easily, increasing conductivity. Doping with boron produces holes in the bonding structure, which may be filled by movement of nearby electrons within the lattice. When a semiconductor in an electric circuit has excess electrons on one side and holes on the other, electron flow occurs more easily from the side with excess electrons to the side with holes than in the reverse direction.

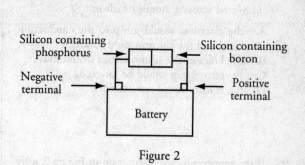

Figure 2

94. Why is iron a good conductor of electricity?

- **A.** Its $3d$ electrons only partially fill the valence band.
- **B.** The band gap is small.
- **C.** The $4s$ and $3d$ orbitals form a filled valence band.
- **D.** The energy levels of the atomic orbitals are closely spaced.

95. How could heat be expected to increase the conductivity of a semiconductor?

- **I.** By reducing collisions between moving electrons
- **II.** By breaking covalent bonds
- **III.** By raising electrons to a higher energy level

- **A.** I only
- **B.** III only
- **C.** I and III only
- **D.** II and III only

96. Why do phosphorus and boron atoms enhance the conductivity of silicon?

- **A.** Their electronegativity differs from that of silicon.
- **B.** They have different numbers of valence electrons.
- **C.** Their semimetallic nature makes them good semiconductors.
- **D.** They are better conductors than silicon even as pure substances.

GO ON TO THE NEXT PAGE.

97. The energy gap for pure silicon is about 1.1 electron volts. If a 1.5 volt electrical potential is connected across a sample of silicon:

    A. the electrons would jump to the conduction band and the silicon would conduct.
    B. the holes in the silicon lattice would move.
    C. the energy gap would be lowered.
    D. the silicon would not conduct.

98. If the semiconductor orientation in Figure 2 were reversed so that the boron-doped silicon were on the left and the phosphorus-doped silicon on the right, what could be said about the electron flow of the new setup?

    A. The electron flow is easier in the new direction than that of Figure 2.
    B. The electron flow is the same in either direction.
    C. The electron flow is harder in the new direction than that of Figure 2.
    D. The electrons cannot flow.

GO ON TO THE NEXT PAGE.

Passage VI (Questions 99–103)

A helium-neon gas discharge laser as shown in Figure 1 below generates a coherent beam of monochromatic light at a wavelength of 632.8 nm.

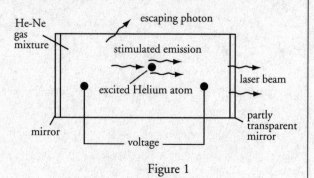

Figure 1

A discharge current of electrons is created in the tube by an applied voltage. When these electrons collide with the helium atoms, they can excite ground-state helium electrons to an energy level of 20.61 eV. The excited electrons cannot decay back to the ground state by emitting a photon because such a transition does not conserve angular momentum. Instead, if the excited helium atom collides with a neon atom, a ground-state electron in the neon atom can be excited to an energy level of 20.66 eV, and the helium electron can return to its ground state.

The above process occurs quite often in the tube until the percentage of neon atoms with electrons in the 20.66-eV energy level is greater than the percentage of neon atoms with electrons in lower levels. This condition is called a population inversion. An excited electron in one of the neon atoms can then spontaneously decay by emitting a photon of wavelength 632.8 nm in a random direction. The photon will stimulate the same transition in another excited atom. The photon radiated by this stimulated emission process travels in the same direction as the original photon. The resulting light is then reflected back and forth inside the tube until it escapes through the partially transparent mirror. (Note: A photon's energy in eV is given by $E = 1240/\lambda$, where λ is the photon's wavelength in nm. The helium and neon ground state energies are both 0 eV.)

99. What is the energy of the photon with wavelength 632.8 nm?

   A.   0.05 eV
   B.   1.96 eV
   C.   20.61 eV
   D.   20.66 eV

100. A population inversion exists when:

   A.   the percentage of neon atoms with electrons in the ground state is greater than the percentage of neon atoms with electrons in higher energy levels.
   B.   the percentage of neon atoms with electrons in a higher energy level is greater than the percentage of neon atoms with electrons in lower energy levels.
   C.   the percentage of neon atoms with electrons in a higher energy level is equal to the percentage of neon atoms with electrons in the ground state.
   D.   all the neon atoms have electrons in the ground state only.

101. A helium atom with an electron in the 20.61-eV energy level collides with a neon atom with an electron in the ground state. The result is that the helium electron returns to the ground state, and the ground state neon electron is excited to an energy level of 20.66 eV. What is the minimum kinetic energy lost by the helium atom?

   A.   0.05 eV
   B.   1.96 eV
   C.   10.3 eV
   D.   20.61 eV

102. A laser produces light with a wavelength of 200 nm at a power of 6.2×10^{15} eV/s. How many photons per second does this laser deliver?

   A. 1.0×10^{15}
   B. 2.0×10^{15}
   C. 4.0×10^{15}
   D. 10.0×10^{15}

GO ON TO THE NEXT PAGE.

103. Why is stimulated emission of photons necessary in order to produce a coherent beam of light instead of spontaneous emission alone?

A. Stimulated emission produces photons of higher energy than those produced by spontaneous emission.

B. Stimulated emission produces photons that travel in the same direction as the photon that induces their emission.

C. Stimulated emission produces photons with longer wavelengths than those produced by spontaneous emission.

D. Either spontaneous or stimulated emission alone would be sufficient to produce laser light.

GO ON TO THE NEXT PAGE.

Passage VII (Questions 104–109)

One of the most common methods that scientists use to determine the age of fossils is known as carbon dating. ^{14}C is an unstable isotope of carbon that undergoes beta decay with a half-life of approximately 5,730 years. Beta decay occurs when a neutron in the nucleus decays to form a proton and an electron which is ejected from the nucleus.

^{14}C is generated in the upper atmosphere when ^{14}N, the most common isotope of nitrogen, is bombarded by neutrons. This mechanism yields a global production rate of 7.5 kg per year of ^{14}C, which combines with oxygen in the atmosphere to produce carbon dioxide. Both the production and the decay of ^{14}C occur simultaneously. This process continues for many half-lives of ^{14}C until the total amount of ^{14}C approaches a constant.

A fixed fraction of the carbon ingested by all living organisms will be ^{14}C. Therefore, as long as an organism is alive, the ratio of ^{14}C to ^{12}C that it contains is constant. After the organism dies, no new ^{14}C is ingested, and the amount of ^{14}C contained in the organism will decrease by beta decay. The amount of ^{14}C that must have been present in the organism when it died can be calculated from the amount of ^{12}C present in a fossil. By comparing the amount of ^{14}C in the fossil to the calculated amount of ^{14}C that was present in the organism when it died, the age of the fossil can be determined.

104. The bones of a living adult human contain about 8 grams of ^{14}C at any given time. If a prehistoric human skeleton is found to contain 1 gram of ^{14}C, how long ago did the person die?

    A.   5,730 years
    B.   17,190 years
    C.   34,380 years
    D.   45,840 years

105. If the production rate of ^{14}C were to increase to 10 kg per year:

    A.   the number of ^{14}C atoms decaying per minute would increase.
    B.   the number of ^{14}C atoms decaying per minute would decrease.
    C.   the weight of ^{14}C on the earth would increase indefinitely.
    D.   the percentage of ^{14}C in living organisms would not change.

106. The method of carbon dating used to determine age depends upon the assumption that:

    A.   the half-life of ^{14}C changes when it is ingested.
    B.   all ingested ^{14}C is incorporated into the body.
    C.   the half-life of ^{14}C depends on the type of molecule in which it resides.
    D.   the half-life of ^{14}C does not depend upon conditions external to the nucleus.

107. In determining the age of the galaxy, a technique similar to carbon dating is used on stars with the radioactive isotope ^{232}Th, which has a half-life of 10^{10} years. ^{14}C is less suitable for this application because:

    A.   its half-life is too long.
    B. ^{14}C is more abundant in stars.
    C. ^{14}C is unstable.
    D.   its half-life is too short.

108. In generating ^{14}C in the upper atmosphere, a ^{14}N nucleus combines with a neutron to form a ^{14}C nucleus and:

    A.   a proton.
    B.   an electron.
    C.   a ^{4}He nucleus.
    D.   a neutron.

GO ON TO THE NEXT PAGE.

109. After a ^{14}C nucleus decays, the electron that is emitted enters lead and is stopped. What percentage of its kinetic energy does the electron transfer to lead?

    A.   25%
    B.   33%
    C.   50%
    D.   100%

GO ON TO THE NEXT PAGE.

Passage VIII (Questions 110–114)

Arsenic is widely distributed in sulfide ores of many metals and is obtained as a by product of copper smelting. The element, as well as many compounds of arsenic—for example, arsine, AsH_3—are extremely poisonous. Arsenic compounds, as might be expected, have found use in herbicides and pesticides, but have also been successful in some pharmacological agents. The first useful antisyphilitic agent, Salvarsan or 3,3'-diamino-4,4'-dihydroxyarsenobenzene dihydrochloride, is an arsenic compound. The element sublimes at 600°C, forming tetrahedral molecules, As_4. Arsenic is a metalloid, possessing properties characteristic of both metals and nonmetals. Ordinarily arsenic is a gray colored metallic-looking solid, but the vapor is yellow in color, has a garliclike odor, and is very poisonous. If the arsenic vapor is cooled rapidly, an unstable yellow crystalline allotrope consisting of As_4 molecules is produced.

The Marsh test, based on the instability of arsine, is a very sensitive test for the presence of arsenic. This test is commonly employed in the detection of arsenic poisoning—either before or after death. The apparatus for the Marsh test is shown in Figure 1.

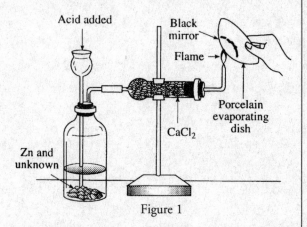

Figure 1

Typically, a sample, usually hair, is taken from a person suspected of being the victim of arsenic poisoning. This sample is then treated in such a way as to produce arsenic oxide, As_4O_6. The oxide is then placed into the apparatus shown in Figure 1 and reacted according to Reaction 1.

$As_4O_6 + 12\ Zn(s) + 24\ H^+(aq) \rightarrow 4\ AsH_3(g) + 12\ Zn^{2+}(aq) + 6H_2O$

Reaction 1

When the evolved arsine is ignited it decomposes into its elements. The arsenic vapor is rapidly cooled when it encounters the porcelain evaporating dish and deposits a black mirror of arsenic on the bottom, indicating the presence of arsenic in the original sample.

110. The phase diagram for arsenic is shown below. At what point does liquid arsenic exist?

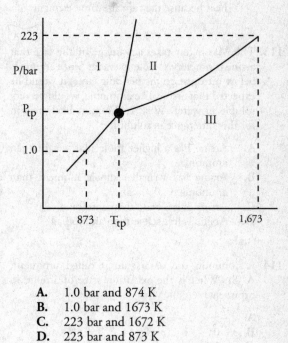

A. 1.0 bar and 874 K
B. 1.0 bar and 1673 K
C. 223 bar and 1672 K
D. 223 bar and 873 K

111. What is the most likely purpose of the calcium chloride in Figure 1?

A. To remove water from the evolved arsine gas.
B. To remove HCl from the evolved arsine gas.
C. To react with the zinc ion making the reaction go to completion.
D. To react with the evolved arsine gas.

GO ON TO THE NEXT PAGE.

112. If equal masses of gray arsenic and yellow arsenic are allowed to completely react with oxygen at 298 K and constant pressure to form As_4O_6, which would produce more heat and why?

   A. The yellow, because it is less stable than the gray.

   B. The gray, because it is more stable than the yellow.

   C. Both would produce the same amount of heat because they form the same product.

   D. Both would produce the same amount of heat because they are the same element.

113. The Marsh test takes advantage of the fact that arsine is not very soluble in water. Since arsenic is below nitrogen on the periodic table, it would be expected that arsine, like ammonia, would be very soluble in water. What is the most likely reason for this difference in solubility?

   A. Arsine has a higher molecular weight than ammonia.

   B. Arsine has a smaller dipole moment than ammonia.

   C. Arsine is less basic than ammonia.

   D. Arsine is less stable than ammonia.

114. A common ore of arsenic is called orpiment, As_2S_3. What is the oxidation state of arsenic in orpiment?

   A. −3

   B. 0

   C. +3

   D. +6

GO ON TO THE NEXT PAGE.

Questions 115 through 119 are **NOT** based on a descriptive passage.

115. What is the shape of a molecule of NH_3?

A. Trigonal planar
B. Pyramidal
C. Tetrahedral
D. Trigonal bipyramidal

116. A deep-sea research module has a volume of 150 m^3. If ocean water has an average density of 1025 kg/m^3, what will be the buoyant force on the module when it is completely submerged in the water? (Note: The acceleration due to gravity is 9.8 m/s^2.)

A. 9.8 N
B. 60 N
C. 1×10^3 N
D. 1.5×10^6 N

117. If a spring is 64 cm long when it is unstretched and is 8% longer when a 0.5 kg mass hangs from it, how long will it be with a 0.4 kg mass suspended from it?

A. 66 cm
B. 68 cm
C. 70 cm
D. 74 cm

118. Which of the following will halve the magnitude of the electrostatic force of attraction between two charged particles?

A. Doubling the distance between the particles
B. Halving the charge on each particle
C. Halving the charge on one of the particles only
D. Placing a positively charged particle midway between the particles

119. Which of the following is true when ice melts?

A. The changes in both enthalpy and entropy are positive.
B. The changes in both enthalpy and entropy are negative.
C. The change in enthalpy is positive; the change in entropy is negative.
D. The change in enthalpy is negative; the change in entropy is positive.

GO ON TO THE NEXT PAGE.

When softball players take batting practice, they often use a machine called an "automatic pitcher," which is essentially a cannon that uses air pressure to launch a projectile. In a prototype automatic pitcher, a softball is loaded into the barrel of the cannon and rests against a flat disk. This disk is locked into place, and a high air pressure is built up behind it. When the disk is released, the softball is pushed along the barrel of the cannon and ejected at a speed of v_0.

Figure 1 shows the batter and automatic pitcher. The angle of the barrel to the horizontal is θ. The unit vectors **i** and **j** point in the horizontal and vertical directions respectively.

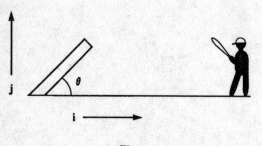

Figure 1

The height above the ground y of the softball as a function of time t is shown in Figure 2, where $t = 0$ at Point A, $t = t_B$ at Point B, and $t = t_C$ at Point C. The softball is ejected from the barrel of the cannon at Point A; it reaches its maximum height at Point B; and the batter hits the softball at Point C. (Note: Assume that the effects of air resistance are negligible, unless otherwise stated.)

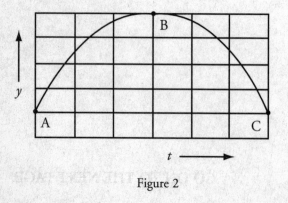

Figure 2

120. What physical quantity is NOT the same at Point C as it is at Point A?

A. The velocity of the softball
B. The speed of the softball
C. The gravitational potential energy of the softball
D. The horizontal component of the velocity of the softball

121. What is the acceleration of the softball t seconds after it exits the barrel?

A. $-g\,\mathbf{j}$
B. $-v_0/t\,\mathbf{i}$
C. $-v_0/t\,\mathbf{j}$
D. $-v_0/t\,\mathbf{i} - g\,\mathbf{j}$

122. How will v_0 change if the impulse on the softball remains the same but its mass is doubled?

A. It will decrease by a factor of 4.
B. It will decrease by a factor of 2.
C. It will not change.
D. It will increase by a factor of 2.

123. What is the ratio of the horizontal distance traveled by the softball at Point B to the horizontal distance traveled at Point C?

A. 5:1
B. 4:1
C. 3:3
D. 1:2

124. How does the work done by the automatic pitcher change as the angle of the barrel to the horizontal increases?

A. The work done increases, because the softball's maximum height increases.
B. The work done decreases, because the softball lands closer to the cannon.
C. The work done does not change, because the air pressure behind the disk is unchanged.
D. The work done does not change, because gravity is a conservative force.

GO ON TO THE NEXT PAGE.

Passage X (Questions 125–130)

There are two opposing theories of light: the particle theory and the wave theory. According to the particle theory, light is composed of a stream of tiny particles that are subject to the same physical laws as other types of elementary particles. One consequence of this is that light particles should travel in a straight line unless an external force acts on them. According to the wave theory, light is a wave that shares the characteristics of other waves. Among other things, this means that light waves should interfere with each other under certain conditions.

In support of the wave theory of light, Thomas Young's double slit experiment proves that light does indeed exhibit interference. Figure 1 shows the essential features of the experiment. Parallel rays of monochromatic light pass through two narrow slits and are projected onto a screen. Constructive interference occurs at certain points on the screen, producing bright areas of maximum light intensity. Between these maxima, destructive interference produces light intensity minima. The positions of the maxima are given by the equation $d\sin\theta = n\lambda$, where d is the distance between the slits, θ is the angle shown in Figure 1, the integer n specifies the particular maxima, and λ is the wavelength of the incident light. (Note: $\sin\theta \approx \tan\theta \approx \theta$ for small angles.)

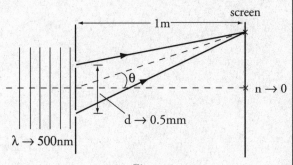

Figure 1

125. What is the angle θ for the third maximum ($n = 3$)?

- **A.** 3×10^{-5} radians
- **B.** 3×10^{-3} radians
- **C.** 0.3 radians
- **D.** 0.3 degrees

126. Which of the following supports the particle theory of light?

- **A.** The energy of light is quantized.
- **B.** Light exhibits interference.
- **C.** Light is subject to the Doppler effect.
- **D.** No particle can have a speed greater than the speed of light.

127. A beam of electrons can also produce an interference pattern. Which one of the following expressions gives a consistent definition of an electron's "wavelength" if it has a total energy given by E? (Note: h = 6.6×10^{-34} J • s is Planck's constant and v is the speed of the electrons.)

- **A.** hvE
- **B.** hE/v
- **C.** hv/E
- **D.** E/hv

128. Which of the following is sufficient information to determine the approximate speed of a ray of light in water?

- **A.** The angle of incidence and the angle of refraction of the light ray as it enters water from air
- **B.** The wavelength in water and the wavelength in air of the light ray as it enters water from air
- **C.** The speed of light in a vacuum and the density of water
- **D.** The speed of light in a vacuum and the index of refraction of water

129. Light waves can be described in terms of frequency f and wavelength λ or in terms of wave number k and angular frequency ω. These quantities are related by the following equations:

$$k = 2\pi/\lambda \text{ and } \omega = 2\pi f$$

Which equation below accurately describes the speed of the wave v in terms of k and ω?

- **A.** $v = f\lambda$
- **B.** $v = \omega + k$
- **C.** $v = \omega/k$
- **D.** $v = \omega k$

GO ON TO THE NEXT PAGE.

130. According to the modern theory of light, a beam of light may be described either as a stream of particles or as a wave, depending on the circumstances. Which of the following correctly states a connection between the two descriptions?

A. The number of light particles that pass by per second is proportional to the frequency of the light wave.

B. The mass of each particle of light is proportional to the intensity of the light wave.

C. The size of each particle of light is proportional to the wavelength of the light wave.

D. The energy of each particle of light is proportional to the frequency of the light wave.

GO ON TO THE NEXT PAGE.

Passage XI (Questions 131–137)

A researcher investigated the equilibrium between CO_2, C, and CO as a function of temperature. The equation is given below.

$$CO_2(g) + C(s) \rightleftharpoons 2\,CO(g)$$

Carbon dioxide, at 298 K and 1 atm, and an excess of powdered carbon were introduced into a furnace, which was then sealed so that pressure would increase as the temperature rose. The furnace was heated to and held constant at a predetermined temperature. The pressure within the furnace chamber was recorded after it had remained unchanged for one hour. The table below shows the pressures recorded for a series of temperatures together with the pressures expected if no reaction had taken place.

Table 1

T(K)	P_r (P recorded after reaction, in atm)	P_e (P expected without reaction, in atm)
900	3.4	3.0
950	3.8	3.2
1,000	4.3	3.4
1,050	5.0	3.5
1,200	7.2	4.0

131. When the system stabilized at 1,200 K, a sample of helium was injected into the furnace. What should happen to the amount of carbon dioxide in the system?

A. It should increase.
B. It should decrease.
C. It should be completely converted to carbon monoxide.
D. It will remain the same.

132. What can be said about the value of $\Delta S°$ of the reaction?

A. It is positive.
B. It is negative.
C. It is zero.
D. It cannot be determined from the information given.

133. How many pi bonds are in the carbon dioxide molecule?

A. 0
B. 1
C. 2
D. 3

134. Which of the following is NOT necessarily true about the equilibrium reaction between CO_2, C, and CO?

A. The standard entropy change is positive.
B. A decrease in pressure at constant temperature would shift the equilibrium to the right.
C. Addition of CO will shift the equilibrium to the left.
D. The standard Gibbs' free energy change is negative.

135. Which of the following shows the correct Lewis structure of carbon monoxide?

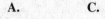

A.   C.

:C=Ö: :C≡O:

B.   D.

:C̈=Ö: :C≡Ö:

GO ON TO THE NEXT PAGE.

136. How are the values of P_e calculated?

    A. $(T/273)(1 \text{ atm})$
    B. $(T/298)(1 \text{ atm})$
    C. $[(T - 273)/273](1 \text{ atm})$
    D. $[(T - 298)/298](1 \text{ atm})$

137. If 0.6 g of elemental carbon are consumed during a trial, how many grams of CO are produced?

    A.   0.8
    B.   1.4
    C.   1.6
    D.   2.8

GO ON TO THE NEXT PAGE.

Questions 138 through 142 are **NOT** based on a descriptive passage.

138. Light traveling from air into a new medium is refracted away from the normal. This medium might be:

    A.   glass.
    B.   water.
    C.   steel.
    D.   a vacuum.

139. Which expression correctly expresses the K_{sp} of a solution of X_mY_n?

    A. $[X^{m+}]^n[Y^{n-}]^m$
    B. $[X^{n+}]^m[Y^{m-}]^n$
    C. $([X^{m+}]^n[Y^{n-}]^m)/X_mY_n$
    D. $([X^{n+}]^m[Y^{m-}]^n)/X_mY_n$

140. Which of the following species exists as a resonance hybrid?

    A. HCN
    B. H_2CO_3
    C. NO_2^-
    D. ClO^-

141. If the reaction between Q and R is third order overall, what is the value of x in the table below?

Trial	Concentration of Q (M)	Concentration of R (M)	Initial rate (M/sec)
1	1.00	1.00	6×10^{-8}
2	2.00	1.00	12×10^{-8}
3	2.00	x	48×10^{-8}

    A.   2.00
    B.   3.00
    C.   4.00
    D.   6.00

142. The temperature of an iron bar is raised, and it expands. If the temperature of a second iron bar, which is initially twice as long as the first bar, is raised by twice as much, what is the ratio of the change in length of the first bar to the change in length of the second bar?

    A.   1:1
    B.   1:2
    C.   1:4
    D.   2:1

STOP. IF YOU FINISH BEFORE TIME HAS EXPIRED, CHECK YOUR WORK. YOU MAY GO BACK TO ANY QUESTION IN THIS PART ONLY.

Writing Sample

Time: 60 Minutes

2 Prompts, Separately Timed:

30 Minutes Each

DIRECTIONS:

You are allotted 60 minutes to work on this part of the exam. You may work only on the Writing Sample part during that time. Should you finish early, you are permitted to check your work in this part of the exam only.

WRITING SAMPLE

DIRECTIONS: The Writing Sample test examines your writing skills. The test contains two assignments, Part 1 and Part 2, and you will have 30 minutes to complete each assignment.

You are permitted to work only on Part 1 during the first 30 minutes of the test and only on Part 2 during the second 30 minutes of the test. Should you finish writing on Part I before the time is up, you may review your work on Part 1, but do not begin writing on Part 2. Similarly, should you finish writing on Part 2 before the time is up, you are permitted to review your work only on Part 2.

Use your time efficiently. Read the assignment carefully before you begin writing a response. Please ensure thorough comprehension of the assignment. Use the space below each writing assignment for notation in planning your responses.

Your response to each part should be an essay composed of complete sentences and paragraphs, as this is a test of your writing skills. Your responses should be as well organized and clearly written as possible given your time restrictions. Corrections or additions should be placed neatly between the lines of your responses.

Please note that illegible essays cannot be scored.

GO TO THE NEXT PAGE AND BEGIN.

Part 1

Consider the following statement:

The pursuit of knowledge is always justified.

Write a unified essay in which you perform the following tasks. Explain what you think the above statement means. Describe a specific situation in which the pursuit of knowledge is not justified. Discuss what you think determines when the pursuit of knowledge is justified and when it is not.

Part 2

Consider the following statement:

True creativity cannot be learned.

Write a unified essay in which you perform the following tasks. Explain what you think the above statement means. Describe a specific situation in which individuals can learn to be truly creative. Discuss what you think determines whether or not true creativity can be learned.

Biological Sciences

Time: 100 Minutes

Questions: 143–219

DIRECTIONS:

You are allotted 100 minutes to work on this part of the exam. You may work only on the Biological Sciences part during that time. Should you finish early, you are permitted to check your work in this part of the exam only.

BIOLOGICAL SCIENCES

DIRECTIONS: The majority of the questions in the following Biological Sciences test are arranged in groups addressing a preceding descriptive passage. Select the single best answer to each question in the group after thorough analysis of the passage. Some discrete questions are not based on a descriptive passage. Similarly, select the best answer to these questions. If you are not certain of an answer, eliminate the answer choices known to be incorrect and select an answer from the remaining alternatives. Indicate your answer selection by blackening the corresponding oval on your answer sheet. A periodic table is provided below for your assistance with the passages and questions.

Periodic Table of the Elements

1 H 1.0																	2 He 4.0
3 Li 6.9	4 Be 9.0											5 B 10.8	6 C 12.0	7 N 14.0	8 O 16.0	9 F 19.0	10 Ne 20.2
11 Na 23.0	12 Mg 24.3											13 Al 27.0	14 Si 28.1	15 P 31.0	16 S 32.1	17 Cl 35.5	18 Ar 39.9
19 K 39.1	20 Ca 40.1	21 Sc 45.0	22 Ti 47.9	23 V 50.9	24 Cr 52.0	25 Mn 54.9	26 Fe 55.8	27 Co 58.9	28 Ni 58.7	29 Cu 63.5	30 Zn 65.4	31 Ga 69.7	32 Ge 72.6	33 As 74.9	34 Se 79.0	35 Br 79.9	36 Kr 83.8
37 Rb 85.5	38 Sr 87.6	39 Y 88.9	40 Zr 91.2	41 Nb 92.9	42 Mo 95.9	43 Tc (98)	44 Ru 101.1	45 Rh 102.9	46 Pd 106.4	47 Ag 107.9	48 Cd 112.4	49 In 114.8	50 Sn 118.7	51 Sb 121.8	52 Te 127.6	53 I 126.9	54 Xe 131.3
55 Cs 132.9	56 Ba 137.3	57 La* 138.9	72 Hf 178.5	73 Ta 180.9	74 W 183.9	75 Re 186.2	76 Os 190.2	77 Ir 192.2	78 Pt 195.1	79 Au 197.0	80 Hg 200.6	81 Tl 204.4	82 Pb 207.2	83 Bi 209.0	84 Po (209)	85 At (210)	86 Rn (222)
87 Fr (223)	88 Ra 226.0	89 Ac† 227.0	104 Unq (261)	105 Unp (262)	106 Unh (263)	107 Uns (262)	108 Uno (265)	109 Une (267)									

	58 Ce 140.1	59 Pr 140.9	60 Nd 144.2	61 Pm (145)	62 Sm 150.4	63 Eu 152.0	64 Gd 157.3	65 Tb 158.9	66 Dy 162.5	67 Ho 164.9	68 Er 167.3	69 Tm 168.9	70 Yb 173.0	71 Lu 175.0
†	90 Th 232.0	91 Pa (231)	92 U 238.0	93 Np (237)	94 Pu (244)	95 Am (243)	96 Cm (247)	97 Bk (247)	98 Cf (251)	99 Es (252)	100 Fm (257)	101 Md (258)	102 No (259)	103 Lr (260)

Passage I (Questions 143–148)

Glycolysis is the sequence of reactions in the cytosol that converts glucose into two molecules of pyruvate with the concomitant generation of 2 ATP and 2 NADH. Under anaerobic conditions, NAD^+ is regenerated from NADH by the reduction of pyruvate to either lactate or ethanol. Alternatively, under aerobic conditions, NAD^+ is regenerated by the transfer of electrons from NADH to O_2 through the electron-transport chain. Glycolysis serves two main functions: it generates ATP and it provides carbon skeletons for biosynthesis.

Phosphofructokinase, which is the enzyme that catalyzes the committed step in glycolysis, is the most important control site. A high concentration of ATP inhibits phosphofructokinase. This inhibitory effect is enhanced by citrate and reversed by AMP. Thus, the rate of glycolysis depends on the cell's need for ATP, as signaled by the ATP/AMP ratio, and on the need for building blocks, as signaled by the concentration of citrate. These relationships are shown in Figure 1.

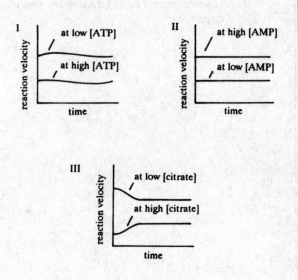

Figure 1

In liver cells, the most important regulator of phosphofructokinase activity is *fructose 2,6-bisphosphate (F-2,6-BP)*. F-2,6-BP is formed by the phosphorylation of fructose 6-phosphate in a reaction catalyzed by *phosphofructokinase 2 (PFK2)*. When blood glucose is low, a glucagon-triggered cascade leads to the phosphorylation of PFK2 and inhibition of phosphofructokinase. The control of the synthesis and degradation of F-2,6-BP is shown in Figure 2.

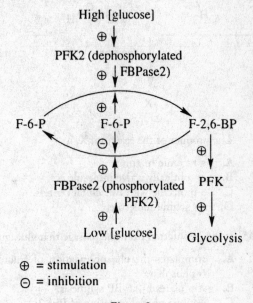

$\oplus$ = stimulation
$\ominus$ = inhibition

Figure 2

143. In an experiment with glycolytic enzymes, 10 mol of glucose produced 2 mol of ATP. This result fails to conform to the theoretical yield from 10 mol of glucose, which should produce:

   A.   1 mol of ATP.
   B.   5 mol of ATP.
   C.   10 mol of ATP.
   D.   20 mol of ATP.

GO ON TO THE NEXT PAGE.

144. One of the reactions of aerobic respiration is the addition of water to fumarate, which is shown below. This reaction is catalyzed by the enzyme fumarase, and occurs stereospecifically with water approaching on only one side of the molecule.

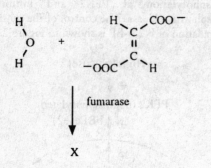

The product of the reaction, X, is:

A. a racemic mixture.
B. an optically active molecule.
C. a molecule with two chiral centers.
D. an achiral molecule.

145. It can be inferred from the passage that glucagon:

A. stimulates the phosphorylation of fructose 6-phosphate.
B. stimulates F-2,6-BP synthesis.
C. inhibits phosphorylation of PFK2.
D. inhibits glycolysis.

146. Which of the following conditions would most enhance the rate of glycolysis?

A. Low concentration of F-2,6-BP
B. High ATP/AMP ratio
C. High concentration of AMP
D. High concentration of citrate

147. A high fructose-6-phosphate concentration will lead to all of the following EXCEPT:

A. increased F-2,6-BP synthesis.
B. decreased F-2,6-BP degradation.
C. stimulation of phosphofructokinase.
D. decreased ATP/AMP ratio.

148. Two bacterial colonies, A and B, are grown anaerobically on separate petri plates containing a glucose-rich medium and are found to be of equal size. The two plates are then incubated for 72 hours in an O_2-rich atmosphere. After incubation, Colony A exhibited growth, and an assay of the medium revealed that most of the glucose in the plate had been consumed; Colony B had nearly disappeared. These results suggest that Colonies A and B most likely contain:

A. facultative aerobes and obligate aerobes, respectively.
B. facultative aerobes and obligate anaerobes, respectively.
C. obligate aerobes and obligate anaerobes, respectively.
D. obligate anaerobes and facultative aerobes, respectively.

GO ON TO THE NEXT PAGE.

Passage II (Questions 149–154)

There are four phases of the *human immunodeficiency virus* (*HIV*) life cycle. In *binding and entry*, the virus binds to the CD4 receptor on CD4$^+$ T-cells via the viral glycoprotein, *gp120*. The binding results in the fusion of the viral and cellular membranes, followed by the entrance of the viral core into the cell. After entry, *synthesis and integration* occurs, during which viral RNA is transcribed into double-stranded DNA by reverse transcriptase. Viral DNA enters the nucleus and integrates into the host genome. Following integration, *expression* of viral genes occurs. Finally, during *assembly and release*, viral structural proteins are synthesized and assemble into particles containing the viral enzymes and two copies of the viral RNA. The particles bud from the cell.

One of the most puzzling cytopathic effects of HIV is the depletion of T-cells, despite the fact that relatively few cells are actually infected. Four models that attempt to account for this effect are summarized below:

Hypothesis 1

HIV particles that fail to integrate into the CD4$^+$ T-cell genome produce a toxic factor that functionally impairs T-cells and eventually leads to cell death.

Hypothesis 2

HIV integration promotes the synthesis of terminal maturation factors in CD4$^+$ T-cells, increasing their susceptibility to the body's normal cell-destruction process.

Hypothesis 3

Viral glycoproteins (gp120 and gp41) expressed on the surface of HIV-infected T-cells fuse with CD4 receptors on healthy cells, forming a nonfunctional cell mass (*syncytia formation*).

Hypothesis 4

gp120 molecules are released into circulation by infected T-cells and bind to the CD4 receptors on healthy T-cells, making the latter subject to an autoimmune attack by anti-gp120 antibodies.

149. A researcher wanting to study the process by which viral mRNA is transcribed in an HIV-infected CD4$^+$ T-cell would add all of the following reagents to her cell culture EXCEPT:

   A. radiolabeled thymine.
   B. radiolabeled guanine.
   C. radiolabeled uracil.
   D. radiolabeled adenine.

150. If Hypothesis 1 were true, which of the following pairs of processes would HIV have to undergo before a toxic factor could be produced?

   A. Binding and entry; synthesis and integration
   B. Reverse transcription and host cell death
   C. Binding and entry
   D. Reverse transcription; synthesis and integration

151. Which of the following supports Hypothesis 3?

   A. Some CD4$^+$ T-cell lines do not form syncytia, but are susceptible to the cytopathic effects of HIV.
   B. Syncytia formation is transient in some CD4$^+$ T-cell lines.
   C. gp120 and gp41 bind almost irreversibly to CD4 receptor molecules *in vitro*.
   D. Syncytia formation does not lead to cell death in some CD4$^+$ T-cell lines.

152. Hypothesis 4 is based on the assumption that:

   A. healthy CD4$^+$ T-cells are not normally subject to autoimmune attacks.
   B. healthy CD4$^+$ T-cells will produce anti-gp120 cells in response to exposure to the HIV virus.
   C. healthy CD4$^+$ T-cells normally synthesize gp120.
   D. proteins travel through the body by way of the immune system.

GO ON TO THE NEXT PAGE.

153. If Hypothesis 3 were true, which of the following cellular organelles would be responsible for directing the newly synthesized gp120 and gp41 molecules toward the plasma membrane, on which they would eventually be expressed?

A. Centrioles
B. Golgi complex
C. Mitochondria
D. Lysosomes

154. HIV infection is detected by the presence of anti-HIV antibodies in the blood. This indicates that during infection:

A. helper T-cells are still able to activate cytotoxic T-cell proliferation.
B. B-lymphocytes are still able to produce antibodies in response to the foreign antigens of HIV.
C. anti-HIV antibodies are effective against the virus.
D. HIV has not infected host macrophages.

GO ON TO THE NEXT PAGE.

Passage III (Questions 155–159)

A chemist investigated the reactivity of four organic compounds; their melting and boiling points are given in Table 1. The compounds were treated with an oxidizing agent and a reducing agent. Their ability to react with Br_2 and HBr was also investigated.

Table 2 records the molecular formulas of the reaction products from these experiments.

Table 1

Compound	I $CH_3CH=CHCH_3$	II $CH_3CH_2CH=CH_2$	III $CH_3C=CCH_3$	IV $CH_3CH_2C=CH$
Melting point, °C	−106/−139	−195	−24	−122
Boiling point, °C	+1/+4	−6	+27	+9

Table 2

Compound	I	II	III	IV
H_2/Pd	C_4H_{10}	C_4H_{10}	C_4H_{10}	C_4H_{10}
Br_2	$C_4H_8Br_2$	$C_4H_8Br_2$	$C_4H_6Br_4$	$C_4H_6Br_4$
HBr	C_4H_9Br	C_4H_9Br	$C_4H_8Br_2$	$C_4H_8Br_2$
Cold, dilute $KMnO_4$	$C_4H_{10}O_2$	$C_4H_{10}O_2$		
Hot, basic $KMnO_4$/H^+	$2C_2H_4O_2$	$C_3H_6O_2$ $^+$ CO_2		

GO ON TO THE NEXT PAGE.

155. Compound I has two melting points because it can exist as either of two:

    A.   anomers.

    B.   enantiomers.

    C.   conformational isomers.

    D.   geometric isomers.

156. What is the name of the product formed when Compound I is reacted with hot, basic $KMnO_4$?

    A.   Acetic acid

    B.   2,3-Butanediol

    C.   Ethanal

    D.   Ethylene glycol

157. The reaction of Compound IV with HBr primarily differs from Compound II in that it proceeds through which of the following intermediates?

    A.   A secondary carbocation

    B.   A vinylic anion

    C.   A vinylic cation

    D.   A tertiary carbocation

158. Hydrogenation and bromination of Compound I occur, respectively, via the mechanisms of:

    A.   *syn* addition and *anti* addition.

    B.   *anti* addition and *syn* addition.

    C.   nucleophilic addition and electrophilic addition.

    D.   electrophilic addition and nucleophilic addition.

159. Why do Compound I and Compound II form the same product in the reaction with HBr?

    A.   Both have equally stable double bonds

    B.   Both have equally reactive double bonds

    C.   Both obey Markovnikov's rule

    D.   Neither obeys Markovnikov's rule

GO ON TO THE NEXT PAGE.

Passage IV (Questions 160–165)

An epidemiologist was called in to investigate an outbreak of illness following a sewage leak into a city's water supply. Blood tests of the affected individuals revealed the presence of an unknown infectious agent, which the epidemiologist determined to be either viral or bacterial. Further examination determined that the infectious agent was bacterial, and when the results were more closely analyzed, it appeared that more than one strain of bacteria was infecting the patients. Four different strains of bacteria, labeled Microbe Q, Microbe R, Microbe S, and Microbe T, were eventually isolated.

Four different types of nutrient plates were prepared, each containing only four amino acids, and the microbes were inoculated onto the plates to determine the essential amino acids of each strain. Those amino acids that an organism cannot synthesize are said to be *essential* to that organism.

Plate 1: cysteine, phenylalanine, serine, threonine
Plate 2: cysteine, phenylalanine, proline, tryptophan
Plate 3: cysteine, proline, threonine, tryptophan
Plate 4: phenylalanine, serine, threonine, tryptophan

The results are shown below in Table 1.

Table 1

Microbe

	Q	R	S	T
Plate 1	+	+	−	+
Plate 2	−	+	+	+
Plate 3	+	−	−	−
Plate 4	−	−	−	+

+ = growth; − = no growth

After the microbes were isolated, it was determined that Microbe R and Microbe S were not pathogenic. Potential antibiotics against Microbe Q and Microbe T were then selected, and the microbes were inoculated onto their respective growth media. Antibiotic discs X, Y, and Z were then placed on each nutrient plate. After 24 hours of incubation (enough time to allow growth), the plates were reexamined. The shaded areas of Figure 1 represent regions of good bacterial growth.

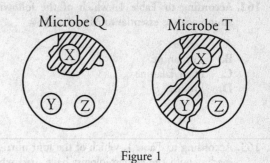

Figure 1

160. Which of the following techniques would have been *most* effective in helping the epidemiologist determine that the infectious agent was bacterial?

- **A.** Hybridize the infectious agent with radiolabeled probes specific for the genes encoding viral structural proteins; only viral genes would hybridize.
- **B.** Analyze a patient's serum in a spectrophotometer to measure its absorption wavelength; the photosynthetic pigments found in all bacteria would distinguish them from viruses, which lack such pigments.
- **C.** Stain the infectious agent for the presence of RNA; only bacteria would stain positive.
- **D.** Stain the infectious agent for the presence of protein; only bacteria would stain positive.

161. Which of the following structures would NOT have been detected when the epidemiologist determined Microbe R's structural composition?

- **A.** Nuclear membrane
- **B.** DNA
- **C.** Cell wall
- **D.** Ribosomes

GO ON TO THE NEXT PAGE.

162. According to Table 1, which of the following amino acids is essential to Microbe Q?

A. Serine
B. Threonine
C. Phenylalanine
D. Proline

163. According to Table 1, which of the four nutrient media could the epidemiologist have used when determining the effectiveness of the antibiotic discs against the pathogenic microbes?

A. The medium from Plate 1
B. The medium from Plate 2
C. The medium from Plate 3
D. The medium from Plate 4

164. Based on the information in Figure 1, which of the following antibiotics would be *most* effective in treating patients infected with both Microbe Q and Microbe T?

A. Antibiotic X
B. Antibiotic Y
C. Antibiotic Z
D. Antibiotic Y and Antibiotic Z are equally effective

165. Which of the following would be the *easiest* method to isolate Microbe Q from Microbe T when they coexist in the same patient?

A. Centrifuge a serum sample from a patient infected with both bacteria; the two strains should layer at different levels and could thus be isolated.
B. Take a blood sample from a patient infected with both bacteria. Put some blood on a nutrient plate containing only phenylalanine, and some on another plate containing only cysteine. Incubate and isolate what grows.
C. Take a blood sample from a patient infected with both bacteria. Put some on a nutrient plate with all the amino acids except cysteine, and some on another plate with all the amino acids except phenylalanine. Incubate and isolate what grows.
D. There is no way to isolate the two bacteria, since all bacteria are similar in their structure and nutritional requirements.

GO ON TO THE NEXT PAGE.

Questions 166 through 170 are **NOT** based on a descriptive passage.

166. The hormone calcitonin acts as a regulator of serum Ca^{2+} levels by promoting the incorporation of Ca^{2+} into bone. Which of the following hormones is antagonistic to calcitonin?

- **A.** Parathyroid hormone
- **B.** Prolactin
- **C.** ACTH
- **D.** Thyroxine

167. In a healthy individual, which of the following blood vessels has the highest partial pressure of carbon dioxide?

- **A.** Pulmonary arteries
- **B.** Pulmonary veins
- **C.** Aorta
- **D.** Coronary arteries

168. Which of the following structures is NOT derived from embryonic ectoderm?

- **A.** Eye lens
- **B.** Pituitary gland
- **C.** Digestive tract
- **D.** Adrenal medulla

169. Transfusion with which of the following blood types would cause severe agglutination in a patient with type B blood, Rh positive?

- **A.** Type B blood, Rh negative
- **B.** Type A blood, Rh positive
- **C.** Type O blood, Rh positive
- **D.** Type O blood, Rh negative

170. The graph below plots the transmembrane diffusion rates for Compound A and Compound B as a function of their extracellular concentrations. Given that both compounds are approximately the same size, and there are no facilitated diffusion sites, it would most likely be inferred that:

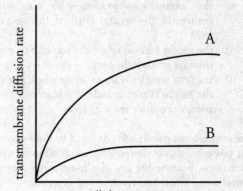

- **A.** Compound A is polar and Compound B is nonpolar.
- **B.** Compound A is nonpolar and Compound B is polar.
- **C.** Compound A is polar and Compound B is polar.
- **D.** Compound A is nonpolar and Compound B is nonpolar.

GO ON TO THE NEXT PAGE.

Passage V (Questions 171–175)

A student working in a laboratory accidentally touches a hot plate with his right hand. An involuntary (reflex) action that operates through a polysynaptic reflex arc involving two synapses causes him to immediately withdraw his hand. This withdrawal is mediated by the following sequence of events:

1) skin receptors sense "hot" pain
2) stimulation of these receptors leads to the transduction of an impulse along a sensory neuron
3) the sensory neuron synapses with an interneuron in the dorsal horn of the spinal cord
4) the interneuron synapses with a motor neuron in the ventral horn of the spinal cord
5) the motor neuron relays the impulse to the muscles in his right arm
6) the arm muscles react in antagonistic pairs: the biceps (flexor muscle) contract and the triceps (extensor muscle) relax

The sensation of pain is also conveyed to the sensory cortex; however, this is slower than conduction to the motor neuron because the impulse must travel along thin myelinated fibers and cross several synapses.

Research has elucidated the chemical and molecular events that produce a reflex contraction. The link between a nerve terminal and the sarcolemma of a muscle fiber is known as a neuromuscular junction; the space between the two is a synapse. The nerve terminal is characterized by the presence of numerous mitochondria and synaptic vesicles containing the neurotransmitter acetylcholine. Transmission of an impulse to the terminal triggers the release of acetylcholine into the synapse via exocytosis. The acetylcholine diffuses across the synapse and then binds to receptors on the muscle sarcolemma. These receptors form the extracellular part of ligand-gated ion channels. Receptor binding causes a change in the conformation of the channels, causing them to open, allowing a rapid influx of Na^+ into the sarcoplasm. This produces an action potential. The action potential is conducted along the sarcolemma and the T system into the muscle fiber, triggering the release of Ca^{2+} into the sarcoplasm and thereby stimulating muscle contraction.

171. Calcium ions stimulate muscle contraction by:

A. binding to the sarcolemma.
B. binding to troponin.
C. causing the formation of permanent actin-myosin cross bridges.
D. binding to actin.

172. Which of the following provides the most plausible explanation for the presence of numerous mitochondria in the nerve terminals?

A. All cells have mitochondria.
B. Neurons are aerobic cells.
C. The diffusion of acetylcholine across a synapse requires ATP.
D. The exocytosis of synaptic vesicles requires ATP.

173. If the student's receptors for the sensation of "hot" pain had been severed, then the student would have:

A. felt no pain, and his hand would have remained on the hot plate.
B. felt no pain, but would have immediately removed his hand from the hot plate.
C. felt pain, but would have been unable to remove his hand from the hot plate.
D. felt pain, but would have slowly removed his hand from the hot plate.

GO ON TO THE NEXT PAGE.

174. Which of the following best explains why the withdrawal of a limb from a burning hot plate occurs faster than the withdrawal of a limb from an uncomfortably warm tub of water?

   A. Intense heat causes a greater amount of acetylcholine to be released into the neuromuscular junction, producing an action potential of greater magnitude.

   B. Intense heat directly stimulates the sensory areas of the brain that respond to temperature, allowing the information to be processed more rapidly.

   C. Intense heat stimulates the secretion of epinephrine from the neuromuscular junction, triggering the "fight-or-flight" responses and decreasing reaction time.

   D. Intense heat stimulates a simple reflex involving only two synapses, allowing the information to be processed more rapidly.

175. When a strong stimulus such as burning heat is applied to a limb, the limb's withdrawal is accompanied by a concomitant extension of the opposite limb; this is known as the crossed extensor reflex. This implies that as the student withdraws his right hand from the hotplate:

   A. his right biceps relax and his right triceps contract.

   B. his right biceps contract and his right triceps contract.

   C. his left biceps relax and his left triceps contract.

   D. his left biceps contract and his right biceps relax.

GO ON TO THE NEXT PAGE.

Passage VI (Questions 176–180)

Alkanes, in the presence of light, react with halogens to produce alkyl halides. The reactions result in the substitution of halogen atoms for hydrogen atoms on the carbon skeleton. The reactions involve free radical intermediates as illustrated in this general mechanism:

Initiation: $X_2 \xrightarrow{\text{light}} 2X\bullet$ (1)

Propagation: $RH + X\bullet \rightarrow R\bullet + HX$ (2)

$X_2 + R\bullet \rightarrow RX + X\bullet$ (3)

(R = alkyl chain, X = F, Cl, Br, I)

The reactivity of an alkane depends on the types of hydrogens that are available to be substituted. Differences in the bond strengths, and in the energies of the transition states, make tertiary hydrogens most reactive, followed by secondary and then primary hydrogens. For instance, in substitution by bromine, tertiary hydrogens are five times more reactive than primary ones.

The order of reactivity of the halogens is:

$$F > Cl > Br > I$$

176. The chlorination of butane is accompanied by which of the following?

I. The formation of chiral products
II. No observed change in optical rotation
III. The formation of achiral products

A. I only
B. III only
C. II and III only
D. I, II, and III

177. Reaction of alkanes containing equal numbers of primary and tertiary hydrogens with fluorine produces approximately equal amounts of each possible product. By contrast, reaction with bromine produces five times as much tertiary product as primary. Which of the following statements is most strongly supported by these facts and the passage?

A. The reactivity of the halogens is inversely related to their selectivity between hydrogens in free-radical substitutions.
B. Bromine is a more efficient halogenating reagent for all classes of alkanes than fluorine.
C. Fluorine is less reactive with respect to substitution of tertiary hydrogens in alkanes than bromine.
D. Fluorine forms stronger bonds to primary carbons than bromine does.

178. Light of low intensity is sufficient to cause the alkanes and halogens to react because:

A. the reactions have low activation energies.
B. only a small, catalytic amount of X radicals must be produced in Step 1.
C. the bonds in the halogen molecules are weak.
D. alkanes are very reactive molecules.

179. Which of the following represents a chain termination step?

A. $Br\bullet + Br_2 \rightarrow Br_2 + Br\bullet$
B. $Br\bullet + R\bullet \rightarrow RBr$
C. $RH + Br_2 \rightarrow RBr + HBr$
D. $Br_2 + R\bullet \rightarrow RBr + Br\bullet$

180. What is the IUPAC name of the product formed when the *most* reactive hydrogen of 2-methylpropane is substituted by a bromine atom?

A. 2-bromomethylpropane
B. 2-bromobutane
C. 1-bromo-2-methylpropane
D. 2-bromo-2-methylpropane

GO ON TO THE NEXT PAGE.

Passage VII (Questions 181–186)

Current theories of carcinogenesis are based on the concept of cellular and viral *oncogenes*. It is believed that the genome of any eukaryotic cell contains DNA segments, called *proto-oncogenes*, that normally code for cell growth-related proteins such as transcription factors, growth factors, growth-factor receptors, and tyrosine kinases (enzymes thought to regulate cell division). These cellular proto-oncogenes can be transformed into tumorigenic oncogenes (*c-onc*) by a number of mechanisms.

A common mechanism by which a cellular proto-oncogene is transformed into a *c-onc* is point mutation, which leads to formation of a defective protein. For example, one well-studied cellular proto-oncogene codes for the *ras* protein. *Ras* proteins have GTPase activity, and their activity is regulated by the presence of GTP or GDP. In the wild-type protein, growth-factor receptors with tyrosine kinase activity stimulate *ras* to exchange GDP with GTP through an indirect process involving intermediate proteins. *Ras* then activates a cytosolic kinase (also an oncogene) *c-raf*. *c-raf* then activates *MAP kinase-kinase*, which in turn activates *MAP-kinase*. MAP-kinase appears capable of phosphorylating transcription factors in the nucleus. After the appropriate genes have been transcribed, *ras* GTPase activity hydrolyzes GTP, converting *ras* to its inactive form. Mutant *ras* proteins are unable to hydrolyze GTP, and therefore remain in the active GTP-bound form.

Alternatively, a proto-oncogene may become an oncogene through a mutation that causes it to produce an excess of a normal protein. Such a mutation may place the gene under the control of a stronger promoter via either chromosomal translocation, or by the integration of a provirus with a strong promoter in the immediate proximity of the proto-oncogene. An excess of a normal protein may also be caused by gene amplification of the proto-oncogene.

Another mechanism of carcinogenesis that also depends on oncogenes is viral carcinogenesis, which is caused by transforming viruses. Transforming viruses, which occur widely in the avian and animal kingdoms, are retroviruses whose genomes contain oncogenes (called viral oncogenes, or *v-onc*) derived from their former eukaryotic hosts. Such viruses can later cause other host cells to become tumorigenic.

181. Which of the following activities would you expect to increase in a tumorigenic cell?

   I. mRNA synthesis
  II. Ribosomal assembly
 III. Cell division

- **A.** I only
- **B.** I and II only
- **C.** II and III only
- **D.** I, II, and III

182. A *c-onc* activated by point mutation differs from the proto-oncogene from which it was derived by:

- **A.** a single base-pair.
- **B.** two base-pairs.
- **C.** a triplet insertion.
- **D.** a triplet deletion.

183. Based on the information in the passage, cellular proto-oncogenes can become tumorigenic oncogenes by all of the following mechanisms EXCEPT:

- **A.** a mutation that results in the synthesis of a faulty protein.
- **B.** a chromosomal translocation that produces an excess of a protein.
- **C.** binding of complementary nucleic acid sequences to proto-oncogene transcripts.
- **D.** a mutation that causes gene amplification of the proto-oncogene.

184. Comparison of a *v-onc* sequence with a corresponding *c-onc* sequence reveals that the organization of the viral gene corresponds to the mRNA of the *c-onc* gene, rather than to its own genomic organization. Which of the following best accounts for this observation?

- **A.** The *v-onc* gene contains only *c-onc* introns.
- **B.** The *v-onc* gene has a greater level of expression than the corresponding *c-onc* gene.
- **C.** The *v-onc* gene was captured from a host cell in the form of RNA during a retroviral infection.
- **D.** Since retroviral DNA is incorporated into the cellular genome, the alternating exons and introns in the *v-onc* gene are spliced by cellular enzymes.

GO ON TO THE NEXT PAGE.

185. Which of the following processes function in an analogous way to *ras* activity?

    A.   Formation of antibody-antigen complexes during an immune response

    B.   Sodium-potassium pump in neurons

    C.   Krebs cycle in mitochondria

    D.   Second messenger system involving cAMP

186. The incorporation of a strong promoter near a proto-oncogene may lead to cancer because the stronger promoter most likely:

    A.   increases the rate of translation.

    B.   increases the rate of transcription.

    C.   increases the rate of translocation.

    D.   increases the rate of point mutations.

GO ON TO THE NEXT PAGE.

Passage VIII (Questions 187–192)

Radioimmunoassay (RIA) is a technique used for measuring hormone concentrations in blood serum based on highly specific antigen-antibody interactions. To carry out an RIA for a particular human hormone, an antibody to that hormone is prepared by immunizing mice or rabbits with an extract from the human endocrine gland that produces the hormone. A measured quantity of this antibody is then mixed with a known concentration of isotopically labeled hormone and the blood sample to be assayed, which contains an unknown concentration of unlabeled hormone. RIA is based on the principle that as long as there is too little antibody to bind both the labeled hormone and unlabeled hormone completely, then the unlabeled and the labeled hormone will compete for antibody-binding sites. Thus, as the concentration of unlabeled hormone in the sample increases, the percentage of antibody-bound radiolabeled hormone decreases.

Hormone concentrations can be calculated by comparing the radioactivity counts obtained from the original RIA to a standard curve, such as the one shown in Figure 1. To generate a standard curve for a particular hormone, RIAs are performed on a series of solutions containing different known concentrations of unlabeled hormone. After the radioactivity of each solution is measured, these concentrations are then plotted against the percentage of antibody-bound radiolabeled hormone.

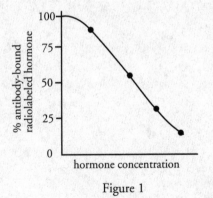

Figure 1

For most hormones, the form that circulates in the blood (the active form) is different from that extracted from the tissues and used to prepare the antibodies and standard curve used for RIAs (the precursor form), though typically, the two forms are very similar in structure and chemistry.

187. According to the passage, an antibody to a particular human hormone is prepared by immunizing laboratory animals with an extract of the human hormone. Which of the following best explains why this technique works?

A. The lab animal's immune system recognizes the human hormone as "foreign," or antigenic, and produces antibodies in response to its presence.

B. Human gland cells must first be injected into a host organism, such as a mouse or rabbit, before they can produce the antibodies.

C. Human hormones will elicit antibody production in mice and rabbits, but not in other animals, such as rats and chimpanzees.

D. Immunization with human hormone, prior to actual exposure to the hormone, protects the lab animal from infection upon second exposure to the hormone.

188. An RIA for antidiuretic hormone (ADH) performed on a healthy person yielded a concentration of 3 pg/mL. If an RIA were performed on a patient suffering from severe blood loss, which of the following ADH concentrations would the RIA most likely yield?

A. 0.5 pg/mL
B. 2 pg/mL
C. 3 pg/mL
D. 5 pg/mL

189. If Figure 1 were the standard curve for FSH, which point on the graph would most likely represent FSH concentration in a woman before pregnancy and in her 16th week of pregnancy, respectively?

A. Point A and Point D
B. Point B and Point D
C. Point C and Point D
D. Point B and Point A

GO ON TO THE NEXT PAGE.

190. RIA is based on the principle that radiolabeled and unlabeled hormone will compete for binding sites on the antibody. Which of the following conditions would NOT compromise the validity of an RIA?

A. The antibody binds the radiolabeled hormone with a greater affinity than the unlabeled hormone.

B. The antibody binds the radiolabeled hormone and the unlabeled hormone with equal affinity.

C. There is enough antibody in the solution to completely bind with the radiolabeled and the unlabeled hormone.

D. The radiolabeled hormone binds to a site on the antibody other than the antigen-binding site, inducing a conformational change that inhibits the binding of unlabeled hormone.

191. If Figure 1 were the standard curve for insulin, which points on the graph would most likely represent the serum insulin concentration calculated from the RIA performed before and 1 hour after glucose infusion, respectively?

A. Point B and Point A
B. Point B and Point D
C. Point C and Point C
D. Point C and Point A

192. Suppose that a researcher who wanted to measure the concentration of a particular *active* hormone unwittingly used its *precursor* form to develop the antibodies and generate the standard curve used for the RIA. If the researcher then performed an RIA on a sample of unlabeled active hormone contaminated with unlabeled precursor hormone, how would this affect the RIA?

A. The standard curve generated for the precursor form would be inaccurate and therefore could not be used to calculate unknown concentrations of that form.

B. The percentage of antibody-bound radiolabeled hormone would be greater than normal, because there would be twice as much unlabeled hormone for the radiolabeled hormone to compete with.

C. The calculated concentration of the active hormone would be greater than its actual concentration, because the antibody would bind to both the active hormone and its precursor form.

D. The calculated concentration of the active hormone would be less than its actual concentration, because the antibody would bind to both the active hormone and its precursor form.

GO ON TO THE NEXT PAGE.

Questions 193 through 197 are **NOT** based on a descriptive passage.

193. Marine and freshwater fish have different problems in maintaining their internal salt and water balances. Osmosis causes freshwater fish to gain water and marine fish to lose water. Based on this information, which of the following must be true?

    A. Marine fish live in an environment hypertonic to their body fluids.
    B. Marine fish live an environment hypotonic to their body fluids.
    C. Freshwater fish live in an environment hypertonic to their body fluids.
    D. Freshwater fish live in an environment isotonic to their body fluids.

194. Myoglobin, which is an oxygen-carrying protein found in muscle tissue, consists of a single polypeptide chain with an attached heme group. In contrast, hemoglobin consists of four heme-carrying polypeptide subunits. Which of the following best accounts for the difference in shape between the hemoglobin and myoglobin oxygen-dissociation curves?

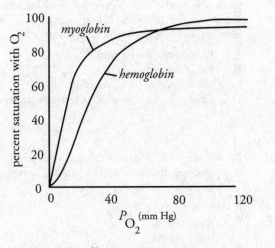

    A. Bohr effect
    B. Cooperative binding of oxygen to myoglobin
    C. Difference in P_{O_2} between blood and muscle
    D. Cooperative binding of oxygen to hemoglobin

195. Which of the following is not a *meta*-directing group in electrophilic aromatic substitution?

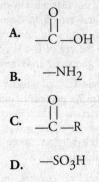

    A. $-\overset{\displaystyle O}{\overset{\displaystyle \|}{C}}-OH$
    B. $-NH_2$
    C. $-\overset{\displaystyle O}{\overset{\displaystyle \|}{C}}-R$
    D. $-SO_3H$

196. An amino acid is subjected to electrophoresis at pH 8.5 and is observed to migrate to the anode. The isoelectric point of this amino acid:

    A. is less than 8.5.
    B. is more than 8.5.
    C. is equal to 8.5.
    D. cannot be determined without more information.

197. It is hypothesized that the binding of testosterone to corticosteroid receptors in the hypothalamus of a developing male fetus accounts for the sexual differentiation of the human brain. This binding causes the hypothalamus to switch from cyclic production of gonadotropin-releasing factors (which is characteristic of females) to acyclic production. This switch, therefore, is likely to affect the release patterns of:

    A. LH.
    B. FSH.
    C. both LH and FSH.
    D. neither LH nor FSH.

GO ON TO THE NEXT PAGE.

Passage IX (Questions 198–203)

Cystic fibrosis (*CF*) is the most common autosomal recessive disease in the Caucasian population. The disease affects 1 in 2,500 newborns, and ranges in degree of severity even within the same family. In some cases, individuals do not survive past the age of five, while in others, adults live full lives through careful management.

It has been determined that CF is caused by a mutation of chromosome 7. In 75 percent of all CF cases, the mutation involves a deletion of three base pairs in a DNA sequence that codes for a transmembrane chloride channel. As a result of the deletion, the chloride channel is unable to operate efficiently.

CF is characterized by sticky, viscous, mucus secretions that impair the normal physiological functions of many organs, most especially the pancreas and lungs. Patients usually suffer from diarrhea, pancreatic exocrine insufficiency, and chronic obstructive pulmonary disease. Breathing is often difficult, and carbon dioxide tends to remain in the blood of CF patients longer than in that of healthy individuals. The diarrhea and pancreatic troubles are treated with enzyme supplementation; the respiratory ailments prove more trying in their treatment. Patients must undergo intense, daily respiratory therapy, and take heavy doses of antibiotics in order to maintain adequate ventilation. One such antibiotic is *cephalosporin C*, which is effective against penicillin-resistant bacteria. Despite the rigorous treatments, individuals with CF usually die as a result of pneumonia or bacterial infections secondary to the respiratory aspects of the disease.

198. One of the most common bacteria to infect patients with CF is *Staphylococcus*. If a sample from a CF patient were cultured, how would *Staphylococcus* appear when stained and viewed under a microscope?

    A.   Helical
    B.   Sickle-shaped
    C.   Rodlike
    D.   Spherical

199. According to the passage, pancreatic insufficiency in CF patients can be effectively treated with enzyme supplementation. Which of the following substances is LEAST likely to be found in such a supplement?

    A.   Lipase
    B.   Trypsin
    C.   Enterokinase
    D.   Chymotrypsinogen

200. What is the probability that a child of two carriers of the CF gene will be affected with CF?

    A.   0%
    B.   25%
    C.   50%
    D.   66%

201. The discovery that the sweat of children with CF contained excessive salt led to the measurement of sodium and chloride in sweat as a means of diagnosing CF. This suggests that, as compared to the chloride channel coded for by the normal gene, the channel coded by the CF gene:

    A.   transports less chloride from surrounding epithelial cells into the sweat ducts.
    B.   transports less sodium from surrounding epithelial cells into the sweat ducts.
    C.   transports more sodium but less chloride from surrounding epithelial cells into the sweat ducts.
    D.   is unable to transport chloride out of the sweat ducts and into surrounding epithelial cells.

202. CF patients suffer from pancreatic exocrine insufficiency as a result of obstruction of the pancreatic ducts leading into the small intestine. Which of the following CF symptoms is most likely caused by this insufficiency?

    A.   Pulmonary obstruction
    B.   Fat malabsorption
    C.   Carbohydrate malabsorption
    D.   Susceptibility to penicillin-resistant bacteria

203. Based on the information in the passage, compared to healthy individuals, CF patients most likely have a blood pH that:

    A.   is more acidic.
    B.   is more basic.
    C.   is the same.
    D.   wildly fluctuates.

GO ON TO THE NEXT PAGE.

Passage X (Questions 204–208)

Ketones are known to readily react with halogens in the presence of acid or base to form alpha-halogenated products. The overall reaction is shown below:

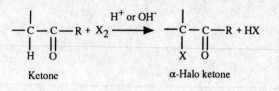

Reaction 1

In basic solution (Figure 1), the hydroxide ion removes a proton from the alpha carbon, yielding a carbanion intermediate (Step 1). Finally, the alpha-halogenated ketone is formed by the addition of a positively polarized bromide to the carbanion (Step 2):

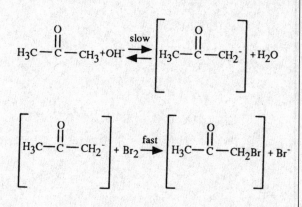

Figure 1

Alpha halogenation under acidic conditions (Figure 2) initially involves protonation of the carbonyl oxygen, resulting in the formation of an enol (Step 2). This molecule then undergoes electrophilic addition to yield another intermediate that can then be deprotonated to form the α-halo ketone (Step 4).

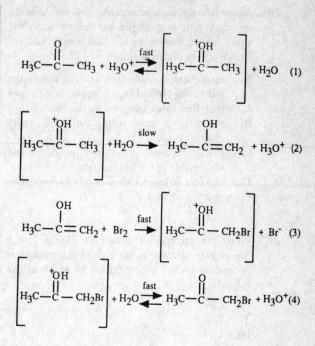

Figure 2

204. What is the function of the hydrogen and hydroxide ions in the acidic and basic solutions, respectively?

- **A.** They both act as catalysts.
- **B.** They are both reactants.
- **C.** The hydrogen ion is a reactant, while the hydroxide ion acts as a catalyst.
- **D.** The hydrogen ion acts as a catalyst, while the hydroxide ion is a reactant.

205. In Figure 2, the first two steps are characteristic of isomerization between which of the following?

- **I.** Tautomers
- **II.** Enantiomers
- **III.** Geometric isomers

- **A.** I only
- **B.** III only
- **C.** I and II only
- **D.** I, II, and III

GO ON TO THE NEXT PAGE.

206. Alpha halogenation of acetone in basic solution usually results in multiple halogenations on the alpha carbon (known as the Haloform reaction). This reaction occurs because:

A. introduction of the first halogen makes the remaining α-hydrogens more acidic and therefore easily removed by the base.

B. the base is very strong and will easily abstract protons.

C. α-halo ketones are highly unstable and susceptible to further reaction.

D. the first halogen stabilizes any carbocations that are formed.

207. From the mechanism drawn in Figure 1, the overall rate of reaction for alpha halogenation is dependent on the concentration of which of the following?

I. CH_3COCH_3
II. Br_2
III. OH^-

A. I only
B. II only
C. I and III only
D. I, II, and III

208. What would be the likely product if acetone was reacted with methylmagnesium bromide and then water?

A. Butanone
B. *tert*-Butyl alcohol
C. *tert*-Butyl bromide
D. Isopropyl methyl ether

GO ON TO THE NEXT PAGE.

Passage XI (Questions 209–214)

Acetylcholine (AC), a vital neurotransmitter of the autonomic nervous system, is released by the presynaptic knob of a neuron in response to an action potential. Once acetylcholine has interacted with the receptors of the postsynaptic membrane, it is quickly inactivated by *acetylcholinesterase* (ACE), the principal enzymatic component of the synaptic cleft.

The active site of ACE consists of two separate regions. The *binding region* contains a carboxylate group, which is responsible for attachment to the quaternary nitrogen atom of acetylcholine. The *catalytic region*, which is responsible for the esterase activity, contains serine (Ser), histidine (His), and tyrosine (Tyr) residues.

Figures 1–8 show how the changes in the active site of ACE are coupled with the breakdown of acetylcholine.

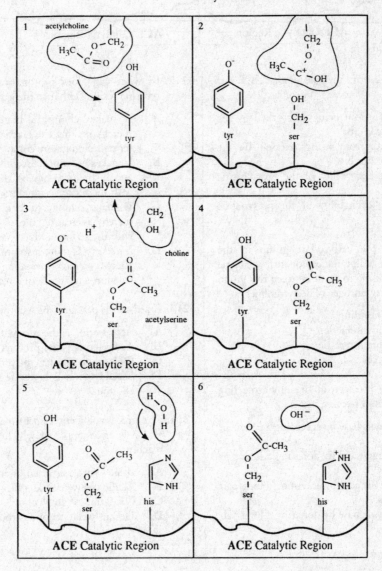

GO ON TO THE NEXT PAGE.

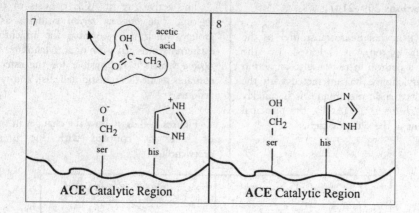

209. It can be inferred from the passage that ACE acts to:

A. prevent AC from being reabsorbed by the presynaptic knob.

B. prevent AC from being released by the presynaptic knob.

C. restore the excitability of the postsynaptic membrane.

D. restore the excitability of the presynaptic knob.

210. Assuming that the carboxylate group in the binding region of ACE is not protonated, what type of interaction is likely to occur between this group and the quaternary nitrogen of acetylcholine?

A. Hydrogen bonding
B. Electrostatic interaction
C. Hydrophobic interaction
D. London forces

211. In Figure 5, the nitrogen in the imidazole ring becomes protonated because it:

A. acts as a Lewis base by accepting a lone pair of electrons.

B. acts as a Lewis acid by donating a lone pair of electrons.

C. acts as a Lewis acid by accepting a lone pair of electrons.

D. acts as a Lewis base by donating a lone pair of electrons.

212. In what way does protonation of AC by the tyrosine residue enhance the activity of ACE?

A. It makes choline a better leaving group, thereby making the reaction of AC with the serine residue more complete.

B. It makes AC more susceptible to nucleophilic attack, thereby making the reaction of AC with the serine residue more complete.

C. It makes choline a better leaving group, thereby increasing the rate of the reaction with the serine residue.

D. It makes AC more susceptible to nucleophilic attack, thereby increasing the rate of the reaction with the serine residue.

213. Based on the passage, which of the following is true?

A. Acetylserine is the product of S_N1.
B. Acetylserine is the product of S_N2.
C. OH^- is a better leaving group than CH_3^-.
D. $SerCH_2O^-$ is a better leaving group than choline$^-$.

214. The process of acetic acid formation in Figures 6 and 7 is an example of which of the following reactions?

A. Basic hydrolysis of an ester
B. Acidic cleavage of an ether
C. Oxidation of an alcohol
D. Decarboxylation of a carboxylic acid

GO ON TO THE NEXT PAGE.

Questions 215 through 219 are **NOT** based on a descriptive passage.

215. Destruction of which of the following organelles would most inhibit intracellular protein digestion?

    A. Lysosomes
    B. Peroxisomes
    C. Rough endoplasmic reticulum
    D. Ribosomes

216. A researcher is trying to determine the contents of a viral genome. Upon chemical analysis, the nucleic acid is found to contain 27% cytosine, 27% adenine, 23% uracil, and 23% guanine. Based on this data, the viral genome most likely consists of:

    A. single-stranded DNA.
    B. double-stranded DNA.
    C. single-stranded RNA.
    D. double-stranded RNA.

217. Which of the following would form the *most* stable carbocation?

    A. $(CH_3)_2CHBr$ dissolved in toluene
    B. $(CH_3CH_2)_3COH$ dissolved in acetone
    C. $(CH_3)_3COH$ dissolved in H_2SO_4
    D. CH_3CH_2I dissolved in diethyl ether

218. Which of the following graphs best corresponds to the optimal pH for pepsin activity?

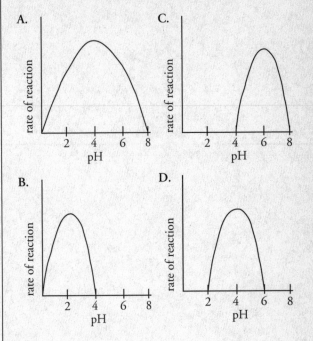

219. Mammalian fetal circulation is similar to amphibian adult circulation in that:

    A. gas exchange occurs only in the lungs.
    B. gas exchange occurs only in the placenta.
    C. the heart has only three chambers prior to birth.
    D. there is a mixing of oxygenated and deoxygenated blood within the heart.

STOP. IF YOU FINISH BEFORE TIME HAS EXPIRED, CHECK YOUR WORK. YOU MAY GO BACK TO ANY QUESTION IN THIS PART ONLY.

ANSWERS AND
EXPLANATIONS

Answer Key

VERBAL REASONING		PHYSICAL SCIENCES		BIOLOGICAL SCIENCES	
1......A	39....A	66.....C	105...A	143...D	182...A
2......A	40....D	67....D	106...D	144...B	183...C
3......C	41....D	68....B	107...D	145...D	184...C
4......D	42....C	69....C	108...A	146...C	185...D
5......B	43....B	70....A	109...D	147...D	186...B
6......D	44....A	71....B	110...C	148...B	187...A
7......B	45....B	72....C	111...A	149...A	188...D
8......C	46....A	73....D	112...A	150...C	189...D
9......C	47....C	74....A	113...B	151...C	190...B
10....D	48....D	75....B	114...C	152...A	191...B
11....C	49....A	76....D	115...B	153...B	192...C
12....D	50....D	77....B	116...D	154...B	193...A
13....A	51....C	78....B	117...B	155...D	194...D
14....D	52....D	79....C	118...C	156...A	195...B
15....C	53....B	80....C	119...A	157...C	196...A
16....D	54....C	81....A	120...A	158...A	197...C
17....C	55....C	82....B	121...A	159...C	198...D
18....A	56....D	83....D	122...B	160...A	199...C
19....B	57....C	84....A	123...D	161...A	200...B
20....D	58....C	85....C	124...C	162...B	201...D
21....B	59....B	86....B	125...B	163...A	202...B
22....D	60....A	87....A	126...A	164...C	203...A
23....A	61....B	88....B	127...C	165...C	204...D
24....B	62....A	89....C	128...D	166...A	205...A
25....D	63....C	90....B	129...C	167...A	206...A
26....D	64....D	91....D	130...D	168...C	207...C
27....C	65....C	92....D	131...D	169...B	208...B
28....B		93....C	132...A	170...B	209...C
29....D		94....A	133...C	171...B	210...B
30....D		95....D	134...D	172...D	211...D
31....B		96....B	135...C	173...A	212...D
32....A		97....A	136...B	174...D	213...B
33....D		98....C	137...D	175...C	214...A
34....D		99....B	138...D	176...D	215...A
35....D		100...B	139...B	177...A	216...C
36....D		101...A	140...C	178...B	217...C
37....A		102...A	141...A	179...B	218...B
38....C		103...B	142...C	180...D	219...D
		104...B		181...D	

Your Score

Now that you've checked your test against the answer key, you can translate the results into an approximation of real MCAT scores and percentile rankings for the Verbal Reasoning, Physical Sciences, and Biological Sciences sections. Simply follow these three steps:

Step 1: Raw Scores
Compute your raw scores by adding the number of correct answers for each section.

Section	Questions	Your Raw Score (Number Correct)
Verbal Reasoning	1–65	
Physical Sciences	66–142	
Biological Sciences	143–219	

Step 2: Score Conversion
Look for your raw scores in the chart below, and pinpoint your estimated scaled scores.

Verbal Reasoning		Physical Sciences		Biological Sciences	
Raw Score	Estimated Scaled Score	Raw Score	Estimated Scaled Score	Raw Score	Estimated Scaled Score
0–9	1	0	1	0–10	1
10–22	2	1–14	2	11–21	2
23–27	3	15–20	3	22–25	3
28–32	4	21–26	4	26–30	4
33–35	5	27–32	5	31–35	5
36–39	6	33–38	6	36–40	6
40–42	7	39–42	7	41–43	7
43–45	8	43–47	8	44–47	8
46–49	9	48–51	9	48–52	9
50–51	10	52–55	10	53–55	10
52–56	11	56–59	11	56–60	11
57	12	60–62	12	61–62	12
58–61	13	63–66	13	63–66	13
62–64	14	67–74	14	67–71	14
65	15	75–77	15	72–77	15

Step 3: Score Distribution

To get an idea of where each scaled score might fall on a standard curve (the curve is different for each MCAT), you can use the score distribution chart below. Refer back to the scoring discussion in the Introduction to the MCAT for a look at an actual score distribution.

Scaled Score	% Achieving Scaled Score	Range of Percentile Ranks
15	1.1	98.8–99.9
14	2.7	97–98.7
13	3.6	93–96
12	4.5	88–92
11	8.6	79–87
10	11.3	68–78
9	12.7	55–67
8	15.0	40–54
7	12.1	29–39
6	9.5	20–28
5	7.4	12–19
4	4.5	7–11
3	3.1	4–6
2	2.7	1.3–3
1	1.2	0–1.2

Scaled Score Mean = 8.0
Standard Deviation = 2.50

VERBAL REASONING

Passage I
Questions 1–8

The first passage in this section is a humanities passage on the topic of nihilism. It's organized in a very orderly fashion, so it should be relatively easy to relocate details when you're answering questions. Paragraph 1 defines nihilism as "the systematic negation of all perceptual orders and assumptions" and then mentions the historical crosscurrents, philosophical skepticism about truth, and the mystical quest for pure truth that led to nihilism. Paragraph 2 delves into the first of these two historical traditions by examining the position of the famous skeptic David Hume, who argued that external reality is unknowable because there is no way to verify that our sense impressions correspond to something real. Paragraph 3 turns to the second historical influence on nihilism, the mystical quest for pure truth. Two examples of mystic thought are discussed, Buddhist meditation techniques and the beliefs of St. John of the Cross. Finally, in Paragraph 4 the author explains how radical skepticism combined with a "near-mystical faith in the power of a new beginning" to form the nihilism of the Russian intelligentsia as well as the nihilistic element in the counterculture of the 1960s.

Let's take a look at the questions.

1 **A**—This question asks you for the author's working definition of *nihilism*. Remember that the author's definition is not the same as the usual definition of nihilism, a form of extremist political thought, so **C** is not correct. The definition that reflects the author's own thinking is provided in the second and third sentences of Paragraph 1. The author says there that nihilism is a complex intellectual stance whose essence is systematic negation of perceptual orders and assumptions. This points to **Choice A** as the correct answer.

Choice B defines the essence of mysticism, not nihilism. **Choice D** is too narrow, being an aspect of political nihilism derived purely from skepticism.

2 **A**—This is an Inference question. The correct answer, **Choice A**, is a restatement of the first sentence of Paragraph 4, which says that the two traditions prepared the ground for the political nihilism of the nineteenth and twentieth centuries. If skepticism and mysticism paved the way for modern political nihilism, then they must be combined in modern political nihilism.

Choice B contradicts the whole thrust of the last paragraph of the passage. **Choice C** goes too far in saying that the two strands of nihilist thought are necessary prerequisites of any positive modern social thought. The second sentence of Paragraph 1 says that nihilism forms the basis for many positive assertions of modern thought, but this doesn't mean that it must form the basis for all of them. **Choice D** is wrong because mysticism appears in both Eastern and Western philosophical traditions.

3 **C**—The third question is in Roman numeral format. You have to decide which statement or statements accurately describe how the author uses quotations from other writers. Let's take the statements one by one.

Statement I is true. There are three quotations used in the passage, two by Stanley Rosen in the second and fourth paragraphs, and one by Novak in Paragraph 3. Rosen's first quote, at the end of Paragraph 2, summarizes Hume's argument, and Rosen's second quote sums up what the author wants to say about the political nihilism of the Russian intelligentsia. Statement I will therefore be part of the correct answer; this eliminates **Choice D**, which does not include Statement I.

Statement II is false because the author never presents any contrasting points of view in the entire passage. This rules out **Choice B. Statement III**, on the other hand, is true. In the opening sentence of Paragraph 4, the author refers to the quote from Novak in the previous paragraph in order to make the transition from the discussion of mysticism to the larger point about how skepticism and mysticism paved the way for nihilism.

Since **Statements I** and **III** are true, **Choice C** is correct.

4 **D**—This question centers on Hume's conclusion in Paragraph 2 that external reality is unknowable. Hume argued that there is no way to verify whether our sense impressions actually correspond to external reality because the only way to check one of our sense impressions is to use other sense impressions. He assumed, therefore, that we have no source of information about external reality other than sense impressions—**Choice D**.

Hume never concluded, at least as far as we know, that "nothing outside the mind exists"; he just said that we couldn't know what was outside the mind. This rules out **Choice A. Choice B** twists Hume's belief that sense impressions are actually part of the contents of the mind; Hume didn't say that sense impressions were **all** that we have in our minds. **Choice C** is a distortion of Hume's conclusion that causality **may** be a subjective projection of the mind.

5 **B**—In the beginning of the last paragraph, the author says that Novak's quote "points to the way [the] philosophical and mystical traditions prepared the ground for the political nihilism of the 19th and 20th centuries." **Choice B** paraphrases this statement and is the correct answer.

Although Novak does characterize St. John's doctrine, this is not why his interpretation is important to the author's argument, so **A** is wrong. Novak does not draw a parallel between Humean skepticism and Christian mysticism, which rules out **Choice C**, nor does he say that St. John's teachings were influential, so **D** is wrong as well.

6 **D**—This Scattered Detail question is in the All-EXCEPT format, so you have to pick the choice that is a technique **not** used by the author to develop his thesis. The best approach to this type of question is simply to go through the choices one by one.

The author discusses David Hume as a representative of skepticism and St. John of the Cross as a representative of mysticism, so **Choice A** is not the answer. **B** is wrong, too; the author contrasts the common definition of nihilism with his own definition in the first three sentences of the passage. It is also in the first paragraph that the author states that skepticism and mysticism are "united by their categorical rejection of the 'known'"—this identification of the common element in the two traditions is **Choice C**.

Eliminating these three choices leaves us with **Choice D** as the correct answer. The author never examines the practical consequences of any social doctrine, let alone those of nihilism.

7 **B**—The author uses Rosen's quote to support his own thesis that the Russian political nihilists combined radical skepticism and the rejection of existing institutions with a faith in the power of a new beginning: "their desire to destroy becomes a revolutionary affirmation." The quote confirms that nihilism is more than just the desire to reject or destroy society (**Choice B**).

Neither the author nor Rosen suggests that the nihilists were impractical, so **A** is wrong. **C** can't be correct because the author never speaks of nihilism as a doctrine that is currently "alive." **Choice D** suggests that the fusion of the skeptical and mystical traditions in nihilism is weighed more heavily towards skepticism than towards mysticism, but the author never says anything to this effect, so it can be eliminated as well.

8 **C**—For the final question of this passage, you have to pick the choice that would best continue the passage's final paragraph. On this type of question, you are looking for a choice that follows logically from the flow of the author's argument. So you can bet that the right answer will somehow refer to the counterculture movement of the 1960s that is mentioned in the passage's final sentence.

Choice A suggests that the negative effects of nihilism are still being felt, but the author never hints that any form of nihilism had a negative effect on anything, so **A** should be tossed out. The nihilistic element of the counterculture movement is not new and different from classical nihilism, so **B** is wrong. **Choice C** would conclude the passage by commenting further on the nihilism of the 1960s revolutionaries—this is more like what you're looking for.

A quick look at **Choice D** confirms that **Choice C** is the best answer. Since the author has obviously been studying nihilism, he isn't going to say that the study of nihilism belongs to the past but not the present.

Passage II
Questions 9–15

The second passage is a rather straightforward one about aggressive behavior in animals. The author gives a working definition of "aggression" in Paragraph 1: it is any action that harms an adversary or compels an adversary to retreat. Paragraph 2 distinguishes between aggression directed at animals of other species and conspecific aggression, which is directed at the members of an animal's own species. The author cites social dominance hierarchies as one of the most common forms of conspecific aggression.

The remaining three paragraphs discuss the two basic types of aggressive behavior—attack and defensive threat. Each involves a pattern of physical and behavioral responses that tends to remain the same regardless of circumstances. The author spends most of Paragraphs 3 and 4 describing these patterns. In the fifthparagraph, the author poses the time-worn question of whether the aggressive patterns of behavior in animals are innate or learned. There is evidence, as the author notes, to support both conclusions.

9 **C**—Question 9 is a Detail question on dominance hierarchies, which are discussed in Paragraph 2. The reason for the stability of these hierarchies is revealed in the final sentence of the paragraph; hierarchies are rarely threatened by disputes because the inferior animal immediately submits when confronted by a superior. **Choice C**, which paraphrases this assertion, is the correct answer.

Choice A doesn't make any sense; even if the behavior responses of the group (whatever those behavior responses are supposed to be) are known by all of the members, this won't automatically make the hierarchy stable. The author never says that the defensive threat posture stops most conflicts (**Choice B**) or that conspecific aggression is inhibited by the need for protection from other species (**Choice D**), so both of these choices can be quickly eliminated.

10 **D**—This Detail question is about the physiological changes a cat experiences when it assumes the defensive threat position. The defensive threat response is discussed primarily in Paragraph 4. An increase in cardiovascular activity (**Choice A**), narrowing of the eyes (**Choice B**), and stomach muscle contraction (**Choice C**) are all mentioned in the paragraph as being part of the defensive threat response. However, the author never says that one of these is more significant than the others, so **Choice D** is correct.

11 **C**—The entire passage is about agonistic, or aggressive, behavior, so you need to rely on your memory of the topics of different paragraphs if you want to go back and verify the statements in this Roman numeral question. **Statement I** is taken practically verbatim from the final sentence of Paragraph 1. Since this statement is true, you can eliminate **Choice B. Statement II** paraphrases the entire final paragraph, so it is true as well and **Choice A** has to be ruled out. **Statement III,** on the other hand, is not supported by anything in the passage; all you know from the second paragraph is that both conspecific and interspecies aggression exist. **Choice C** is the correct answer.

12 **D**—Question 12, an Inference question, centers on the nature-versus-nurture argument discussed in the final paragraph. Keep the author's conclusion—that aggressive patterns are

both innate and learned—in mind when you're looking for the right choice. It allows you to rule out **Choice C** immediately, since it is clear that scientists have not resolved the question in favor of genetics.

The only thing the passage says is controversial is the definition of aggression, so **Choice A** is wrong. **Choice B** is wrong because the author never says that the experiments on mice were the first investigations done to answer the nature–versus–nurture question. This leaves **Choice D** as the only possible correct answer, and it seems reasonable to infer from the author's remark, "copious evidence suggests that animals learn and practice aggressive behavior," that there has been a lot of study devoted to this subject.

13 **A**—By now you should have a pretty good idea of what's in the passage. Scan the choices and eliminate the ones that look familiar. **Choice B**, the evolutionary purpose of aggression, is explicitly addressed in the final sentence of Paragraph 1. Conspecific aggression occurring in dominance hierarchies, **Choice C**, is discussed in Paragraph 2. The relationship between play and aggression, **Choice D**, is mentioned in the final two sentences of the passage.

Choice A seems to be the winner by the process of elimination. Indeed, the physiological changes that accompany aggressive behavior were discussed in detail only with respect to the defensive threat response and not with respect to attack behavior in cats. **A** is the correct answer.

14 **D**—This is an Application question. You already know a considerable amount from the passage about aggressive behavior in animals;

you just have to decide which new assertion fits in with what you already know.

The author doesn't say anything about a link between aggressive behavior and breathing (the real reason a shark has to stay in motion), so **Choice A** is out. The inability of newborn mice to exhibit the attack response is NOT proof that aggressive behavior must be learned, as **Choice B** claims. On the contrary, mice attack after only one month, too short a time to have learned this behavior—which is why the author cites this as evidence that aggressive behavior must be partially genetic. **Choice C** is wrong because the author never discusses animal species that don't exhibit aggressive behavior.

That leaves us with **Choice D**, which says that certain hawks use the same means of attack on both squirrels and gophers. This fits right in with the facts of the passage, since the second sentence of Paragraph 3 states that the physiological and behavioral patterns that make up aggressive behavior change very little regardless of the stimuli that provoke them (the stimuli here being the squirrels and the gophers). Thus **Choice D** is the correct answer.

15 C—This Main Idea question shouldn't be that difficult. The very first words of the passage telegraph what it is all about: agonistic behavior in animals. Each paragraph covers a different aspect of aggressive patterns of behavior. The author never focuses on one thing closely for very long, so **Choice C** is the one you want.

Eliminate **Choices A** and **B** right away. The author never "analyzes the differences" between attack and defensive threat behavior, and the only thing mentioned in the passage as being debatable is the exact definition of "aggression." **Choice D** is wrong for two reasons. First, the author is writing about all animals, not just mammals—note the example of the pecking order among domestic fowl.

Second, the illustrations of agonistic behavior are merely the author's way of achieving his greater purpose, which is to give a quick overview of animal aggression.

Passage III
Questions 16–24

On now to the third passage in this test. As the first paragraph indicates, this one is about the proposed "Clean Air Act" and the reaction of the mass transit authorities to the proposal. Paragraph 2 explains the aims of the act and specifies the types of pollutants that it hopes to combat. Some of the concerns of the transit authorities are brought forward in Paragraph 3, while Paragraph 4 discusses the development and implementation of alternative fuel sources, which would help in reducing the level of pollutants in the atmosphere. In Paragraph 5, the author outlines the drawbacks of the use of alternative fuels. Paragraph 6 highlights the position of transit authorities that perhaps the best way to contend with the pollution problem is to build more mass transit systems and encourage people to use them rather than personal transportation.

16 D—In the third paragraph, the author states that transportation agencies will find it challenging to strike a balance between complying with the government's new standards and continuing to fulfill the transportation needs of the general public (**Choice D**).

Choice A is incorrect because it contradicts the whole theme of the passage, i.e., that compliance with the provisions of the Act will be difficult for transit agencies. **Choice C** can be ruled out because government funding for mass transit is not discussed anywhere in the passage. Similarly, **Choice B**

is wrong because the abilities of wealthy private corporations to change their methods of business is not discussed by the author.

17 **C**—The correct answer to this Inference question can be found by looking at the first two sentences of the last paragraph. Transit authorities believe that unless the Clean Air Act acknowledges that people need some form of mass transportation, the problems of pollution might not be significantly altered. **Choice C** paraphrases this idea.

It is stated in the first paragraph that compliance with the Act might make it difficult for transit agencies to continue to operate within realistic budgets. However, one can not infer from the information given in the passage that transportation costs will rise to a prohibitive level. **Choice A** is therefore incorrect. **B** is out because private automobile manufacturers aren't mentioned anywhere in the passage. Finally, **Choice D** is wrong because there is no reason to think that the use of public transportation would decrease from the present level if nothing were done to affect it.

18 **A**—According to the fifth paragraph, transit officials believe that developing new ways to fuel mass transit will take at least 50 years to realize. In other words, alternative fuel development is an unrealistic goal for the short term (**Choice A**).

Choice B is out because restrictions on petroleum products are not discussed in the passage. Nor is there any mention of federal and state subsidies of alternative fuel development, so **Choice C** can be eliminated. As for **Choice D**, the passage never says that developing alternative fuels will increase the cost of transportation to consumers.

19 **B**—The answer to this Detail question can be found in the first sentence of Paragraph 2: The aim of the Clean Air Act is to reduce the level of sulfur dioxide by at least 10 million tons (**Choice B**).

Choices A and **C** are incorrect because they're too extreme; the second paragraph doesn't say anything about "completely eradicating" pollution or "eliminating" toxic air emissions (the latter will just be "strictly regulated"). Finally, although penalties for transgressors of the regulations would be enforced by the Act, the main goal of the Act is not to punish people for polluting but to reduce the level of pollution, so **Choice D** is wrong.

20 **D**—The Clean Air Act makes a lot of proposals, which are in the second and fourth paragraphs. You have to go through the answer choices and pick out the one mentioned in either of these two paragraphs.

Choice A is wrong because one of the major criticisms of the Act (in the last paragraph) is that it does not emphasize the use of mass transit over private transportation. Neither does it (as far as we know) attempt to increase public awareness of the effects of pollution (**Choice B**), which would be a way to encourage people to use mass transportation. **C** goes too far: it would be impossible to propose the "total eradication" of pollutants.

Choice D is the only one remaining. The fourth paragraph states that provisions contained in the Act are aimed at encouraging the development and practical use of alternative fuel sources. In fact, the Act states that mass transit in certain cities should run on "clean-burning fuels" by the year 2000. **Choice D** is therefore correct.

21 **B**—The last sentence of Paragraph 1 provides the answer to this Detail question: Transit authorities are "concerned that it would be difficult to comply with the pollution and emissions control standards while continuing to operate within realistic budgets." **Choice B** paraphrases this nicely.

There is no evidence that the Clean Air Act would discourage the use of mass transit, so **A** is wrong. Nor is the cost of switching to new sources of energy ever discussed, which rules out **C**. The transit officials do point out that there will be "political and social ramifications of usurping the role of the petroleum industries" (**Choice D**), but **B** is the correct answer because transit authorities are obviously more worried about themselves than about the petroleum industries.

22 **D**—When answering a question that asks for the one false statement among true ones, see if one particular answer choice jumps out at you. If that does not happen, then your best bet is to carry out a process of elimination.

Choice A in this question is taken from the last sentence of the first paragraph. It is a true statement and is therefore an incorrect response to the question. **Choices B** and **C** are also true statements. The former is taken word-for-word from Paragraph 5, while the latter is a synopsis of information given in the first two sentences of the last paragraph.

This leaves us with **Choice D,** which is a false statement and is therefore the correct answer. The statement is a distortion of information given in the last sentence of Paragraph 4. It is true that the Act proposes that new buses in major cities must run on clean-burning fuel; however, there is no suggestion here nor elsewhere in the passage that transit authorities feel incapable of complying with that particular provision of the Act.

23 **A**—In the third sentence of Paragraph 4, the author states that the goal of the mobile resources section of the Act is to eradicate fuel emissions in order to provide cleaner air and a more favorable environment. **Choice A** is therefore the correct response.

Choice B is a distortion of the author's assertion that provisions in the mobile resources section are meant to encourage the development and practical use of alternative fuel sources. **Choice C** is also incorrect; transit officials criticize the Act for failing to convince the public of the environmental benefits of mass transit. And the last sentence of paragraph 5 says that the ACT does not mention redevelopment of the oil industries' method of production, so **D** is out as well.

24 **B**—Look at the first two sentences of the last paragraph. Transit authorities contend that unless the Act acknowledges the need for some form of public transportation and takes steps to encourage mass transit, pollution levels might not be significantly altered by the Act. **Choice B** is therefore the correct response.

Nothing is said in the passage about lead emissions, financial incentives to encourage the use of mass transit, or the role of private industry in the global warming crisis, so **A, C**, and **D** can all be eliminated.

Passage IV
Questions 25–33

The next passage is a social science passage about the historian Fernand Braudel. The first paragraph introduces us to Braudel and the *Annales* historians, who assumed that history must be interpreted in the context of the forces and material conditions that influence human behavior.

Paragraph 2 outlines Braudel's conception of the three temporalities that interact to make history: short-lived dramatic events, larger half-century cyclical processes, and the *longue duree*, the aspects of everyday life that remain unchanged for centuries and define the limits of potential social change. Paragraph 3 focuses on Braudel's doctoral thesis on the Mediterranean in order to present an example of the way geographical features can impact on human populations over a long span of time even more than national borders do. The final paragraph mentions a few of the criticisms that have been lodged against Braudel, but concludes that he asked significant questions that traditional historians had overlooked.

25 **D**—The main idea of the passage is outlined in the first paragraph. The author states that Braudel's writing has made significant contributions to historical theory and research and that it departs from traditional historical approaches. The author goes on in the rest of the passage to illustrate Braudel's contribution by defining his ideas and distinguishing them from conventional historical techniques. So, **Choice D** is the correct answer.

Choice A is wrong because Braudel's historical analysis of Mediterranean life is just an example the author uses to support the main idea. **Choice B** is incorrect because there is nothing in the passage to indicate that Braudel criticized Marxist historiography. And since the perspective of *longue duree* is never contrasted with the actions of major historical figures, **C** is clearly wrong.

26 **D**—The reason that the author refers to Febvre and Bloch is explained in the parentheses at the end of Paragraph 1. The author states that Febvre and Bloch had anticipated

Braudel by originating the historical approach that emphasized economics. **Choice D** therefore is the correct answer.

Choice A is wrong because the limitations of the *Annales* approach are not discussed until the end of the passage. The relevance of economics to history is not mentioned in relation to Febvre and Bloch, so **Choice B** is wrong. **Choice C** is incorrect because the need for combining various sociological approaches is not debated in the first paragraph or elsewhere.

27 **C**—**Choice C** is the correct answer to this All-EXCEPT question because nationalism is never mentioned in the passage. All the other choices are aspects of Braudel's approach to history. **A** is mentioned in Paragraph 1. Paragraph 3 explains that Braudel ignored national boundaries in favor of geographical features in his work on the Mediterranean (**Choice B**). In the same paragraph, you find out that unchanging aspects of everyday life (**Choice D**) were what the French historian studied most closely.

28 **B**—This is a paragraph Main Idea question, so the right answer has to cover the entire paragraph. Beware of choices that are just details from the paragraph in question (in this case, the third paragraph), like **Choice C**. The author mentions the geography of the Mediterranean only in the context of discussing his real subject: Braudel's depiction of the role of geography in human history (**Choice B**) when a long view of history is taken.

Choice A should be eliminated because Braudel's use of obscure facts does not mean that he was "fascinated" with them. **D** is wrong because the author never says that national borders are irrelevant; they were just less significant to Braudel than geographical boundaries.

29 **D**—The author states in Paragraph 1 that unlike conventional historians, the *Annales* historians emphasized understanding history in the context of the forces and material conditions that underlie human behavior. **Choice D** paraphrases this.

Annales historians are interested in synthesizing data from social sciences in order to understand history, but they aren't more interested in other social sciences than in history, so **Choice A** is wrong. Braudel incorporated the study of great figures into his framework of the three temporalities, so there is no reason to think *Annales* historians would be critical of the achievements of historical figures (**Choice B**). **Choice C** is incorrect because the author states in Paragraph 1 that the *Annales* historians advocate using economic data in historical research.

30 **D**—The author ends the passage by affirming the value and influence of Braudel's approach; he cites the number of similarly designed studies as evidence. The next sentence will most likely refer to these studies in some way and be similarly upbeat about Braudel's work. **Choice D** fits the bill.

Choice A, on the other hand, is wrong because it contradicts the positive tone the last sentence of the passage established. **Choice B** is incorrect because it does not continue the thought from the last sentence and is inconsistent with the main ideas of the passage as a whole. **Choice C** is wrong because it too is negative in tone when a positive sentence is appropriate.

31 **B**—The author voices the possible criticisms of Braudel in the last paragraph. One of them is that he minimized the differences among the social sciences, so **Choice B** looks like the correct answer here.

The author is never critical of Braudel's "structures," so **A** is out. The relationship between short-term events and long-term social activity is not mentioned by the author at all, so **C** is wrong, and **Choice D** can be eliminated because Braudel is criticized for having no boundaries for social analysis, not for having rigid boundaries.

32 **A**—The *longue duree* is the aspects of daily life—what people eat, what they wear, how they travel—that remain unchanged for centuries. **Statement I**, then, is certainly an example of what Braudel would consider the *longue duree*. **Statement II**, however, falls into the category of *evenementielle*, the short-lived dramatic events of a region, whereas the reduction in the population of a region (**Statement III**) from a disease might last a half-century or so, would fall into the category of *conjonctures*. Since **Statement I** is the only one that exemplifies *longue duree*, **Choice A** is correct.

33 **D**—**Choice D** is the correct answer to this Application question because the author suggests in the first paragraph that one fundamental principle of Braudel's work is that history must be understood in the context of forces and material conditions that underlie human behavior. So the assertion that historical actions are influenced by forces of which individuals may be unaware is perfectly consistent with Braudel's principles.

Choice A, on the other hand, is off base because neither written history nor social elites are mentioned in the passage. **Choice B** is incorrect; defining the limits of potential social change in the *longue duree* was but one aspect of Braudel's work, and was certainly not the historian's most important task. **Choice C** is a cliché and not particularly relevant to nor descriptive of Braudel's analysis.

Passage V
Questions 34–39

This passage is about Neanderthals and their connection, or perhaps lack of connection, to modern humans. The first and second paragraphs explain why Neanderthals are no longer thought of as subhuman or prehuman but as a fully human species. As Paragraph 3 says, however, anthropologists do not believe that there was enough time for Neanderthals to evolve into modern human beings. The differences between Neanderthals and modern human were simply too great, according to this view. Paragraph 4 puts forth the alternative theory that modern humans could have evolved quickly from a segment of the Neanderthal or some other ancestral population by the process of localized evolution that would then "displace or absorb" the Neanderthals. In Paragraph 5, the author discusses the puzzle of the disappearance of the Neanderthals.

34 **D**—The characteristics that Boule took as evidence that the Neanderthals were subhuman are listed in Paragraph 2. **Choice D** is correct because Boule never cites the use of tools as evidence of subhuman development.

35 **D**—Let's examine the choices one by one and try to eliminate the wrong answers. **Choice A** is wrong because the intelligence of the Neanderthals is never compared to that of humans. **B** may have been true of the Neanderthals, but only after the onset of the Ice Age, so there must be a better answer. **Choice C** is incorrect because explanations of the disappearance of the Neanderthals posit that modern humans wiped them out or displaced or absorbed them.

Choice D is the correct answer; the author states in Paragraph 1 that the Neanderthal's burial of their dead is regarded as an indication that they had capacity for religious and abstract thought.

36 **D**—According to the third paragraph, Neanderthals inhabited a vast area from 100,000 to 35,000 years ago and then disappeared within a period of five to ten thousand years. If they actually took the whole 10,000 years to disappear, that means the latest any Neanderthal could have existed was 25,000 years ago (**Choice D**).

37 **A**—The evidence that the Neanderthals did not evolve into modern humans is laid out in the second half of Paragraph 3. The author says that the anatomical differences between Neanderthals and modern humans (**Choice A**) are major enough that evolution could not have taken place in a span of ten thousand years.

B is a close wrong answer choice, since the brief time frame of 10,000 years **is** part of the reason that scientists think humans did not evolve from Neanderthals. But the time frame isn't evidence enough; presumably, if Neanderthals and humans were close enough anatomically, 10,000 years would have been enough time for evolution to take place. It's the anatomical differences that seem to make the whole thing impossible.

Choices C and **D** aren't mentioned in the passage at all.

38 **C**—The hypotheses about the disappearance of the Neanderthals are all in Paragraph 5. Of the choices listed, only **Choice C** is not put forward in this paragraph as a possible explanation. Even if humans did evolve from an isolated group of Neanderthals, as Trinkaus and Howells suggest, knowing this would not shed light on the mystery of the disappearance of the entire population of Neanderthals.

39 **A**—According to the fourth paragraph, interbreeding in a concentrated population can produce more pronounced genetic effects in a shorter period of time than interbreeding in a sparser population would. From this it can be inferred that the rate of evolution is directly related to the concentration of the species population (**Choice A**).

Changes in the anatomical features of a species (**Choice B**) might be a way to measure the rate of evolution, but anatomical features do not directly affect the rate of evolution. The rate of environmental change (**Choice C**) and the adaptive capabilities of a species (**Choice D**) may both affect a species' survival, but they, too, do not speed up evolution in the way that concentrating the population can.

Passage VI
Questions 40–45

This passage is a brief history lesson about the political struggles in Russia just after its 1917 revolution. The first paragraph describes how the postrevolutionary situation fell short of the socialist vision. As a result, as we learn in the second paragraph, a certain amount of debate about long-range policy took place among the Bolsheviks, with several groups of varying perspectives and programs emerging. The third and fourth paragraphs sketch out the programs advocated by Bukharin and Trotsky, while the fifth paragraph explains that Stalin's program did not become clear until he gained control of the party. Stalin's political maneuvers in the quest for power and his campaign to "build up heavy industry on the backs of the peasants" are the subjects of Paragraphs 6 and 7.

40 **D**—This is an All-EXCEPT question, so you have to pick out the choice that did **not** contribute to the weakness of the Bolshevik regime. The author discusses the problems facing the Bolshevik regime in 1921 in the first paragraph. These problems included a collapse of industrial production stemming from the civil war (**Choices A** and **B**), and persistent peasant revolts (**Choice C**). A lack of democracy (**Choice D**), however, did not hurt the Bolsheviks; rather, they were able to monopolize power by refusing to legalize other political parties. **D** is correct.

41 **D**—The author describes the details of the New Economic Policy at the end of Paragraph 1. The author lists the permission of private trade—which was previously banned—as one feature of the policy. Forced requisitions were eliminated and trade unions were allowed to be active again. In other words, the New Economic Policy relaxed economic controls—**Choice D**.

Economic centralization (**Choice A**) and deliberate inflation (**Choice B**) can be ruled out because they are not mentioned in the first paragraph. **C** directly contradicts the fact that trade unions were once again allowed to fight for higher wages and benefits and to strike.

42 C—The features of Bukharin's program are listed in Paragraph 3. At the end of the paragraph, the author states that one of Bukharin's policies was to form alliances with nonsocialist foreign regimes that were favorable to Russia. This makes **Choice C** the correct answer.

Choice A is one of Trotsky's policies, not Bukharin's. Avoiding confrontations with the trade unions (**Choice B**) was presumably the idea behind the New Economic Policy's lifting of restrictions; this wasn't Bukharin's policy either. **Choice D** was not a feature of anyone's program.

43 B—Details of Trotsky's and Stalin's policies and attitudes can be found in Paragraphs 4 and 7, respectively. Trotsky called for rapid industrialization and Stalin sought to build up heavy industry, so it's clear that industrialization was important to both of them (**Choice B**).

Choice A is incorrect; the author states that Trotsky was critical of the elite, but Stalin's attitude toward them is left unstated. Similarly, you don't know how either of them felt about democracy within the party (**Choice C**) or how Trotsky felt about trade unions (**Choice D**), so these choices are wrong.

44 A—You can throw out **Choices B** and **D** right away—Trotsky had control of the Red Army, not Stalin, and there is no reason to think that Stalin's initially neutral appearance helped him at all once he began to maneuver. Trotsky's misjudgment of threats (**Choice C**) enabled Stalin to force him out of Red Army leadership, but control of the party helped Stalin much more. He was able to use his powers to remove Zinoviev and Kamenev from Party leadership and to expel Trotsky from the Party and have him murdered. Thus **Choice A** is correct.

45 B—You know from the second paragraph that disputes over the long-range direction of policy led to the struggles within the Bolshevik party. This rules out **Choices A** and **D**, and all you have to figure out is whether the policy was foreign or economic. Since foreign policy is mentioned only once in the passage, the differences were clearly over economic policy (**Choice B**).

Passage VII
Questions 46–53

This is a passage on the ecological balance between food and population size. The first paragraph points out that while the interrelationship between food availability and population size is a basic ecological principle, recent work reveals that the interrelationship may be more complex than ever before imagined. That is, some plant food sources seem to regulate the size of rodent populations through biochemical signals. The second paragraph presents the example of 6-MBOA in young mountain grasses, which encourages reproduction in the mountain vole. The third paragraph gives another example: Common forest trees in Alaska discourage browsing by the *Lepus* hare by producing shoots that contain an unpalatable substance; this is thought to cause a decline in the hare population. The final paragraph then suggests the need for further research.

46 A—The answer to a Main Idea question has to be broad enough to cover the entire passage without being *too* broad. **Choice C**, for example, is wrong because although the author does summarize some data on the relationship between food sources and population size, it would be impossible for the passage to cover all available data on the subject. **Choice B**, on the other hand, is not broad enough; 6-MBOA is discussed in only one of the paragraphs. **Choice D** is off base because the author never argues against the conclusions of earlier researchers. She just says that things are more complex than was previously thought, and leaves it at that.

A summarizes the passage nicely and is the correct answer.

47 **C**—This Inference question contains a line reference that leads you to the end of Paragraph 2. The biological adaptation to which the sentence is referring is the "phytochemical triggering of copulatory behavior" in voles—that is, the chemical 6-MBOA in young mountain grasses causes voles to reproduce at just the right time, when there is a lot of grass for voles to feed on. This is important because the amount of available grass varies considerably. 6-MBOA, then, ensures the survival of voles in a situation of fluctuating food supply (**Choice C**).

6-MBOA doesn't limit reproduction; it encourages reproduction, so **A** is wrong. Use your common sense to eliminate **Choice B:** Seeking available food resources comes pretty naturally to animals. **Choice D** is wrong because a biological adaptation maximizes the survival of the entire species, not just individual voles.

48 **D**—The author recommends research on the reproductive behavior of lemmings because lemmings are similar in kind and in habitat to voles. Knowing whether lemmings have a reproductive trigger mechanism similar to that of voles would allow us to determine whether Berger's findings about voles are true of other species as well. This idea is captured by **Choice D**.

Choices B and **C** contradict this notion entirely. **Choice A** goes way too far: There is no way one study of lemmings could tell us all there is to know about the interrelationship between food supply and reproductive behavior in northern rodent populations.

49 **A**—Ecologists have long thought, according to the first sentence of the paragraph, that population size is a function of available food (this, by the way, rules out **Choice D**). They just didn't realize that the interrelationship of food and population size was so complex. In other words, they thought that the amount of available food was the only food factor that affected population (**Choice A**); they didn't know about food that biochemically encouraged or discouraged reproduction (which eliminates **Choice C**). **Choice A** is the correct answer.

We don't know what scientists formerly thought about the link between environmental factors and reproductive behavior, so **B** is not an option.

50 **D**—In this All-EXCEPT question, you have to identify the choice that is **not** an element of either experiment. **Choice A** is mentioned in the middle of Paragraph 2 as part of the vole experiment. **Choice B** was part of that experiment as well, as indicated at the beginning of Paragraph 2. Measuring consumption of treated and untreated foods (**Choice C**) was the method used in the experiment on hares.

Choice D is the one choice that was not an element of either experiment discussed in the passage. The passage does discuss the use of a control group in the 6-MBOA experiment, but this experiment was not measuring changes in the birth rate of the animals, so **D** is the correct answer.

51 **C**—This question asks for the assumption upon which rests Bryant's interpretation. Bryant concluded from his experiment that avoidance of unpalatable resins in the natural food source of *Lepus* may play a role in the decline in the *Lepus* population. He is assuming that hares will not eat anything at all, and thus starve to death, if they find resin on their food. The gist of this is captured in **Choice C**.

Certainly **Choice A** is not an underlying assumption. Bryant's experiment would be worthless if the hares' behavior in the experiment didn't give us an idea of how they behaved in nature. **Choice B** is out because Bryant's experiment does not investigate the reasons for the decennial rise in hare population. **Choice D** makes no sense because if the hares learned to look for new sources of food once they couldn't eat the resinous shoots, their population wouldn't decrease.

52 **D**—This Roman numeral question is a bit reminiscent of Question 50 in that you are once again considering what was or was not part of both studies. **Statement I** is not true because the effect of diet on reproduction is part of Berger's study only. Both studies investigate the relationship between food source and population size, so **Statement II** is true. **Statement III** is clearly true as well, so **Choice D** is the correct answer.

53 **B**—This is a very general question about the passage, so let's look at the answer choices to see if some of them can be ruled out. **Choices A** and **D** are wrong because we never find out why 6-MBOA forms in response to browsing (that is, how it helps the plant to do this) or exactly how it triggers reproductive activity in the vole. Nor do we know whether phytochemical reactions can be found anywhere besides northern environments, which eliminates **Choice C**. That leaves us with **Choice B**, and, sure enough, the importance of the timing of the voles' reproductive effort is explained in the last sentence of Paragraph 2. **Choice B** is the correct answer.

Passage VIII
Questions 54–58

The eighth passage on this test is a humanities passage about the portrayal of women in Stendhal's work and Simone de Beauvoir's reactions to Stendhal's images. De Beauvoir appreciated Stendhal's idea that the ideal woman was man's equal—intelligent, cultivated, free; she also, as we find out in the third paragraph, was relieved that Stendhal rejected the mystification of women. She did not agree, according to the fourth paragraph, with his idea that women can only realize and fulfill their own selves by having a man as an objective and a justification for living. Nevertheless, de Beauvoir was compelled by Stendhal's character Lamiel, who is the subject of the final three paragraphs of the passage. Despite her disadvantaged background, Lamiel gains a freedom of mind that allows her to "shape a destiny worthy of herself in a mediocre world." She is a great soul with no comfortable place in society and thus an equal to Stendhal's men.

54 **C**—This Inference question has to do with Stendhal's view of self-realization. In the first paragraph, the author says that in Stendhal's view, the ideal woman is one that reveals a man to himself, and in order to do so she must be his equal. Self-realization can be attained, then, through an equal (**Choice C**). Muses (**Choice A**), God (**Choice**

B), and family (**Choice D**) are not mentioned in the passage.

55 **C**—Go back to the sentence in question and read the surrounding sentences. Stendhal projected himself into Lamiel, his female character, de Beauvoir notes; he "assumed Lamiel's destiny." This is why Lamiel is "somewhat speculative"; Stendhal takes on the identity of a woman (**Choice C**), which means he had to rely on speculation.

Choice **A** is wrong. We know from the third paragraph of the passage that Stendhal rejected myth, rejected the mystification of women. Nothing in the passage indicates that Stendhal sensationalized his plots (**Choice B**) or exaggerated the aspirations of his female characters (**Choice D**).

56 **D**—This is an easy Detail question in the All-EXCEPT format. According to the third paragraph, de Beauvoir rejected the mystification of women in "fury, nymph, morning star . . . siren." The choice missing here is **D**, "mistress."

57 **C**—This is an Inference question regarding Stendhal's requirement for love. The answer appears both in the second paragraph—"love . . . will be more true if woman, being man's equal, is able to understand him more completely"—and in the last paragraph—"two who may have the chance to know each other in love . . . defy time" etcetera. The key is clearly understanding of each other (**Choice C**).

There is no mention in the passage of faithfulness or of a blessing of the union, which means **A** and **D** are out. Stendhal rejected the mystification of women, so **B** is wrong as well.

58 **C**—The line reference leads you to the middle of Paragraph 4; read the surrounding lines. Stendhal's belief that the fulfillment of women is dependent upon total dedication to men is what disappoints de Beauvoir. **Choice C** is correct.

A is wrong because Stendhal does believe that women can use their spiritual and creative powers if they have a worthy objective. Similarly, Stendhal does acknowledge the aspirations of women, as seen in his character Lamiel (contrary to **Choice D**). **B** is incorrect because de Beauvoir was happy that Stendhal "lived among women of flesh and blood."

Passage IX
Questions 59–65

The final passage is about the so-called "graying" of America, that is, the aging of the American population. The first and second paragraphs explain that the elderly population in America is growing rapidly due to increased life expectancy and to the aging of the baby boomers. From Paragraph 3 to the end of the passage, the author considers the ramifications of this aging of America. Paragraph 3 considers the possible effect on family structure. Paragraph 4 suggests that the elderly will become more attractive as employees and work longer. Paragraphs 5, 6, and 7 discuss the impact of the growing elderly population on Social Security and health care, which will have to be the focus of major government policy decisions.

59 **B**—The answer to this Detail question is a direct quote from the first sentence of Paragraph 6: The elderly population will double in the next forty years. No current housing shortage (**Choice A**) is discussed in the passage, nor does the author ever state that the elderly represent 30 percent of the U.S. population, **Choice D. Choice C** contradicts the second sentence in Paragraph 5, which notes that only 3 percent of today's elderly Americans make more than $50,000 a year.

60 **A**—The second sentence in Paragraph 5 states that according to government figures, 77 percent of elderly Americans earn less than $20,000 per year (**Choice A**). None of the other choices are drawn from the passage.

61 **B**—Since the first sentence of Paragraph 7 says that the Medicaid/Medicare system is already threatened by the continuous upward spiral of medical costs, you can infer that the projected doubling of the cost of care for disabled elderly Americans will represent a further drain on the system. In other words, Medicaid and Medicare will probably become even more expensive in the future, so **Choice B** is the correct answer.

 Choice A is never implied. In fact, it seems that a national health care system might be less expensive than the current system. **Choice C** distorts Paragraph 6's reference to the fact that the government has borrowed against the Social Security system to pay interest on the national debt. **Choice D** is too pessimistic. The author says that aging "boomers" may well demand that national health care be provided.

62 **A**—The second sentence of Paragraph 1 says that elders now outnumber teenagers for the first time in American history (**Choice A**). Since the boomers are the largest generation in U.S. history, numbering 75 million, **Choice B** is highly unlikely. Finally, the author never actually states

how many elderly people there are in the current U.S. population, but the current number must surely be greater than the number in 1950, **Choice C**, or in 1970, **Choice D**.

63 **C**—Speculation on the nature of the family of the future is in Paragraph 3. The second sentence of that paragraph states that one likely development will be a gradual restructuring towards an extended multigenerational family, making **Choice C** correct.

64 **D**—Since you don't know where the answer will come from in the passage, you have to go through the choices one by one. **Choice A** contradicts the statement from the middle of Paragraph 4 that only 15 percent of 65-year-old men still work. There is no evidence that any elderly people have lost their Social Security benefits, so **B** is out. **Choice C** distorts the second sentence of the final paragraph, which says that the cost of caring for disabled elderly Americans is expected to double in the next decade alone. **Choice D**, therefore, must be the correct answer; in fact, the author does say at the end of Paragraph 5 that elderly Americans have come to depend on government subsidies.

65 **C**—The last question in this set is based on the last paragraph of the passage. As the author says, the medical establishment and various special interest groups have so far blocked legislation aimed at creating a national health care system. **Choice C** is correct.

 The institution of a national health care system is never tied in the passage to the elimination of the federal deficit, so **A** is wrong. **Choice B** contradicts the suggestion in the passage that a national health care program may be less expensive than the current system. **Choice C** is wrong because it is the problems with Medicare/Medicaid that may make a national health care program necessary.

PHYSICAL SCIENCES

Passage I
Questions 66–70

66 C—To answer this question, you need to use Wien's law, which is given in the passage. It states that $\lambda = 2.9 \times 10^6/T$, where λ is the most intense wavelength emitted in nanometers and T is the temperature in kelvins. Since the temperature of the Sun's photosphere is 5,800 K, the most intense wavelength emitted is given by $\lambda = 2.9 \times 10^6/5,800 = 500$ nm, which is **Choice C**.

67 D—When an electron makes a transition from a higher energy state to a lower energy state, a photon is emitted with energy equal to the difference between the energies of the two states. The table in the passage provides energies for photon transitions from energy state $n = 2$ to various higher energy states in hydrogen. The absolute energy difference between states $n = 4$ and $n = 3$ is equal to the difference between their energies relative to the $n = 2$ state. Therefore, the energy of the photon emitted in the transition from $n = 4$ to $n = 3$ is $4.08 \times 10^{-19} - 3.02 \times 10^{-19} = 1.06 \times 10^{-19} \approx 10^{-19}$ J.

The energy of a photon E is given by $E = hc/\lambda$, where h is Planck's constant, c is the speed of light in a vacuum, and λ is the photon's wavelength. Rearranging to solve for λ gives $\lambda = hc/E$. Using $E = 10^{-19}$ J from above, we find:

$$\lambda = (6.6 \times 10^{-34})(3 \times 10^8)/(10^{-19}) \text{ m.}$$

Rounding to the nearest integer gives $\lambda = 20 \times 10^{-34+8+19}$ m $= 2 \times 10^{-6}$ m. Since 1 nm = 10^{-9} m, $\lambda = 2,000$ nm, which is **Choice D**.

68 B—The binding energy of an electron is by definition the energy required to detach an electron from an atom in its ground state. Hydrogen's ground state is the $n = 1$ state. When the atom is ionized, the electron is separated from the atom and makes a transition to the highest energy state, the $n = \infty$ state. This is not a distinct energy state, but rather it defines the minimum energy that must be transferred to the electron to free it from the atom. Hence, the energy difference between the $n = \infty$ and the $n = 1$ state is the binding energy of the electron in the hydrogen atom, and **Choice B** is correct.

Choices A, C, and D can all be ruled out based on the data presented in the passage that indicates that the energy increases as n increases. This implies that the energy of the $n = 2$ state is greater than that of the $n = 1$ state by some finite, positive amount E_{12}. Furthermore, according to the table, the energy of the $n = \infty$ state is 5.44×10^{-19} J greater than the energy of the $n = 2$ state. Since the energy difference between $n = \infty$ and $n = 1$ is the sum of these two finite, positive quantities ($E_{12} + 5.44 \times 10^{-19}$ J), it must also be finite and positive. Therefore, **Choice A** is wrong. **Choice C** is wrong because a zero frequency photon would correspond to zero energy, as shown by the formula $E = hf$, but, as discussed above, the energy absorbed must be positive. **Choice D** is also wrong because the sum $E_{12} + 5.44 \times 10^{-19}$ J is clearly greater than 5.44×10^{-19} J, the energy absorbed in the $n = 2$ to $n = \infty$ transition.

69 C—This question asks for the frequency f of light given its wavelength λ. If you didn't remember the relationship between the two, you could have figured it out from the formula $hf = hc/\lambda$ given in the passage. Dividing both sides by h, we obtain $f = c/\lambda$, where c is the speed of light in a vacuum. Plugging in λ = 550 nm, we obtain:

$$f = \frac{3 \times 10^8 \text{m/s}}{555 \times 10^{-9}\text{m}} = 5 \times 10^{14} \text{ Hz}$$

which most closely corresponds to **Choice C**.

70 **A**—This question asks you to apply Wien's law to the case of a star changing its size and temperature. Wien's law, $\lambda = 2.9 \times 10^6 / T$, indicates that the wavelength of the peak intensity depends only on temperature. Therefore, if the star's temperature doesn't change when it doubles in size, the wavelength of the peak intensity of the star's radiation will not change. **Choice A** is therefore the correct answer, and **Choices B** and **C** are wrong. Since the shape of the spectrum, like the location of the peak, is also a function of temperature **Choice D** is wrong as well.

Passage II
Questions 71–77

71 **B**—When the half-reactions are written as reductions—as they are here—the cell voltage is determined by the equation

$$E_{\text{cell}} = E_{\text{cathode}} - E_{\text{anode}}$$

(Remember that E_{cell} must be greater than zero for the reaction to be spontaneous.) The cell voltage is therefore 2.05 V:

$$1.69 \text{ V} - (-0.36 \text{ V}) = 2.05 \text{ V}$$

Since the potentials of cells connected in series are additive, a 20 V battery needs ten 2.05 V cells. **Choice B** is the correct answer. **Choice A** is a 10 V

battery, **Choice C** is a 30 V battery, and **Choice D** is a 40 V battery.

72 **C**—Oxidation—the loss of electrons— occurs at the anode. When both half-reactions are written as reductions, the following equation is used to determine the cell potential:

$$E_{\text{cell}} = E_{\text{cathode}} - E_{\text{anode}}$$

(Again, remember that E_{cell} must be greater than zero for the reaction to be spontaneous.) The cell potential is positive when the reduction potential of the second reaction in Table 1 is subtracted from the first reaction, making the first reaction the cathode and the second reaction the anode. Since oxidation occurs at the anode, the reaction must proceed to the left, making **Choice C** the correct answer. **Choice A** and **Choice B** are wrong because the first reaction is the cathode reaction, not the anode reaction. **Choice D** is wrong because the second reaction proceeds to the left, not to the right.

73 **D**—Oxidation occurs when a species' oxidation number increases; reduction occurs when a species' oxidation number decreases. Also discussed earlier, oxidation occurs at the anode and reduction occurs at the cathode. From the answer choices, it can be seen that lead oxide and lead are the only species that have to be investigated. In Reaction 1, Pb^{4+}, in lead oxide, is going to Pb^{2+}, in lead sulfate. Since lead's oxidation number has decreased, it has been reduced. **Choice A**, **Choice B**, and **Choice C** can, therefore, all be eliminated, leaving **Choice D** as the correct answer. **Choice D** is correct because lead is being reduced at the anode—where oxidation occurs—from Pb to Pb^{2+}.

74 A—The battery is being recharged, so Reaction 1 is proceeding to the left. Since aqueous sulfuric acid, H_2SO_4, is one of the products of recharging, the concentration of H^+ will increase, making **Choice A** the correct answer. **Choice B** is wrong because $PbSO_4(s)$ is serving as a reactant during recharging, and is therefore consumed during the reaction. **Choice C** is wrong because water is also a reactant during recharging. **Choice D** is wrong because the amount of lead oxide increases, not decreases as the battery is being recharged.

75 B—As can be seen in Reaction 1, when the lead-acid battery is being discharged, sulfuric acid, a reactant, is being consumed. Since it is stated in the passage that sulfuric acid is the electrolyte, the density will decrease as the discharge progresses, so the density at point A is less than that at point B. **Choice B** is, therefore, the correct answer. **Choice A** is wrong because at point A there is less electrolyte present, not more. **Choice C** is wrong because the density decreases as the discharge progresses. **Choice D** is wrong because there is a direct relationship between the density of the electrolyte and the state of discharge.

76 D—Remembering that a $k\Omega$ is 10^3 Ω and using the relationship that $V = IR$, a current of 0.1 A times a resistance of 10,000 Ω gives a voltage of 1,000 V. **Choice D** is therefore the correct answer. **Choice B** would have been chosen if you did not convert kiloohms to ohms. **Choice A** or **Choice C** could have been chosen if you made other conversion errors.

77 B—The reason that the battery "goes dead" with decreasing temperature is that the viscosity of the electrolyte increases. At higher viscosities the ions are moving much slower, which leads to an increase in resistance and a decrease in the power output. Roman numeral I states that the resistance of the electrolyte has decreased. This is not true, the resistance of the electrolyte increases with decreasing temperature. Since **Choice A**, **Choice C**, and **Choice D** all contain Roman numeral I, they can be eliminated, leaving **Choice B** as the correct answer.

Passage III
Questions 78–82

78 B—The question stem states that the voltage source, which, according to the passage, has negligible internal resistance, is replaced by a battery with a small, but significant internal resistance. A battery with significant internal resistance can be modeled as a voltage source connected in series with a resistor. Hence, the new circuit is the same as the one in Figure 1, except for the addition of a second resistor (call its resistance R_{int}) in series with the original resistor (call its resistance R_0). To determine how this additional resistance affects the circuit, use Ohm's law $V = IR$, where V is the voltage, I is the current, and R is the resistance. Solving for I gives $I = V/R$. Thus, in the original circuit, the voltage source supplies a voltage V and the ammeter measures a current $I_{original} = V/R_0$. In the new circuit, the total resistance is given by the addition rule for resistors in series, $R_{total} = R_0 + R_{int}$. Therefore, the current measured by the ammeter in the new circuit will be $I_{new} = V/(R_0 + R_{int})$, which is clearly smaller than $I_{original}$ since its denominator is larger. So **Choice B** is correct, and **Choice A** is wrong.

Choices **C** and **D** are wrong because the resistance of a resistor is a property that does not change with the addition of other resistors to the circuit. The resistance of a resistor remains constant when the voltage across it or the current through it changes.

79 **C**—Like charges repel each other and opposite charges attract each other. Since electrons have negative charge, they will move away from a negative terminal and move towards a positive terminal. This corresponds to the counterclockwise direction. So **Choices A** and **B** can be ruled out.

By convention current flows in the direction that positive charge would flow. This means that in the circuit in Figure 1, the current flows in the clockwise direction, from the positive terminal to the negative terminal, and **Choice C** is the correct answer. If you couldn't figure out the direction of current flow or the direction that the electrons travel, but you knew they were opposite directions, you could have eliminated **Choices B** and **D**.

80 **C**—Ammeters, like all components of electric circuits, have some internal resistance. Therefore, adding an ammeter to the circuit is like adding another resistor in series. If the ammeter has a large resistance, then the current flowing through the resistor will be significantly reduced when it is added to the circuit. If it has a small resistance, the current will be only slightly affected; so **Choice C** is correct.

Choice A is wrong. Insulated wires are wires surrounded by a nonconducting material, which prevents unintended contact with the current. Insulating the wires won't directly affect the current through the resistor and won't affect the way that the ammeter works. **Choice B** is wrong as well. The current in the wire to the right of the resistor is the same as the current to the left of the resistor, so an ammeter will function identically at either location. In both cases, the ammeter is in series with the resistor. **Choice D** is also wrong. An ammeter that can detect current in either direction may be useful. But whether it can or not is unrelated to the ammeter's effect on the current flowing through the resistor.

81 **A**—When the electrons collide with the atoms of the resistor, the vibration of the atoms increase, and the atoms' kinetic energy, which is the energy of motion, increases as well. By definition, the temperature of a gas, liquid, or solid is a measure of the average kinetic energy of the atoms that make up the substance. Thus, the increase in the kinetic energy of the atoms is directly related to the increase in temperature. **Choice A** is correct.

Since temperature is related to the average kinetic energy and not the potential energy, **Choices B** and **D** are wrong. As for **Choice C**, the passage states that the atoms vibrate as a result of the collisions. A moving electron hits an atom that is basically stationary and starts it in motion. This means that the electron transfers some of its kinetic energy to the atom. So the electron's kinetic energy actually decreases as a result of the collisions, and **Choice C** is wrong.

82 **B**—The energy delivered to a piece of toast must be equal to the energy dissipated by the toaster's resistor. The rate of energy dissipation, or the energy released per unit time, is known as the power. Mathematically, this can be expressed as $P = E/t$, where P is the power, and E is the energy released in time t. The passage gives the relation $P = I^2R$, where P is the power, I is the current, and R is the resistance of the resistor. Equating the two expressions for power and solving for E, gives $E = I^2Rt$. Now we substitute the values given in the question stem into the last equation for the energy and obtain $E = (4 \times 10^{-3} \text{ A})^2(10 \times 10^3 \ \Omega)(1 \text{ s}) = 0.16 \text{ J}$, which is **Choice B.**

As is often the case with questions involving calculations, the wrong answer choices are the results of math errors. For example, you would have obtained **Choice D** if you had forgotten to square the current.

Passage IV
Questions 83–88

83 **D**—If the pH of blood increases to 7.6, it becomes more alkaline, and the pH of blood must be kept at approximately pH 7.4. Since it is stated in the second sentence of the last paragraph that blood pH can be adjusted rapidly by changes in the rate of CO_2 exhalation, **Choice A** and **Choice B** can be eliminated. In order to bring the pH of blood back to its normal value of 7.4, it must become more acidic; it becomes more acidic by increasing the concentration of H^+. Reaction 1 has H^+ as a product, and according to Le Châtelier's principle, you should know that a reaction will proceed in a direction that will consume an added reactant or product. In other words, the concentration of a product can be increased by increasing the concentration of a reactant. If the concentration of carbon dioxide is allowed to increase, it will react to produce more H^+, resulting in a lowering of the pH. The concentration of carbon dioxide will increase if it is not exhaled, making **Choice D** the correct response.

84 **A**—Carbonic acid, H_2CO_3, is the intermediate formed when carbon dioxide and water combine, making **Choice A** correct. You should recognize that when the products of Reaction 1 combine, carbonic acid result. **Choice B** is incorrect because it is just not a logical intermediate: water and carbon dioxide would not react to form H^+ and CO_3^{2-}. **Choices D** and **C** can be eliminated because they both contain carbon dioxide, which is one of the two reactants.

85 **C**—You should know that the smaller the pK_a the stronger the acid. Looking at Table 1, it can be seen that the histidine side chains buffer has a stronger conjugate acid than both the organic phosphates buffer and the ammonium buffer. **Choice C** is therefore the correct response. **Choice A** is wrong because the pK_a of the histidine side chains buffer is not equal to the organic phosphates buffer. **Choice B** is wrong because it is the reverse of what it should be. **Choice D** is wrong because, again, the pK_a of the histidine side chains buffer is not equal to the organic phosphates buffer.

86 **B**—In Region I the following reaction takes place:

$$H_3PO_4(aq) + OH^-(aq) \rightarrow H_2PO_4^-(aq) + H_2O$$

As OH^- is added, $H_2PO_4^-$ is formed and a buffer is realized. So, in this region, there is a point at which the concentration of H_3PO_4 will equal that of $H_2PO_4^-$. In Region II there is a point at which exactly enough base has been added to react with all of the H_3PO_4; this point is called an equivalence point. In Region III the following reaction takes place:

$$H_2PO_4^-(aq) + OH^-(aq) \rightarrow HPO_4^{2-}(aq) + H_2O$$

Again, this system constitutes a buffer, and there is a point in this region at which—after enough base has been added—the concentration of $H_2PO_4^-$ will equal that of HPO_4^{2-}. **Choice B** is therefore the correct response. In Region IV, at another equivalence point, exactly enough base has been added to react with all of the $H_2PO_4^-$. In Region V the following reaction takes place:

$$HPO_4^{2-}(aq) + OH^-(aq) \rightarrow PO_4^{3-}(aq) + H_2O$$

This system is, of course, a buffer as well.

87 A—When a weak acid is reacted with a strong base, the equivalence point will be in the basic region. Consider the titration of equimolar solutions of acetic acid and NaOH. Before the equivalence point, the following reaction takes place:

$$C_2H_4O_2(aq) + OH^-(aq) \rightarrow H_2O + C_2H_3O_2^-(aq)$$

At the equivalence point, only $C_2H_3O_2^-$ exists. When $C_2H_3O_2^-$ undergoes hydrolysis (i.e., reacts with water), hydroxide ions are formed according to the following equilibrium:

$$C_2H_3O_2^-(aq) + H_2O \rightleftharpoons C_2H_4O_2(aq) + OH^-(aq)$$

The numerical value of the equilibrium constant along with the initial concentration of acetate is all that is needed to determine the hydroxide ion concentration. When equimolar solutions of a strong acid and a strong base are titrated, the equivalence point will be neutral. It is neutral because neither of the ions present at the equivalence point can undergo hydrolysis. **Choice A** is therefore the correct response. **Choice B** would be correct if a weak base was titrated with a strong acid.

88 B—As the passage states, the immediate buffering effect of bicarbonate is controlled by changes in the breathing rate. When acidosis occurs, the concentration of H^+ is too high. As discussed earlier, Le Châtelier's principle applies:

To decrease the concentration of H^+, the concentration of carbon dioxide must decrease. If the breathing rate increases, more carbon dioxide is exhaled and its concentration in the blood decreases. Since the effect of this rapid breathing is to remove carbon dioxide from the body, the ultimate effect is to decrease the total CO_2/HCO_3^- concentration in the blood. So **Choice B** is correct. **Choice A** is wrong because the ratio of CO_2 to HCO_3^- would decrease, not increase. **Choices C** and **D** are wrong because the breathing rate would increase, not decrease.

Discrete Questions 89–93

89 C—Since rotation about a point is at issue, an understanding of torques is needed to solve the problem. The torque τ, or rotational force on a rigid body resting on a pivot point, is given by $\tau = rF$, when a force F acts at a distance r from the pivot in a direction perpendicular to the axis of rotation. Balance is achieved when the net torque is zero, i.e., the clockwise torque equals the counterclockwise torque.

Draw a little sketch of the telephone handset, balanced horizontally on a pivot point. The weight of the mouthpiece is (100 grams)g, where g is the acceleration due to gravity. Call the distance between the point where this force acts and the pivot r_m. Similarly, the weight of the earpiece is (150 grams)g, and acts a distance r_e from the pivot. To achieve balance, the opposing torques must be equal to each other, so $(100 \text{ grams})gr_m = (150 \text{ grams})gr_e$. Solving for r_m and canceling out g gives $r_m = (3/2)r_e$. So the mouthpiece must be (3/2) times farther from the pivot than the earpiece, and **Choice C** is correct.

90 B—The relationship between ΔG, ΔH, ΔS, and temperature is

$$\Delta G = \Delta H - T\Delta S$$

For a reaction to be spontaneous, ΔG must be less than zero. If a reaction is not spontaneous at any temperature, ΔH must be positive and ΔS must be negative. No matter what the temperature, ΔG will always be positive and the reaction will be non-spontaneous. **Choice B** is therefore the correct response. **Choice A** is for a reaction that would be spontaneous if the temperature was sufficiently high. **Choice C** is for a reaction that is spontaneous at ALL temperatures. **Choice D** is for a reaction that would be spontaneous if the temperature was sufficiently low.

91 D—To achieve boiling, intermolecular forces holding the liquid together have to be overcome so that the molecules of the substance can enter the vapor phase. Boiling points of substances, therefore, often reflect the strength of the intermolecular forces operating among the molecules. **Choice D** is correct because the intermolecular hydrogen-oxygen bonds in water are stronger than the intermolecular hydrogen-sulfur bonds in hydrogen sulfide. When hydrogen is bonded to a strongly electronegative element such as nitrogen, oxygen, or fluorine, very strong intermolecular forces exist. These forces are called hydrogen bonds. **Choice A** is wrong because, even though it is true that intramolecular oxygen-hydrogen bonds are stronger than intramolecular sulfur-hydrogen bonds, it is not the reason that water boils at a higher temperature than hydrogen sulfide. **Choice B** is wrong because if the enthalpy of vaporization of water is less than that of hydrogen sulfide, less energy is required to evaporate a given quantity of water at a constant temperature than for hydrogen sulfide. This is not what happens: the heat of vaporization of water is greater than that of hydrogen sulfide, so water boils at a higher temperature. **Choice C** is wrong because it is the ability of water to hydrogen bond that makes it boil at a higher temperature.

92 D—A semipermeable membrane allows the movement of solvent molecules, but not solute molecules. This means that water molecules can move through the semipermeable membrane and that glucose molecules cannot. **Choice A**, **Choice B**, and **Choice C** can all be eliminated, leaving **Choice D** as the correct response. You should be aware that osmosis is the net movement of solvent molecules through a semipermeable membrane from a pure solvent or a dilute solution to a more concentrated solution. In this case, solution A, which is 5 percent glucose, is more concentrated than solution B, which is only 1 percent glucose. So, there will be a movement from the more dilute solution, solution B, to one of higher concentration, which is solution A.

93 C—Normality is defined as the number of equivalents of solute per liter of solution. An equivalent of an acid is the amount of acid required to give one mole of H^+. Phosphoric acid, which contains three moles of protons per mole of acid, therefore contains three equivalents per mole. A one-molar solution of phosphoric acid is said to be 3 normal. The solution in question contains 49 grams of phosphoric acid, and the molar mass of phosphoric acid is 98. Since 49 is half of 98, the amount of phosphoric acid in this sample is half of the three equivalents in each mole of the acid. So there are 1.5 equivalents of phosphoric acid in this solution. Now, the total volume of the solution is 2,000 milliliters, or 2 liters. So this solution contains 1.5 equivalents of acid per 2 liters. This comes to 0.75 equivalents per liter, which is a 0.75 N solution.

Passage V
Questions 94–98

94 A—The passage mentions that metals have partially filled valence bands. This means that there are low energy unoccupied atomic orbitals in metals through which electrons may move freely. Therefore, the valence band for metals is the conduction band, and consequently, there is no band gap. Metals such as iron are good conductors of electricity because of these unoccupied low energy orbitals. All of this information is contained in the passage and requires little or no background knowledge. **Choice A** is therefore the correct response. **Choice B** is incorrect because metals, unlike semiconductors, do not have a band gap. **Choice C** is wrong because iron's 3*d* orbital is not filled; it has only six electrons, not ten. **Choice D** is true of many solids including metals, semiconductors, and insulators, but it does not answer the question and so is incorrect.

95 D—**Statement I** says that heat could be expected to reduce the frequency of collisions between moving electrons. This is not true: heat increases the kinetic energy of electrons, thereby increasing, not decreasing, the frequency of collisions. **Choice A** and **Choice C** can be eliminated. **Statement II** says that heat breaks covalent bonds. This is true: sufficient energy—in this case supplied by heat—will break covalent bonds. The passage doesn't tell you explicitly that heat breaks covalent bonds in semiconductors, but it is implied in the description of the semiconductive properties of silicon. In the first sentence of the second paragraph, you are told that silicon forms tetrahedral covalent bonds, and that when heated, it will conduct. Since silicon is *sp*³ hybridized—forming a filled valence band—bonds must be broken in order to promote electrons to the conduction band. **Choice B** can therefore be eliminated, making **Choice D** the correct response. The truth of **Statement III** should then be obvious: in order for the freed electrons to "jump" to the higher energy band gap, they must gain energy. Heat supplies the energy and permits this to happen.

96 B—The passage states that phosphorus atoms increase the conductivity of silicon because phosphorus provides the crystal with unbonded electrons, while boron atoms produce holes in the bonding structure. From the periodic table, we note that boron has three valence electrons, silicon has four, and phosphorus has five. Since the bonds in the silicon crystal are tetrahedral, a phosphorus atom surrounded by silicon atoms will be able to form covalent bonds with only four of its valence electrons, leaving the fifth one unbonded. Boron has only three valence electrons, so a boron atom surrounded by silicon atoms will be able to form only three covalent bonds, leaving a hole in the bonding structure of silicon. It is the presence of these unbonded electrons and holes that enhances the conductivity of phosphorus. **Choice B** is therefore the correct answer. **Choice A** is wrong because the difference in electronegativity between boron, phosphorus, and silicon is quite small. **Choice C** is wrong for two reasons: phosphorus isn't a semimetal, and even if these two elements were both semimetals and good semiconductors, this in itself wouldn't explain the enhancement of silicon's conductivity produced by doping silicon with some of these elements. **Choice D** is wrong because, like **Choice C**, it wouldn't explain the phenomenon the question asks about even if it were true.

97 A—Since the band gap is 1.1 eV, an applied voltage in excess of 1.1 V would give the electrons enough energy to cross the band gap and populate the conduction band. (You should know that an electron volt is equal to the energy required to move an electron through a potential difference of one volt.) **Choice A** is therefore the correct response. **Choice B** is wrong because pure, undoped silicon doesn't have any holes. The passage states that holes are produced when the silicon is doped with boron. **Choice C** is wrong because there is no information in the passage that suggests that the band gap is affected by an external potential. **Choice D** is wrong because the electrons do have enough energy to overcome the band gap and would move into the conduction band.

98 C—The passage provides almost all the necessary information to answer this question. The only piece of background information needed is that electrons flow from the negative terminal to the positive terminal. The passage states that phosphorus-doped silicon has more electrons than pure silicon and that boron-doped silicon has fewer electrons than pure silicon. In addition, it is stated that electrons flow more easily from a side with excess electrons—the phosphorus-doped silicon—to a side with fewer electrons—the boron-doped silicon. So, if the semiconductor orientation were switched, electron flow would not be as easy as the original configuration. **Choice C** is therefore the correct response.

Passage VI
Questions 99–103

99 B—This question is a straightforward application of the equation given in the passage, $E = 1{,}240/\lambda$. In this equation, E is the energy in electron-volts of a photon having a wavelength λ in nanometers. Note that this formula is a variant of the more familiar equation $E = hc/\lambda$. Plugging $\lambda = 632.8$ nm, we obtain $E = 1{,}240/632.8 \approx 2.0$ eV, which is closest to **Choice B**. It is a good idea to save time by estimating because the answer choices are relatively far apart.

100 B—To answer this question, you have to refer back to the passage to find the description of the condition called a population inversion. The passage states that a population inversion exists when the percentage of neon atoms with electrons in the 20.66 eV energy level is greater than the percentage of neon atoms with electrons in lower levels. The distinctive characteristic of this distribution is that the percentage of atoms with electrons in a higher energy level is greater than the percentage of atoms with electrons in lower levels. The only choice that is consistent with this is **Choice B**, so it is the correct answer.

101 A—To solve this problem, apply the law of conservation of energy to atomic systems. In the absence of dissipative forces, the total energy of a system, which is the sum of the kinetic and potential energies, is conserved. In the case of atoms, the potential energy is the energy stored when the electron moves to a higher energy state by absorbing a photon.

In the collision between the helium and neon atoms, the helium atom loses 20.61 eV of potential energy because its electron returns to the ground state and the neon atom gains 20.66 eV of potential energy. Since energy is conserved, the helium atom must have lost some kinetic energy as well. The neon atom cannot gain more energy than the helium atom loses. Therefore, the minimum amount of kinetic energy that the helium atom must lose is equal to the difference between the two potential energies. This is equal to $20.66 - 20.61 = 0.05$ eV, which is **Choice A**. If the helium atom loses only this amount of kinetic energy, then the neon atom's kinetic energy will not change during the collision. If the helium atom loses more than 0.05 eV, then the neon atom's kinetic energy will increase.

102 A—The power of the laser is 6.2×10^{15} eV/s, which means that the laser produces 6.2×10^{15} eV of energy each second. This energy takes the form of photon energy. To solve for the number of photons produced per second, figure out how many photons correspond to an energy of 6.2×10^{15} eV. The formula given in the passage states that the energy (in eV) of one photon is given by $E = 1{,}240/\lambda$, where λ is the photon's wavelength in nm. Hence, the energy of n photons must given by $n(1{,}240/\lambda)$. Setting this expression equal to 6.2×10^{15} eV and solving for n, we obtain $n = \lambda(6.2 \times 10^{15}/1{,}240)$. The question stem states that for this laser, $\lambda = 200$ nm. Substituting in, we calculate $n = 200(6.2 \times 10^{15}/1{,}240) = 1.0 \times 10^{15}$, which is **Choice A**.

103 B—To answer this question, you have to figure out the difference between stimulated and spontaneous emission. The passage states that a photon is emitted in a random direction when an atom spontaneously decays. This process is called spontaneous emission. It also states that a photon can stimulate an electron transition in an atom. The photon that is emitted in this process, called stimulated emission, travels in the same direction as the stimulating photon. Therefore, spontaneous emission produces photons that travel in random directions, whereas stimulated emission produces photons that travel in the same direction as the stimulating photon. A coherent beam of light consists of photons traveling in the same direction. **Choice B** is correct.

Choices A and **C** are wrong because, as stated in the third paragraph, the photon produced by spontaneous emission causes stimulated emission by inducing the *same* electron transition in another excited atom. Since the electron transition is the same, the photon energy released by the transition is the same, and the photon wavelengths must be the same because energy and wavelength are related by the formula $E = 1{,}240/\lambda$.

Choice D is incorrect because stimulated emission is necessary to obtain a large number of photons traveling in the same direction.

Passage VII
Questions 104–109

104 B—The passage states that after death, the ^{14}C in a skeleton that beta decays is not replaced by new ^{14}C. Consequently, as time passes, the amount of ^{14}C in the skeleton decreases.

The half-life quantifies the rate of this decrease. The half-life of an isotope is the length of time it takes for half of the atoms in a sample of that isotope to decay. A skeleton starts out with 8 g of ^{14}C, and the half-life of ^{14}C is 5,730 years. Therefore, after 5,730 years, 8 g of ^{14}C will decay to 4 g. After another 5,730 years, 4 g will decay to 2 g, and after yet another 5,730 years, 2 g will decay to 1 g, which is the amount present in the prehistoric skeleton.

Hence, the prehistoric skeleton must be 3(5,730) = 17,190 years old, and **Choice B** is correct.

105

A—The number of atoms decaying per unit time is directly proportional to the number of atoms present. To see this, recall that the definition of half-life is the time required for half of a sample to decay. The half-life is a constant for a given material regardless of the sample size. Therefore, if the initial amount of material is greater, then a larger amount of material will decay during each half-life. If the production rate of ^{14}C increases, then there will be more ^{14}C present. Hence, the number of ^{14}C atoms decaying per unit time will increase. So **Choice A** is correct and **Choice B** is incorrect.

The second paragraph describes how a balance between ^{14}C production and decay is reached, so that the total amount of ^{14}C on Earth approaches a constant. If ^{14}C production is increased, then the weight of ^{14}C on Earth will initially increase. However, as this ^{14}C begins to decay, the total amount of ^{14}C will approach a new constant as a new balance is reached between the production and decay processes. Hence, **Choice C** is wrong.

If the production of ^{14}C increases, then a larger fraction of the carbon on Earth will be ^{14}C, and living organisms will ingest a larger fraction of ^{14}C. Therefore, the percentage of ^{14}C in living organisms will increase, and **Choice D** is wrong.

106

D—Carbon dating uses the fact that ^{14}C is unstable and decays over time, while ^{12}C is stable and does not decay. Let's say the ratio of ^{14}C to ^{12}C in an organism is known at the moment of death. By measuring the ratio of ^{14}C to ^{12}C in a fossil, the age of the fossil can be determined because the ^{14}C in the dead organism decays over time in a quantifiable way.

Although it is not explicitly stated in the passage, **Choice D** is an assumption of carbon dating. It correctly states that the half-life of ^{14}C does not depend upon conditions external to the ^{14}C nucleus. This means that the half-life does not depend on the weather, the amount of ^{14}C present, etcetera. Because the half-life is a constant with respect to conditions external to the nucleus, it can be used to measure elapsed time accurately. Since measuring time is the goal of carbon dating, **Choice D** is a necessary assumption.

Choice A is wrong because ingestion is an event that is external to the nucleus. **Choice C** is wrong because the type of molecule in which ^{14}C is incorporated is also a condition external to the nucleus. **Choice B** is wrong because we know from biology that some carbon leaves the body as waste. This does not affect carbon dating, however, because what matters is the ratio of ^{14}C to ^{12}C left in the body, not the specific amount of ^{14}C left in the body.

107

D—The age of the galaxy is much greater than that of fossils on the earth. Therefore, in determining the age of the galaxy, it makes sense to use an isotope with a longer half-life than ^{14}C, which is used in determining the age of Earth fossils. This is because ^{14}C will decay to undetectable quantities more quickly than an isotope with a longer half-life, like ^{232}Th. Hence, **Choice D** is correct, and **Choice A** is incorrect.

Choice B is wrong because there is no reason to think that ^{14}C is more abundant in stars. And if it were true, ^{14}C would be *more* suitable for this application because the larger abundance would be easier to measure. **Choice C** is wrong because the instability of ^{14}C, and ^{232}Th for that matter, is precisely what makes them useful as dating tools.

108

A—To answer this question, you have to balance a nuclear reaction. The question stem suggests the reaction

$$^{14}_{7}N + ^{1}_{0}n \rightarrow ^{14}_{6}C + ^{a}_{b}?,$$

which has a nitrogen nucleus and a neutron on the left side and a carbon nucleus and the unknown particle on the right.

Two things must be balanced in a nuclear reaction: the charge of the nucleus (which corresponds to the number of protons), and the number of nucleons (which is the number of protons plus the number of neutrons). Balancing nuclear charge, we obtain $7 + 0 = 6 + b$, which implies $b = 1$. Balancing the number of nucleons, we obtain $14 + 1 = 14 + a$, which implies $a = 1$. Thus, the unknown particle is a nucleon with a charge of +1. The only particle that fits both criteria is the proton, **Choice A**. **Choice B** is wrong because an electron is not a nucleon and it has a charge of –1. **Choice C** is wrong because a helium nucleus has 4 nucleons and a charge of +2. **Choice D** is wrong because a neutron has a charge of 0.

109

D—Kinetic energy, the energy of motion, is given by K.E. = $(1/2)mv^2$, where m is the mass of the object and v is its speed. The electron emitted when a ^{14}C nucleus decays is emitted with some initial speed and thus has kinetic energy. After it enters lead and is stopped, the electron's speed is zero so its kinetic energy is also zero. In other words, all the electron's kinetic energy is gone. Since energy is conserved, 100 percent of the electron's kinetic energy must have been transferred somewhere, and in this case, it is transferred to the lead. Hence, **Choice D** is correct.

Passage VIII
Questions 110–114

110

C—This question is testing your knowledge of phase diagrams. You should know that Region I—the lower temperature region—is where the solid state exists, Region II—the higher temperature and pressure region—is where the liquid phase exists, and that Region III—the higher temperature and lower pressure region—is where the vapor phase exists. **Choice C** is correct because at this temperature and pressure the liquid phase exists. **Choice A** and **Choice B** are wrong because the vapor phase exists at these points. **Choice D** is wrong because the solid phases exists at this point.

111

A—Calcium chloride, by forming solid hydrates with water, is often used as a desiccant, or drying agent. It is used in this experiment because the presence of water might prevent the arsine gas from igniting. **Choice A** is therefore the correct response. **Choice B** is wrong because calcium chloride is not basic, rendering it ineffective in removing HCl. **Choice C** is wrong because—as seen in Figure 1—calcium chloride and zinc ion do not have any contact. **Choice D** is wrong because arsine gas is the analyte, removing it would defeat the purpose of the test.

112

A—It is stated in the last sentence of the first paragraph that yellow arsenic is unstable. Since it is less stable than gray arsenic, meaning that it is at a higher potential energy, more energy will be released when it converts to As_4O_6. **Choice A** is the correct response. **Choice B** is wrong because gray arsenic, being more stable than the yellow, will release less energy. **Choice C** and **Choice**

D are wrong because, as was just discussed, they release different amounts of energy.

113 B—The solubility of one compound in another is usually governed by the rule that "like dissolves like." Water and ammonia, both being polar, are quite soluble in each other. Arsine has a similar geometry to that of ammonia, but the electronegativity of arsenic is substantially less than that of nitrogen, and remember: ammonia can hydrogen bond with water, arsine cannot. In fact, the electronegativity of arsenic is very close to that of hydrogen. Because of arsenic's electronegativity, arsine has a small dipole moment, rendering it insoluble in polar solvents such as water. **Choice B** is the correct response. While **Choice A, Choice C,** and **Choice D** are true statements, they are less important factors in influencing the solubility of compounds, especially in the case of arsine.

114 C—Because there are three sulfides in orpiment and the molecule has no charge overall, the total negative charge of the sulfides, minus six, must be balanced by the positive charges of the arsenics. The two arsenics, therefore, have a collective charge of +6, and each arsenic has a charge of plus three. **Choice C** is the correct response.

Discrete
Questions 115–119

115 B—Ammonia has a central nitrogen atom that is bonded to three hydrogen atoms. According to the valence-shell electron-pair repulsion theory, or VSEPR theory, a central atom surrounded by three bonded pairs of electrons and

one lone pair of electrons has a pyramidal geometry. **Choice A** is wrong because a trigonal planar molecule has the central atom surrounded by three bonding pairs of electrons and no lone pairs, such as BF_3. **Choice C** is wrong because a tetrahedral molecule has the central atom surrounded by four bonding pairs of electrons and no lone pairs, such as CH_4. **Choice D** is wrong because a trigonal bipyramidal shape has the central atom surrounded by five bonding electron pairs and no lone pairs, such as PF_5.

116 D—Archimedes' principle states that the buoyant force exerted by a fluid on a submerged object is equal to the weight of the fluid displaced. In this case, the submerged object is the research module and the fluid is ocean water. Mathematically, the buoyant force is given by $F = m_w g$, where m_w is the mass of the water and g is the acceleration due to gravity. Since we are not given the mass of the water displaced, we express it as $m_w = \rho_w V_w$, where ρ_w is the density of the water and V_w is the volume of the water displaced. But the volume of the water displaced is identical to the volume of the submerged module, V_0. Hence, $m_w = \rho_w V_w = \rho_w V_0$, and $F = m_w g = \rho_w V_0 g$. Since the answer choices are far apart, we round off the values given in the question and calculate

$$F = \rho_w V_0 g \approx (1,000 \text{ kg/m}^3)(150 \text{ m}^3)(10 \text{ m/s}^2)$$
$$= 1.5 \times 10^6 \text{ N},$$

which is **Choice D.** Note that no conversions are necessary since all the values are given in SI units.

117 B—To solve this problem, apply Hooke's law $F = kx$, where F is the force applied to the spring, x is the distance the spring stretches, and k is the spring constant. The forces applied in this case are weights. Since weight is proportional to mass, the distance the spring stretches is also proportional to the mass of the object attached to the spring.

The spring starts out with a length of 64 cm. When the 0.5 kg mass is attached, it stretches 8% longer, or 64(0.08) = 5.12 cm. Since the distance stretched and the mass attached are proportional, the ratio of the distance stretched to the mass attached is (5.12 cm)/(0.5 kg) ≈ 5/(0.5) = 10 cm/kg. In other words, each kilogram attached to the spring stretches it 10 cm. Thus, when the 0.4 kg mass is attached, the spring is stretched a distance (0.4 kg)(10 cm/kg) = 4 cm. Therefore, the total length of the spring is its original length plus the distance it stretches, or 64 + 4 = 68 cm. This is **Choice B**.

118
C—The electrostatic force between two charged particles is given by $F = kq_1q_2/r^2$, where k is a constant, q_1 and q_2 are the charges on the particles, and r is the distance between the two charges. Since the force is proportional to each of the charges, halving the charge on one of the particles will also halve the force, and **Choice C** is correct. Halving the charge on both particles will reduce the force by one-fourth, so **Choice B** is wrong. Since the force is inversely proportional to the square of the distance, doubling the distance will reduce the force by one-fourth, and **Choice A** is wrong. Watch out for **Choice D**. It is wrong because the presence of a third charge will not change the force of attraction between the first and second charges. The third charge, however, will change the net force on the first and second charges because it interacts with each separately.

119
A—When heat is absorbed during a reaction, ΔH is positive; when heat is released, ΔH is negative. The melting of ice requires absorption of heat to disrupt the attrac-

tions between molecules, so the change in enthalpy is positive, and you can eliminate **Choice B** and **Choice D**. Now, entropy is the measurement of the disorder in a system; the change in entropy is expressed as ΔS. When the disorder of a system increases, ΔS is positive; when disorder decreases, ΔS is negative. When ice melts, the individual molecules of water become freer to move around, so there is an increase in disorder and ΔS is positive. Therefore, **Choice C** is wrong and **Choice A** is the correct answer.

Passage IX
Questions 120–124

120
A—The velocity of the softball is a vector, which means that it has both a magnitude and direction. At Point A, the velocity vector points up and to the right, because the softball is traveling in this direction. At Point C, however, the velocity vector points down and to the right. Since the velocity's direction has changed, it is not the same at Points A and C, and **Choice A** is correct.

You should know that the gravitational potential energy of the softball is given by $U = mgy$, where m is the mass, g is the acceleration due to gravity, and y is the height above the Earth. Since Points A and C are at the same height y, the gravitational potential is the same and **Choice C** is incorrect.

The passage says to ignore air resistance, so the total mechanical energy, which is the kinetic plus potential energy, is conserved in this system. Since the gravitational potential is the same at Points A and C, the kinetic energy $(1/2)mv^2$ must be the same as well. Because the mass m does not change, the speed v must be the same at both points also, and **Choice B** is wrong.

Since air resistance is negligible, the only force present is that of gravity, which acts in the vertical direction. Consequently, there is no horizontal force on the softball, which means there can be no horizontal acceleration. Therefore, the horizontal component of the velocity must remain the same throughout the softball's flight, and **Choice D** is wrong.

121 A—Newton's second law $F = ma$ states that a force produces an acceleration in the same direction as the force. In the absence of a force, there is no acceleration. In this situation, the only force present is the force of gravity, which is the same at all times during the softball's flight. Near the earth's surface, the gravitational force is directed downward and its magnitude is given by $F = mg$, where m is the softball's mass and g is the acceleration due to gravity. Putting the gravitational force into Newton's second law, we obtain $ma = mg$. Canceling the masses, we obtain $a = g$. In other words, the acceleration of the softball is the same as the acceleration due to gravity.

Figure 1 shows that the unit vector **j** points upwards, which means that −**j** points downwards. Because **j** is a unit vector, its magnitude is 1. Since the softball accelerates downward with a magnitude of g, the acceleration is symbolically given by g(−**j**) = −g**j**. Thus, **Choice A** is correct. **Choice C** is incorrect because it has the wrong magnitude. **Choices B** and **D** are wrong because they both include an acceleration in the horizontal direction −**i**.

122 B—You should know that the change in momentum of a body is equal to the impulse applied to that body. The magnitude of the momentum of a body is given by mv, where m is its mass and v is its speed. In this situation an impulse is applied to the softball to launch it from the cannon. Before the impulse the speed of the softball is zero, so we can write $J = \Delta(mv) = mv_0 − m(0) = mv_0$,

where J is the impulse. Solving for v_0, we obtain $v_0 = J/m$. Since m is inversely proportional to v_0, doubling the mass will halve v_0, so **Choice B** is correct.

123 D—Figure 2 shows that the curve is symmetric around $t = t_b$. Since the axes of graphs are always linear unless otherwise stated, the time elapsed at Point C is twice the time elapsed at Point B. There are no horizontal forces because air resistance is negligible. Therefore, the horizontal speed is the constant v_0 throughout the softball's flight. The horizontal distance traveled is then given by $x = v_0t$, where t is the time elapsed. Since the time elapsed at Point C is twice the time elapsed at Point B, the horizontal distance traveled at Point C is twice that traveled at Point B, and **Choice D** is correct.

124 C—The softball starts off at rest and acquires a speed v_0 as it is launched from the cannon. The work-energy theorem states that the work done equals the change in the kinetic energy. Since the softball acquires a kinetic energy equal to $(1/2)mv_0^2$, the automatic pitcher must have done work on it. The pitcher uses air pressure, which builds up behind a disk, to do the work when the disk is released. The angle of the barrel to the horizontal will not affect this mechanism, and the softball will still be ejected with the same kinetic energy. Hence, the work done by the pitcher does not change and **Choice C** is correct.

Although it is true that the softball's maximum height increases and that the distance it lands from the cannon decreases, the work done by the pitcher does not change, so **Choices A** and **B** are wrong. Although it is also true that gravity is a conservative force, it is irrelevant because the question asks about the work done by the pitcher, not the work done by gravity. Hence, **Choice D** is incorrect as well.

Passage X
Questions 125–130

125 B—To solve this problem, apply the formula given in the passage that quantifies the positions of the intensity maxima. The formula is $d\sin\theta = n\lambda$, where d is the distance between the slits, θ is the angle, and λ is the wavelength. The note in the passage says that $\sin\theta \approx \theta$ when θ is small. You have to know that this approximation is valid only when θ is measured in *radians*. Making this approximation, we obtain $d\theta = n\lambda$, and solving for θ we obtain $\theta = n\lambda/d$. Note that the distance units of λ and d can be anything as long as they are the same. n is given in the question stem, and λ and d are given in Figure 1. Substituting, we obtain

$$\theta = \frac{3(500 \times 10^{-9} \text{ m})}{(5 \times 10^{-4} \text{ m})} = 3 \times 10^{-3} \text{ radians,}$$

which is **Choice B**.

126 A—If a quantity is quantized, it means that there is a fundamental unit of that quantity that cannot be further divided. For example, charge is quantized, so charges appear in nature only as multiples of the fundamental charge e. There is not a continuous range of values for the possible charge on an object. Similarly, light energy is quantized. The fundamental unit of light energy is called a photon. The photon, because it cannot be subdivided, is similar to other elementary particles. Thus, quantization implies particle-like characteristics, and **Choice A** is correct.

The passage states that the wave theory, not the particle theory, predicts that light will exhibit interference, so **Choice B** is incorrect. The Doppler effect refers to the change in frequency observed when a wave source or detector is in motion. That the

Doppler effect occurs with light as well as sound waves indicates that light has wave, not particle, characteristics and **Choice C** is wrong. Neither particles nor waves can travel faster than the speed of light, so the fact that particles cannot travel faster than light does not support or weaken the particle theory and **Choice D** is wrong.

127 C—The easiest way to solve the problem is to check the units of each of the answers, a process called dimensional analysis. Since wavelength is measured in meters, the correct answer will be in meters as well. First, note that h has the units of J·s, and v, a speed, has the units of m/s. Then, **Choice C** has the units of $hv/E = $ (J·s)(m/s)/J = m, so it is correct. The other choices are incorrect. **Choice A** has the units of $hvE = $ (J·s)(m/s)(J) = J^2m. **Choice B** has the units of

$$\frac{hE}{v} = \frac{(J \cdot s)(J)}{(m/s)} = \frac{(J \cdot s)(kg \cdot m^2/s^2)}{(m/s)} = (J \cdot kg)m.$$

Choice D has the units of $E/hv = $ J/[(J·s)(m/s)] = m^{-1}.

Another way to solve the problem is to recall that the photon energy E is given by $E = hc/\lambda$, where c is the speed of light, and λ is the photon's wavelength. Solving for λ, we obtain $\lambda = hc/E$. To find the "wavelength" of an electron, replace the speed of light c with the speed of the electron v, and obtain $\lambda = hv/E$, where E is now the energy of the electron. Again, this is **Choice C**.

128 D—You should know that the speed of light is different in different media. The formula associated with this concept is $n = c/v$, where n is the index of refraction of a given medium, c is the speed of light in a vacuum, and v is the speed of light in the given medium. Hence, if the index of refraction and the speed of light in a vacuum are known, we can solve for the speed of light in the medium. Thus, **Choice D** is correct.

We would need the air's index of refraction, along with the variables in **Choice A**, to calculate the water's index of refraction using Snell's law. Even if we could calculate the water's index of refraction, we would need the speed of light in a vacuum to calculate the speed of light in water, so **Choice A** is wrong. Similarly, the variables in **Choice B** allow the calculation of the index of refraction, but the speed of light is still required, so **Choice B** is wrong. **Choice C** is incorrect because while density might play an indirect role in the index of refraction, the density is not sufficient information to determine the index of refraction.

129 C—You should know that the speed v of a wave is given by $v = f\lambda$, where f is the frequency of the wave, and λ is its wavelength. This makes sense, since λ is the distance traveled by the wave in one cycle, and frequency is the inverse of the period, which is the time it takes for one wave to cycle. Now solve the relation in the question stem $k = 2\pi/\lambda$ for λ to obtain $\lambda = 2\pi/k$. Also solve $\omega = 2\pi f$ for f to obtain $f = \omega/2\pi$. Substituting these expressions into the speed equation, we obtain $v = f\lambda = (\omega/2\pi)(2\pi/k) = \omega/k$, which is **Choice C**. **Choice A**, while a correct relation, is not the right answer because it does not express v in terms of ω and k. **Choices B** and **D** can be eliminated on the basis of dimensional analysis because they do not have the units of speed, m/s. k has units of m^{-1} and ω has units of s^{-1}, so **Choice B** is nonsensical and **Choice D** has units of 1/(ms).

130 D—A particle of light is known as a photon. You should know the formula

$E = hf$, which states that the energy E of a photon is equal to Planck's constant h times the frequency f of the light. The photon energy is thus proportional to the frequency of the light. Since the photon energy is a property of a particle and frequency is a property of a wave, this relationship successfully connects the particle and wave descriptions of light, and **Choice D** is correct.

Choice A is incorrect because the number of particles passing by per unit time is related to the intensity of the light, not its frequency. **Choice B** is wrong because photons have zero mass. **Choice C** is wrong because photons are thought of as pointlike particles without size.

Passage XI
Questions 131–137

131 D—You should know that helium, a noble gas, is very unreactive and would almost certainly not react with any of the species in the furnace. Because the helium does not react with any of the species that participate in the equilibrium, the equilibrium is unaffected by the addition of helium. According to Le Châtelier's Principle, if any of the reactants or products were added or removed, either physically or by reacting with an added substance, the concentrations would change, and the equilibrium would shift to counteract the stress. Such a situation does not exist here. The correct choice is therefore **Choice D**.

132 A—The entropy of a reaction is a measure of the disorder of the system. The sign of the value of the entropy indicates whether the products of a reaction are more or less disordered than the reactants. A reaction that experiences an increase in disorder in going from reactants to products would have a positive ΔS for the reaction. Similarly, a reaction that decreases its disorder would have a negative ΔS for the reaction. In this reaction, 1 mole of carbon dioxide, a gas, reacts with 1 mole of solid carbon to give two moles of carbon monoxide gas. Since there are more moles of gas in the products than in the reactants, there is an increase in entropy, meaning that the sign of the change is positive. **Choice A** is therefore the correct response.

133 C—The carbon dioxide molecule has a central carbon bonded to two oxygen atoms: carbon shares two electrons with each oxygen, and each oxygen shares two electrons with carbon. As a result of this sharing pattern, two double bonds are formed. You should know that a double bond consists of one sigma bond and one pi bond. Since there are two double bonds, there are two pi bonds, making **Choice C** the correct choice.

134 D—You should know the relationship $\Delta G = \Delta H - T\Delta S$. ΔS for this reaction is positive, because there are more moles of gaseous products than reactants, but there is no information about the sign of ΔH. Since ΔH cannot be determined, neither can ΔG. **Choice D** is the correct response. **Choice A** is wrong (that is, the statement is certainly true) because, as was just stated, the entropy change is positive. **Choice B** is wrong because, according to Le Châtelier's principle, a decrease in pressure will favor the side of the reaction with more moles of gas. In this case, it is the products side, and the equilibrium is said to have shifted to the right. **Choice C** is wrong because, again, according to Le Châtelier's principle, addition of a product will shift the equilibrium to the left, that is, the reactants side.

135 C—The first thing that should be done is to determine which choices have the proper number of valence electrons. Carbon monoxide must have a total of ten electrons: six from the oxygen and four from the carbon. **Choice B** and **Choice D** can be eliminated because they both have twelve electrons. In **Choice A**, the carbon has one pair of unbonded electrons, plus four more electrons in the double bond. This gives the carbon a total of only six electrons in its valence shell, so the carbon doesn't have a complete octet, and **Choice A** must be wrong. **Choice C** shows the correct Lewis structure for carbon monoxide: each atom has a complete octet, and there is a total of ten electrons.

136 B—P_e, as the table explains, is the expected pressure at each temperature if no reaction had taken place. When the carbon dioxide is introduced into the furnace chamber, it is at a pressure of 1 atmosphere and a temperature of 298 K. Above 298 K, P_e is greater than 1 atmosphere because, at constant volume, the pressure increases as the temperature increases. Since P_e is the pressure if no reaction had taken place, any change in the number of moles of gas present does not have to be considered. Since the pressure of a gas is directly proportional to its temperature in Kelvins, the ratio of the EXPECTED pressure to the original pressure of 1 atmosphere must be equal to the ratio of the temperature of the trial to the original temperature of 298 K. The equation is as follows:

$$P_e/(1 \text{ atm}) = T/298$$

Solving for P_e yields answer **Choice B**.

137 D—Since carbon has a molar mass of 12 grams, a tenth of a mole would be 1.2 grams, and the 0.6 grams stated in the question is one-twentieth of a mole. The equation given in the passage shows that for every one mole of carbon consumed, two moles of CO are produced. So, if one-twentieth of a mole of carbon is consumed, two-twentieths, or one-tenth, of a mole of CO will be produced. One-tenth of the molar mass of CO, 28 grams, is 2.8 grams. Therefore **Choice D** is the correct response.

Discrete
Questions 138–142

138 D—The question is about refraction, which is the process that bends light as it travels from one medium into another. Snell's law—$n_1 \sin\theta_1 = n_2 \sin\theta_2$—describes this process, where n_1 and n_2 are the indices of refraction of the two media, and θ_1 and θ_2 are the angles that the light rays make with the normal to the interface between the two media. This law predicts that light traveling into a medium with a higher index of refraction will be refracted towards the normal. Light traveling into a medium with a lower index of refraction will be refracted away from the normal. In the question, the light is refracted away from the normal, so the new medium must have an index of refraction lower than air. The vacuum has the lowest index of refraction possible, $n = 1$, so **Choice D** is correct.

Steel is opaque, so light will not travel through it at all. The steel surface will absorb or reflect light, not refract it, so **Choice C** is wrong. Water and glass both have indices of refraction that are higher than air, so both **Choices A** and **B** are wrong. Note that even if you did not remember whether higher indices cause refraction towards or away from the normal, you could have eliminated **Choices A** and **B** because they both would bend the light in the same direction, and both cannot be right.

139 B—The K_{sp}, or solubility product constant, is found by multiplying together the concentrations of the dissociated ions, each raised to a power equal to the number of ions in one formula unit of the salt. When a mole of the salt, X_mY_n, dissolves, m moles of X^{n+} ions and n moles of Y^{m-} ions enter solution. So, the coefficient of X is m, and the coefficient of Y is n. The expression is as follows:

$$K_{sp} = [X^{n+}]^m [Y^{m-}]^n$$

Choice B is therefore the correct answer. **Choice A** is wrong because it has the coefficients reversed. **Choice C** and **Choice D** can be eliminated because the K_{sp} is not a fraction.

140 C—A resonance hybrid is a molecule that cannot be represented by just one Lewis structure; the molecule is said to be a composite of the possible structures. **Choice A** is wrong because all the atoms have a complete octet—hydrogen having its two electrons—and only one Lewis structure is possible:

$$H\!-\!C\!\equiv\!\overset{\cdot\cdot}{N}$$

Choice B is wrong because it too has only one structure:

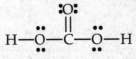

Choice C is correct because it does exist as a resonance hybrid:

$$:\ddot{O}-N=\ddot{O} \quad \longleftrightarrow \quad \ddot{O}=N-\ddot{O}:^{-}$$

Keep in mind that the nitrite ion does not exist as one or the other of the above resonance structures but is a composite of them, having a structure somewhere between the two. **Choice D** is wrong because it has only one Lewis structure as well:

141 A—A comparison of trials 1 and 2 in the table shows that if the concentration of R is held constant and the concentration of species Q is doubled, the reaction rate also doubles. So, the rate of the reaction is proportional to the concentration of Q, and, thus, the reaction is first order for Q. Now, if the reaction is third order overall, then it must be second order for R. Now that we know that the reaction is second order for R, we can proceed to figure out what concentration of R would result in the observed rate for trial 3. Looking at the table, you can see that the concentration of Q in trial 3 is equal to that of Q in trial 2. Therefore, the difference in rate between trial 2 and trial 3 must be due entirely to the change in the concentration of R. Now, the rate in trial 3 is 4 times the rate in trial 2. But, since the reaction is second order with respect to R, the rate will be quadrupled simply by doubling the concentration of R. So, the concentration of R in trial 3 must be double its concentration in trial 2, and, therefore, the concentration of R in trial 3 is 2.00. Thus, **Choice A** is correct.

142 C—To answer the question, apply the formula for the thermal expansion of a solid. This formula is given by $\Delta L = \alpha L \Delta T$, where ΔL is the change in length, L is the original length, ΔT is the change in temperature, and α is some constant that depends on the type of material. This formula makes sense intuitively: as the length increases, there is more material available to expand, and as the temperature increases, the more vigorously the material expands.

Compared with the first iron bar, the second iron bar is twice as long, so $L_2 = 2L_1$, and is raised twice as much in temperature, so $\Delta T_2 = 2\Delta T_1$. Note that α is the same for both bars because they are made of the same material. Therefore, the ratio of the first bar's length change to the second bar's length change is

$$\frac{\Delta L_1}{\Delta L_2} = \frac{\alpha L_1 \Delta T_1}{\alpha L_2 \Delta T_2} = \frac{\alpha L_1 \Delta T_1}{\alpha (2L_1)(2\Delta T_1)} = \frac{\alpha L_1 \Delta T_1}{4(\alpha L_1 \Delta T_1)} = \frac{1}{4}$$

so **Choice C** is correct.

WRITING SAMPLE

Stimulus 1: "The pursuit of knowledge is always justified."

Stimulus 2: "True creativity cannot be learned."

On the following pages you'll find sample responses to the above essay prompts and critiques of the sample essays. Reviewing this information will help you to better understand the MCAT Writing Sample section. The particular essays presented (two for each statement) were chosen because they each exhibit strengths and weaknesses that had a clear effect on the writer's scores. Your critical understanding of what constitutes a good essay will be sharpened once you read both the teacher's comments on each essay and the detailed discussion. Once finished, you'll be able to review your own essays and thoroughly critique them. (Of course, if you can find another MCAT student with whom to trade essays, that's even better; it is always more difficult to criticize your own work than someone else's work.)

Read the sample essays for Stimulus 1 and Stimulus 2 after you've written your own essays and evaluate how effectively they fulfill the three tasks and the scoring criteria. Keep in mind the instructions for the essays:

1) explain what the statement means;

2) describe a specific situation that illustrates a point of view opposite to the one expressed by the statement; and

3) explain how the conflict between the viewpoints might be resolved.

Try giving the essays holistic scores before you look at the given scores or at the teacher's comments. If your score doesn't match that of the MCAT readers, don't worry. Your job is not to score these essays well, but to recognize the ways in which the writers did a good job and the ways in which they could have done a better job.

A Recap

Here's a chance to review the essentials before you evaluate your essays and the sample essays.

THE THREE TASKS

Task One

Analyze a given statement. Define and explore its deeper meaning, and describe the implications of the statement.

Task Two

Describe an example that contrasts with the statement as you developed it in the first task.

Task Three

Derive and articulate a method of deciding when the statement should be applied and when it shouldn't.

Characteristics of Holistic Scores

Score: 6

- Fulfills all three tasks
- Offers an in-depth consideration of the statement
- Employs ideas that demonstrate subtle, careful thought
- Organizes ideas with coherence and unity
- Shows a sophisticated use of language that clearly articulates ideas

Score: 5

- Fulfills all three tasks
- Offers a well-developed consideration of the statement
- Employs ideas that demonstrate some in-depth thought
- Organizes ideas effectively, though less so than a Level 6 essay
- Shows above-average command of word choice and sentence structure

Score: 4

- Addresses all three tasks
- Offers a consideration of the statement that is adequate but limited
- Employs ideas that are logical but not complex
- Organizes ideas with coherence but may contain digression(s)
- Shows overall control of word choice and sentence structure

Score: 3

- Overlooks or misinterprets one or more of the three tasks
- Offers a barely adequate consideration of the statement
- Employs ideas that may be partially logical, but also may be superficial
- Shows a fundamental control of word choice and sentence structure
- May present problems in clear communication

Score: 2

- Significantly overlooks or misinterprets one or more of the three tasks
- Offers a flawed consideration of the statement
- Organizes ideas with a lack of unity and/or coherence
- May show repeated mistakes in grammar, punctuation, etcetera
- Contains language that may be hard to understand

Score: 1

- Exhibits significant problems in grammar, punctuation, usage, and/or spelling
- Presents ideas in a confusing and/or disjointed manner
- May completely disregard the given statement

SAMPLE ESSAYS

FIRST SAMPLE RESPONSE TO STIMULUS 1

"The pursuit of knowledge is always justified."

With the application of the scientific method in fields ranging from atomic physics to social psychology, the human pursuit of knowledge has proved particularly fruitful. The benefits we have derived from science are readily visible now in our everyday lives, not just in the labs of physicists and chemists: we use computers to process information at amazing speeds, we use television to tap into vast electronic and satellite networks to receive news from around the globe, we receive treatment at local hospitals for diseases that would have been fatal mere decades ago. That such success from the scientific pursuit of knowledge has been possible could be evidence to support the argument that "the pursuit of knowledge" in this manner "is always justified."

It is clear, however, after one considers only a couple of the negative aspects of science, that the pursuit of knowledge is not always justified. It should not be allowed, for example, for humans to experiment on other humans in order to gain knowledge, whether or not the experimenter is attempting research for "the good of mankind." This is a sticky problem in medical science because researchers can often only be sure of the effects of a particular drug after testing it out on a sample of humans—animal models can only provide so much information. It certainly is not justifiable, however, to try out new drugs on humans when the possible outcome is so unknown.

In cases such as this, when the pursuit of knowledge could adversely impact on another human or group of humans, the justifiability of research is possible only under certain circumstances: when those whom research could negatively affect have acquiesced after being fully informed of the possible consequences of research. Otherwise, if scientific activity in any way endangers the humans it is intended to help, it thereby loses its purpose and its justifiability and should not be sustained.

ANALYSIS OF FIRST SAMPLE RESPONSE TO STIMULUS 1

Holistic Score: 4

needs some explanation or definition

Task 1

With the application of **the scientific method** in fields ranging from atomic physics to social psychology, the human pursuit of knowledge has proved particularly fruitful. The benefits we have derived from science are readily visible now in our everyday lives, not just in the labs of physicists and chemists: we use computers to process information at amazing speeds, we use television to tap into vast electronic and satellite networks to receive news from around the globe, we receive treatment at local hospitals for diseases that would have been fatal mere decades ago. **That such success** from the scientific pursuit of knowledge has been possible could be evidence to support the argument that "the pursuit of knowledge" **in this manner** "is always justified."

good details

nice connection

the scientific method?

Task 2

It is clear, however, after one considers only a couple of the negative aspects of science, that the pursuit of knowledge is not always justified. It should not be allowed, for example, for humans to experiment on other humans in order to gain knowledge, whether or not the experimenter is attempting research for "the good of mankind." This is a sticky problem in medical science because researchers can often only be sure of the effects of a particular drug after testing it out on a sample of humans—animal models can only provide so much information. It certainly is not justifiable, however, to try out new drugs on humans when the possible outcome is so unknown.

clarify

Task 3

In cases such as this, when the pursuit of knowledge **could adversely impact** on another human or group of humans, the justifiability of research is possible only under certain circumstances: when those whom research could negatively affect have acquiesced after being fully informed of the possible consequences of research. Otherwise, if scientific activity in any way endangers the humans it is intended to help, it thereby loses its purpose and its justifiability and should not be sustained.

complex sentence structure

Your organization of ideas and your use of details in this essay are very good. However, the ideas themselves often lack clarity and depth. In particular, you never explain why you focus solely on scientific knowledge, nor do you clarify what "the scientific method" is. Thus, paragraph 1 is weaker than it would be otherwise, given its admirable details. Also, your example for Task 2 needs to be more specific to make sense. You say experimentation on humans "should not be allowed" and trying out new drugs "is not justifiable." Yet in paragraph 3, you say such things can be allowed (under certain conditions). What then, exactly, is the example you mean to describe in paragraph 2?

SECOND SAMPLE RESPONSE TO STIMULUS 1

"The pursuit of knowledge is always justified."

Human beings have a natural instinct to explore the surrounding environment. Rather than simply reacting to stimuli, we seek to understand facts, patterns, and events in the world around us, often in order to change or control our environment.

It can be argued that this pursuit of knowledge is what makes us uniquely human, and therefore is not only justifiable but inescapable. We seek to understand everything from the cosmos to the inner workings of the atom. And, again uniquely among animals, we seek to understand ourselves. The analysis of human behavior, whether of individuals or of groups, has occupied a preeminent place in our intellectual life throughout recorded history.

However, the pursuit of knowledge, instinct-driven as it is, leads some in directions that are difficult to justify from any standpoint except individual power. Perhaps the most frequently cited example of overzealous pursuit is the nearly complete license claimed by contemporary journalists to unearth the private financial and sexual activities of individuals who are in the public eye. In such cases, journalists raise a familiar rallying cry: "The public has a right to know!"

The public has an undeniable right to know whether an elected or appointed official is misappropriating public monies. One could even make a case for the right to know whether such an official is a tax delinquent or a scofflaw who has amassed thousands of dollars in parking fines. But journalists tread on thin ice when they infringe on an individual's private life, revealing personal vices, mishaps, mistakes, or tragedies. The only purpose served by gaining and disseminating such knowledge is to pass group judgment on private matters that have no bearing on the public good.

To determine what kinds of knowledge can justifiably be pursued, and to decide to what depth and in what manner the investigation may justifiably be conducted, journalists should consider two things. First, would they condone a similar investigation of a private individual by a private individual, for the latter's personal knowledge and towards the exercise of personal power? Second, will a large segment of society benefit from this knowledge? Journalists must tread softly on individual rights and not trample them for the sake of a frivolous or lascivious readership.

ANALYSIS OF SECOND SAMPLE RESPONSE TO STIMULUS 1

Holistic Score: 6

Task 1

Human beings have a natural instinct to explore the surrounding environment. Rather than simply reacting to stimuli, we seek to understand facts, patterns, and events in the world around us, often in order to change or control our environment.

It can be argued that this pursuit of knowledge is what makes us uniquely human, and therefore is not only justifiable but inescapable. We seek to understand everything from the cosmos to the inner workings of the atom. And, again uniquely among animals, we seek to understand ourselves. The analysis of human behavior, whether of individuals or of groups, has occupied a preeminent place in our intellectual life throughout recorded history.

nice summary of your response to Task 1

However, the pursuit of knowledge, instinct-driven as it is, leads some in directions that are difficult to justify from any standpoint except individual power. Perhaps the most frequently cited example of overzealous pursuit is the nearly complete license claimed by contemporary journalists to unearth the private financial and sexual activities of individuals who are in the public eye. In such cases, journalists raise a familiar rallying cry: "The public has a right to know!"

very nice transition

Task 2

The public has an undeniable right to know whether an elected or appointed official is misappropriating public monies. One could even make a case for the right to know whether such an official is a tax delinquent or a scofflaw who has amassed thousands of dollars in parking fines. But journalists **tread on thin ice** when they infringe on an individual's private life, revealing personal vices, mishaps, mistakes, or tragedies. The only purpose served by gaining and disseminating such knowledge is to pass group judgment on private matters that have no bearing on the public good.

cliché

Task 3

To determine what kinds of knowledge can justifiably be pursued, and to decide to what depth and in what manner the investigation may justifiably be conducted, journalists should consider two things. First, would they condone a similar investigation of a private individual by a private individual, for the latter's personal knowledge and towards the exercise of personal power? Second, will a large segment of society benefit from this knowledge? Journalists must tread softly on individual rights and not trample them for the sake of a frivolous or lascivious readership.

complex sentence structure

This essay merits the highest score on four counts: (1) Your ideas are expressed with admirable thoroughness and clarity of thought; (2) all three writing tasks are synthesized into a compelling, unified argument; (3) your language shows variety and complexity of expression, while maintaining its overall clarity; (4) your vivid example from journalism allows you to narrow the given topic without losing focus on the assigned task.

Discussion

Essays for Stimulus 1: "The pursuit of knowledge is always justified."

Upon review of the first essay, it becomes apparent that all three of the tasks are clearly addressed. Also, as the teacher's comments point out, both the essay's organization and its use of details are quite good. The writer effectively ties together the paragraphs, making sure that the separate parts come together as a unified and coherent whole. That's important. The first sentence of paragraph two, for instance, makes a clear transition from paragraph one's discussion of the positive side of the pursuit of scientific knowledge to paragraph two's discussion of the negative side. Similarly, the first sentence of paragraph three further clarifies the example in paragraph two and presents a concluding point about that example.

The author also uses details effectively. Specifics give an argument substance and supply something concrete to which the reader can attach the general ideas being discussed.

Another positive aspect of this essay is its use of language and sentence structure. The words aren't elaborate, but in general they show a genuine facility with language. Remember, it is not important to impress people with a phenomenally large vocabulary—using clear and precise language is much more vital. The variety of sentence structures used in the essay also demonstrates the writer's skills. A number of the sentences are quite complicated, yet the writer avoids unnecessary complexity and showing off. The result is a varied rhythm to the sentences that keeps the essay from merely plodding along. All of these good characteristics are what garnered this essay a four. Now let's examine why it didn't get a higher score.

Why does the writer zero in on the scientific method, and what exactly is "the scientific method"? We're never really told. Hence, the essay's overall thesis, that the application of the scientific method is mostly beneficial but can lead to problems, is a bit hazy.

Furthermore, in light of what paragraph three says, you would expect the writer to fulfill the second task by discussing scientific experimentation without known consent. As it stands, paragraph three contradicts paragraph two somewhat, as the teacher has noted. A bit more specificity would help. For example, what kind of experimentation is the student worried about? Finally, paragraph three's conclusion is confusing: Having informed consent does not mean that there is no danger involved.

Overall, the writer has some good ideas, but he needs to clarify them a bit more before putting them down on paper.

Evaluating the second essay, one can see that it's not perfect, but it is very good given the author's time constraints. The first two paragraphs serve to discuss the stimulus statement thoroughly. Many students forget this important first task and breeze through with a sentence or two paraphrasing the statement. Here we are given an in-depth, precise introduction that fulfills the first task—a good model to follow.

The writer completely satisfies task two as well. The author offers a clear and convincing opposing viewpoint. The counter argument grows naturally out of the last two sentences of paragraph two—an indication that the writer knew the direction in which the essay was going. Obviously, the author did a good job of prewriting: mentally preparing and outlining the essay before taking pencil to paper.

Finally, a word of praise about this student's ability to handle language. The teacher takes note of a good, complex structure in the first sentence of the last paragraph, and there are certainly other sentences to applaud. The vocabulary is varied without being overdone.

The writer could have been a bit clearer about what is meant by the exercise of personal power. The initial implicit point is that journalists write about personal matters purely to increase their own readership and to add to their fame; that is, to revel in an exercise of personal power. Then the author makes a slightly different generalization at the end of paragraph four, where it is noted that the only purpose served by disseminating such knowledge is to pass group judgment on private matters that have no bearing on the public good. That's different from simply reveling in one's own personal power. Don't worry: We're being more critical about the writer's reasoning than the MCAT scorers would be. After all, you have only thirty minutes to come up with an organized and convincing essay. This one clearly merited a six.

FIRST SAMPLE RESPONSE TO STIMULUS 2

"True creativity cannot be learned."

As individuals, all human beings have within them creative abilities. There is some quality in every person to imagine and then create that cannot be completely described or explained. These abilities cannot be learned, as they already exist in each and every one of us.

Some of us, however, may find that we have difficulty accessing our creativity. In this way, creativity <u>can</u> be "learned." Everyone, whether privileged or disadvantaged, can, with help, unlock creative capacities in themselves. Take, for example, the process of learning to draw. So often, people are "taught" to be "creative" by being told that they must function like someone else. In a typical art class, students are shown models of "good" drawings, given a paper and pencil, and told to produce an equivalent work of art. Then their attempts are criticized, and the novice artists become frustrated and discouraged, losing all sense of their own abilities. This technique serves only to kill whatever natural creative impulses the students might have. Another technique, outlined in the book <u>Drawing on the Right Side of the Brain</u>, has students begin with exercises that create a supportive environment. In one exercise, students look at an object while they draw it, never lifting pencil from paper, and never looking at what they're doing. In another, students reproduce a drawing which has been turned upside down. In both cases, the point is to draw students' attention away from how "real" the drawing looks and put their attention on what the object they're drawing actually looks like. Thus, students are encouraged to do what they, as individuals, can do.

Creativity requires innovation, and innovation requires risk-taking. No one will take a risk when the result may be severe criticism and humiliation. The quality of creativity rests on positive self-esteem. In the case of those learning to draw, an approach that doesn't seek to criticize what they do seems to work better than one that compares their work to "successful art." So being in a supportive and non-judgmental atmosphere in which they are totally accepted is the way to encourage people to take the risk of trying to do something they have never done before and thus unlock their creative capacities.

ANALYSIS OF FIRST SAMPLE RESPONSE TO STIMULUS 2

Holistic Score: 4

Task 1

As individuals, all human beings have within them creative abilities. There is some quality in every person to imagine and then create that cannot be completely described or explained. These abilities cannot be learned, as they already exist in each and every one of us.

Task 2

Some of us, however, may find that we have difficulty accessing our creativity. In this way, creativity <u>can</u> be "learned." Everyone, whether privileged or disadvantaged, can, with help, unlock creative capacities in themselves. Take, for example, the process of learning to draw. So often, people are "taught" to be "creative" by being told that they must function like someone else. In a typical art class, students are shown models of "good" drawings, given a paper and pencil, and told to produce an equivalent work of art. Then their attempts are criticized, and the novice artists become frustrated and discouraged, losing all sense of their own abilities. This technique serves only to kill whatever natural creative impulses the students might have. Another technique, outlined in the book <u>Drawing on the Right Side of the Brain</u>, has students begin with exercises that create a supportive environment. In one exercise, students look at an object while they draw it, never lifting pencil from paper, and never looking at what they're doing. In another, students reproduce a drawing which has been turned upside down. In both cases, the point is to draw students' attention away from how "real" the drawing looks and put their attention on what the object they're drawing actually looks like. Thus, students are encouraged to do what they, as individuals, can do.

this changes the focus of your argument from "Can creativity be learned" to the simpler question of, "What's the best way to teach it?"

good details

Task 3

Creativity requires innovation, and innovation requires risk-taking. No one will take a risk when the result may be severe criticism and humiliation. The quality of creativity rests on positive self-esteem. In the case of those learning to draw, an approach that doesn't seek to criticize what they do seems to work better than one that compares their work to "successful art." So being in a supportive and non-judgmental atmosphere in which they are totally accepted is the way to encourage people to take the risk of trying to do something they have never done before and thus unlock their creative capacities.

Your essay addresses all three tasks clearly, but you tend to oversimplify by not focusing specifically on whether or not creativity can be learned. This weakness is shown in particular by your sketchy treatment of Task 1. Your main point appears to be that "true creativity" is an inherent ability, but you don't explain this thoroughly. Thus, your example in paragraph 2 leaves us wondering: Is drawing a picture without looking at the paper "truly creative" in the way the statement means? And in paragraph 3 we wonder: Is self-esteem all we need to become truly creative?

SECOND SAMPLE RESPONSE TO STIMULUS 2

"True creativity cannot be learned."

Certain individuals are endowed with such creativity that this quality sets them apart from the rest of society. Painters, poets, musicians, playwrights—their lives revolve around the cultivation of their creative talent. It would seem that these individuals possess creativity as part of their nature, for they operate at a level at which the average person could not, even with extensive training. How many of us could produce a work to equal the worst of William Shakespeare, though we might have taken years of "creative play-writing" classes? Perhaps this means that creativity is heritable. A gene or set of genes for the trait of "creativity" have not been isolated yet, and may not be, because our word creativity may only be a category for many different specific talents. Despite the lack of a defined biological origin, however, creativity is thought by many to be something that cannot be learned.

Creativity is not an all-or-nothing phenomenon; most people will not display the creative genius of da Vinci, but they do have a measure of creativity that they should be encouraged to develop. This could, for example, have positive results in a class on writing. Exposing students to different styles of writing and then urging them to write about their personal experiences will often reveal creative impulses that the teacher can guide. Learning to be truly creative for these students is merely a matter of overcoming inhibitions and finding an outlet for previously unused or stifled creativity.

It is not, therefore, whether creativity can be learned that is important; it is finding out how to bring creativity out of a person. Clearly not everyone will be able to compose musical masterpieces, but this should not hinder one from attempting to develop one's own creative resources.

ANALYSIS OF SECOND SAMPLE RESPONSE TO STIMULUS 2

Holistic Score: 5

Task 1

Certain individuals are endowed with such creativity that this quality sets them apart from the rest of society. Painters, poets, musicians, playwrights—their lives revolve around the cultivation of their creative talent. It would seem that these individuals possess creativity as part of their nature, for they operate at a level at which the average person could not, even with extensive training. How many of us could produce a work to equal the worst of William Shakespeare, though we might have taken years of "creative playwriting" classes? Perhaps this means that creativity is heritable. A gene or set of genes for the trait of "creativity" have not been isolated yet, and may not be, because our word creativity may only be a category for many different specific talents. Despite the lack of a defined biological origin, however, creativity is thought by many to be something that cannot be learned.

Task 2

Creativity is not an all-or-nothing phenomenon; most people will not display the creative genius of da Vinci, but they do have a **measure of creativity** that they should be encouraged to develop. This could, for example, have positive results in a class on writing. Exposing students to different styles of writing and then urging them to write about their personal experiences will often reveal creative impulses that the teacher can guide. Learning to be **truly creative** for these students is merely a matter of overcoming inhibitions and finding an outlet for previously unused or stifled creativity.

is this still "true creativity"?

Task 3

It is not, therefore, whether creativity can be learned that is important; it is finding out how to bring creativity out of a person. Clearly not everyone will be able to compose musical masterpieces, but this should not hinder one from attempting to develop one's own creative resources.

are you changing your definition?

With a bit more depth, this essay could have scored a 6. On the one hand, your handling of Task 1 demonstrated superior rhetorical and reasoning skills. On the other, your treatment of Tasks 2 and 3 grows increasingly less complex and thorough. Paragraph two requires more explanation of what true creativity means in your example of a writing class; you seem to be using this key phrase in a different sense than in paragraph 1. Paragraph 3 begins very well but, again, requires more fleshing out. I'm left feeling that you could have scored a 6 had you spent some prewriting moments clarifying what you meant by true creativity—is it for artists or for most people or for both?

DISCUSSION

Essays for Stimulus 2: "True creativity cannot be learned."

The first response is a strong four. The writer has handled the tasks well and confidently (although he did skimp a bit on the first task), and he used an adequate number of details to buttress his case. The author also managed to hook various examples and ideas together by relying on logical transitions. Paragraph two, for instance, is overflowing with details, yet you always have a clear idea of where the author is heading due to the use of appropriate connectors like *however*, *for example*, and *thus*. Finally, there is a solid conclusion to the ideas set forth. Though you may find some problems with those ideas, as the teacher does, the essay ends in a logical fashion.

The major problem with this response is that the essay doesn't really focus on the given statement. This is a common problem, so beware of it. Look at paragraph one, for example. Does it really explain what it means to say that true creativity cannot be learned? Does the fact that we all have creative abilities mean that there is not some creativity that can be learned? The student would have benefited from spending just a few moments working out some ideas about what "true creativity" means. Then the student would have been able to use that terrific example about the right side of the brain to illustrate his idea.

Instead, as the teacher noted, the student switches his focus from the idea that creativity seems to be something all of us have within us to the topic of how best to teach it. The writer thus changes the question being discussed and sets up an easier problem for himself. We are looking for clear fulfillment of the three tasks in response to the given statement. Unfortunately, this student failed to deliver.

The last essayist received a five. If you compare the beginning of this essay with the prior one, you can see that this student's opinions regarding "true creativity" are far more apparent. In this student's mind, the people who are truly creative, like William Shakespeare, can produce work that very few of us could equal. The student clearly differentiates the creative people from those who don't have creativity. The argument at this point is quite cogent.

Problems arise in the following paragraphs because the student doesn't stick to the aforementioned characterization of creativity. As the teacher notes, the student goes on to say, "well, people don't always have to be da Vincis; they can still have a measure of creativity that they should be encouraged to develop. . . ." The teacher notices this and asks, "Is this still true creativity?"—a key question. If you spend the first paragraph discussing what your idea of true creativity is and then change your definition, you are not presenting a unified argument. The teacher highlights this point with the commentary at the bottom of the page reading, "[this] paragraph requires more explanation. You seem to be using this key phrase in a different sense than in the prior paragraph." This problem could have been solved with just a little bit more initial thinking and prewriting. Remember, it is important to maintain consistency in your ideas.

Finally, take note of the fact that this student backs away from the stimulus statement and claims that "it's not whether creativity can be learned that's important, it's blah blah blah." The statement is there for you to work with; stick with it and don't disparage it if you think it's silly. The best writing sample scores are obtained by students who address all three tasks clearly and logically, regardless of personal feelings or bias toward the stimulus statement.

BIOLOGICAL SCIENCES

Passage I
Questions 143–148

143
D—The complete catabolism of a mole of glucose yields a net of 36 moles of ATP. The glycolytic portion of this pathway, however, yields only a net of 2 moles of ATP. Therefore, if 10 moles of glucose were to undergo glycolysis, then the total ATP produced would be 10 times the amount formed from the glycolysis of one mole, so 10×2 moles of ATP = 20 moles of ATP. Therefore, **Choice D** is correct and **Choice A**, **Choice B**, and **Choice C** are wrong.

144
B—If the reaction was not stereospecific, water could add to the double bond of fumarate to form two enantiomers:

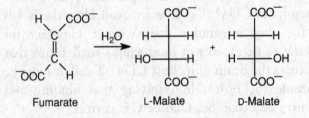

Fumarate   L-Malate   D-Malate

However, the question stem states that the reaction is stereospecific. Therefore, fumarate, which is a *trans* isomer, will react differently to its *cis* counterpart, forming a stereochemically different product. As a result, only one enantiomer will be formed, which is an optically active molecule: **Choice B** is the correct response. A racemic mixture consists of an equal quantity of enantiomers. This would be produced only if the reaction was not stereospecific. Therefore, **Choice A** is wrong. **Choice C** is wrong because only one chiral center is produced in the reaction. An achiral molecule is

one which doesn't contain any chiral centers, or if it does, it possesses an internal plane of symmetry. Since the product has a chiral center and no internal plane of symmetry, **Choice D** is wrong.

145
D—According to the passage and Figure 2, a low blood glucose concentration stimulates a glucagon-triggered cascade that leads to the phosphorylation of PFK2 to form the enzyme FBPase 2 which degrades F-2,6-BP into fructose 6-phosphate, inhibiting phosphofructokinase activity in the process. Since phosphofructokinase catalyzes the committed step in glycolysis, its inhibition will in turn inhibit glycolysis. **Choice D** is thus correct, since glucagon inhibits glycolysis.

Choice A and **Choice B** are wrong, since glucagon does not stimulate the production of F-2,6-BP, it promotes its degradation. **Choice C** is wrong, since according to Figure 2, the phosphorylation of PFK2 occurs when blood glucose levels are low. Glucagon, therefore, promotes the phosphorylation of PFK2.

146
C—According to Figure 1, a high AMP concentration results in a greater glycolytic reaction velocity than a low AMP concentration. Therefore **Choice C** enhances the rate of glycolysis, and is correct.

Choice A is wrong; a low concentration of fructose 2,6-bisphosphate inhibits phosphofructokinase activity, which leads to an inhibition of glycolysis. **Choice B** is wrong since a high ATP to AMP ratio corresponds to a high ATP concentration or a low AMP concentration, and since Graphs I and II tell you that a high ATP concentration and a low AMP concentration reduces the rate of glycolysis, **Choice B** can be eliminated. **Choice D** is wrong since, as seen in Graph III, a high citrate concentration reduces the rate of glycolysis.

147

D—A high fructose-6-phosphate concentration will lead to increased phosphofructokinase activity and enhanced glycolysis, so there will be more ATP. Greater ATP concentration will raise the ATP/AMP ratio, so **Choice D** is correct, since the ATP/AMP ratio will not decrease with high concentrations of fructose 6-phosphate.

Choice A and **Choice B** can be eliminated, since according to Figure 2, fructose 6-phosphate stimulates the synthesis of F-2,6-BP and inhibits its degradation. **Choice C** can also be discarded, since high concentrations of F-2,6-BP stimulate phosphofructokinase.

148

B—Colony A survived under both anaerobic and aerobic conditions, and demonstrated considerable growth and glucose consumption under aerobic conditions. This implies that the Colony A bacteria are facultative aerobes. That Colony B practically disappeared when incubated under aerobic conditions implies that Colony B bacteria must be obligate anaerobes. Thus, Colonies A and B are, respectively, facultative aerobes and obligate anaerobes, so **Choice B** is correct and **Choice A**, **Choice C**, and **Choice D** are all incorrect. You should have eliminated **Choice A** and **Choice C** right away, since the fact that the bacteria from both colonies existed for some time under anaerobic conditions implies that neither of them could be obligate aerobes, since obligate aerobes require molecular oxygen for existence.

Passage II
Questions 149–154

149

A—The transcription of viral mRNA in an HIV-infected CD4+ T-cell requires the same reagents as does the transcription of eukaryotic mRNA in a healthy CD4+ T-cell: RNA polymerase, ribose, phosphate, and adenine, cytosine, guanine, and uracil. Unlike DNA, RNA doesn't contain thymine. So, if the researcher wanted to study mRNA synthesis (transcription), then she would add radiolabeled adenine, guanine, cytosine, and uracil, but not radiolabeled thymine, since it wouldn't be incorporated into the mRNA transcripts. Thus, **Choice A** is correct and **Choice B**, **Choice C**, and **Choice D** are incorrect.

150

C—Hypothesis 1 is based on the premise that HIV fails to integrate. These unintegrated viruses produce a factor that results in CD4+ T-cell death. So if Hypothesis 1 is true, then integration doesn't occur. However, for HIV to be capable of producing a toxic factor that causes the death of its host CD4+ T-cell, it must be inside the host cell, implying that binding and entry do occur. So, **Choice C** is correct.

You can immediately eliminate **Choice A** and **Choice D**, since they both include integration. Reverse transcription is the process by which DNA is synthesized from an RNA template with the enzyme reverse transcriptase. There's not enough information in the description of Hypothesis 1 to determine whether or not reverse transcription must occur before the toxic factor can be produced. Furthermore, it would be virtually impossible for HIV to produce a toxic factor after it had already induced the death of its host cell. Thus, **Choice B** is wrong.

151 C—According to Hypothesis 3, HIV-infected cells express the viral proteins gp120 and gp41 on their surfaces, and these proteins bind to the CD4 receptors on healthy T-cells, yielding a mass of immune-impaired cells known as syncytia. The net result is an effective depletion of T-cell activity. If gp120 and gp41 bound almost irreversibly to CD4 receptors, then syncytia formation would account for the depletion of T-cells associated with HIV infection. Therefore, **Choice C** supports Hypothesis 3 and is correct.

Choice A is wrong, because it contradicts Hypothesis 3 by saying that some CD4$^+$ T-cell lines do not form syncytia yet are still susceptible to depletion due to HIV infection. Hypothesis 3 states that syncytia formation is the cause of the T-cell depletion. **Choice B** doesn't support Hypothesis 3, either. If syncytia formation were transient, these T-cells would be only temporarily nonfunctional, and the supply of T-cells would not be depleted. **Choice D** neither supports nor contradicts Hypothesis 3. Although syncytia formation does lead to cell death, the cell death is not necessary for syncytia formation to render the T-cells nonfunctional.

152 A—According to Hypothesis 4, gp120 molecules are released by HIV-infected CD4$^+$ T-cells and bind to healthy CD4$^+$ T-cells. According to the passage, gp120 binds to the CD4 receptor molecules expressed on the surface of other T-cells. Since CD4 receptor molecules are a normal part of CD4$^+$ T-cell structure, they are recognized by the immune system as "self." However, CD4 receptor molecules bound to gp120 molecules are recognized as "foreign," since the gp120 molecules are not normally present in the body. In response to the presence of gp120, the immune system produces anti-gp120 antibodies, thereby attacking its own CD4$^+$ T-cells. This is known as an autoimmune response. Therefore, Hypothesis 4 makes sense only

if healthy CD4$^+$ cells are not normally subject to autoimmune attacks, and so **Choice A** is correct.

Choice B is wrong because the B-cells are the antibody-producing components of the immune system. **Choice C** is wrong because healthy CD4$^+$ T-cells don't synthesize gp120 molecules. **Choice D** is wrong because it would be impossible for gp120 to travel through the body via the immune system, since the immune system is not a system in the traditional sense of the word. The immune system refers to a group of nonspecific and specific defense mechanisms mediated by specialized cells, such as B-cells, T-cells, and macrophages, that travel through the body via the circulatory system.

153 B—The Golgi complex (Golgi apparatus) is the organelle responsible for the packaging and distribution of newly synthesized proteins, including viral proteins, such as gp120 and gp41. Thus, **Choice B** is correct.

Choice A is wrong because centrioles are cylindrical structures whose role, if any, in animal cell mitosis is unclear to date. **Choice C** is wrong because mitochondria are the sites of cellular respiration in eukaryotic cells. **Choice D** is wrong because lysosomes are responsible for the digestion of various cellular and extracellular metabolites as well as the degradation of unwanted toxins.

154 B—According to the question stem, the test for the presence of HIV is the detection of anti-HIV antibodies circulating in the blood. HIV depletes the body's supply of T-cells, which are crucial for the proliferation and activity of the B-cells that produce the anti-HIV antibodies detected in the blood. This means that at some point during HIV infection, there are enough healthy T-cells in circulation to allow for the production of anti-HIV antibodies by B-cells, and so

Choice B is correct.

Though **Choice A** is most likely a true statement, it is wrong because cytotoxic T-cells are not the cells responsible for the presence of anti-HIV antibodies in the blood of an HIV-infected person. **Choice C** is wrong because, even if it were true, it still wouldn't account for the presence of circulating anti-HIV antibodies. **Choice D** is wrong, since the presence of anti-HIV antibodies would not imply that macrophages have not been infected. Macrophages are phagocytic mononuclear white cells that serve accessory roles in cellular immunity; they are not directly involved in antibody production. **FYI:** Macrophages have been shown to harbor HIV *in vivo*, yet they are relatively resistant to HIV cytopathic effects, most likely due to their low level of CD4 expression. Some studies have suggested that these cells may be the basis of the neurological abnormalities seen in some AIDS patients.

Passage III
Questions 155–159

155 **D**—In Compound I, there is no rotation of substituents attached to the double bond. Therefore, the methyl substituents can be located on the same side of the double bond (*cis*) or on opposite sides (*trans*)

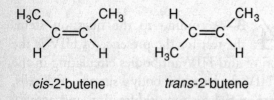

cis-2-butene   trans-2-butene

The *cis/trans* arrangement of substituents around a double bond is known as geometric isomerism, making **Choice D** the correct response. *Cis* and *trans* isomers have different physical properties, attributed to a difference in their dipole moments and symmetry. **Choice A** is wrong since anomers are

cyclic forms of carbohydrates that differ in the configuration about the anomeric carbon (usually carbon 1). Enantiomers are chiral molecules that are non-superimposable mirror images of each other. In addition, they have identical chemical and physical properties (except the ability to rotate plane-polarized light). Compound I is achiral and its isomers have different physical properties, so **Choice B** is wrong. Conformational isomers arise by the rotation around a single bond, not a double bond. At normal temperatures, these isomers cannot be isolated, therefore **Choice C** is also wrong.

156 **A**—In hot basic potassium permanganate, nonterminal alkenes will be oxidatively cleaved to form 2 molecules of carboxylic acid. Compound I is symmetrical, so cleavage and subsequent oxidation will result in the formation of two molecules of acetic acid:

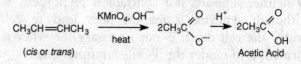

The molecular formula of acetic acid is $C_2H_4O_2$, and, since two molecules are formed, the overall result is $2C_2H_4O_2$, which corresponds exactly with Table 2. **Choice B** and **Choice D** are incorrect because these molecules are diols and are formed when alkenes are treated with cold dilute potassium permanganate. **Choice C** is wrong because the molecular formula doesn't match that in the table. Also, aldehydes will not form under these conditions.

157 **C**—The addition of HBr to Compound II follows Markovnikov's rule: H^+ adds to the least substituted, double-bonded carbon first to form a carbocation intermediate $-CH_3CH_2CH^+CH_3$. Br^- then adds to this molecule to form 2-bromobutane:

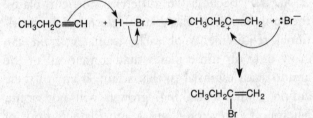

HBr adds to Compound IV in much the same way as Compound II. H^+ adds to the least substituted carbon, but this time the intermediate $CH_3CH_2C^+=CH_2$ is formed. This is called a vinylic cation—an intermediate in which the positive charge is adjacent to a double bond. Therefore **Choice C** is the correct answer. After the vinylic cation is formed, Br^- adds to form $CH_3CH_2CBr=CH_2$:

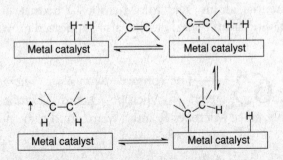

The double bond can then add another molecule of HBr to form a *gem*-dihalide $-CH_3CH_2CBr_2CH_3$. **Choice A** and **Choice D** are incorrect because carbocations are formed when HBr adds to alkenes, not alkynes. **Choice B** is wrong since the positive charge on the vinylic intermediate means that it is a cation not an anion.

158 A—Catalytic hydrogenation of alkenes is always a *syn* process, because the alkene molecules collide with the surface of the solid catalyst bearing hydrogen in such a way that only one side of the double bond is left exposed to attack by hydrogen:

On the other hand, the addition of bromine to an alkene occurs through an *anti* addition mechanism. A cyclic bromonium ion is initially formed; bromide then adds to the molecule 180° to the first bromine, i.e., on the opposite face of the molecule. Hence, the hydrogenation and bromination of Compound I are respectively, *syn* and *anti* addition; **Choice A** is therefore the correct response. **Choice B** is incorrect because this states that the opposite occurs. **Choice C** is wrong because hydrogenation does not occur through nucleophilic addition. **Choice D** is wrong because bromination is classified as electrophilic addition, not nucleophilic addition.

159 C—Markovnikov's rule is followed in the addition of HBr to Compound I and Compound II. Hence, the following carbocation is formed:

$$CH_3CH_2\overset{+}{C}H-CH_3$$

Br^- then adds to this carbocation to produce 2-bromobutane; **Choice C** is therefore correct. **Choice D** is wrong because Markovnikov's rule is only disobeyed when radical initiators such as peroxides or ultraviolet light are present. **Choice A** is wrong because internal, more highly substituted double bonds are stabilized by their alkyl groups. Thus the double bond in Compound I is more stable than the double bond in Compound II. **Choice B** is also wrong because if the double bond in Compound I is more stable, it will be less reactive.

Passage IV
Questions 160–165

160 **A**—All viruses have a protein coat consisting of protein subunits. Since all viruses are so closely related, there will be homology between the viral genes coding for the protein coats of different viruses. This means that probes specific for proteins present in the protein coats of almost all viruses can be created. By hybridizing the unknown infectious agent with probes specific for the few major variants of viral protein coats, the nature of the infectious agent can be determined. If the probes hybridize with the genes of the infectious agent, the agent must be a virus. If the probes do not hybridize with the genes, this means that the infectious agent does not contain the viral genes coding for the protein coat, which means that the agent must be bacterial. Thus, **Choice A** is correct.

Choice B is wrong because, while viruses do not have any photosynthetic pigments, only some bacteria do have them. Only the cyanobacteria, or blue-green algae, are photosynthetic, and cyanobacteria are not infectious agents in humans. **Choice C** is wrong because although most viruses are DNA viruses, RNA viruses also exist. And since all bacteria have RNA, if the infectious agent was an RNA virus, both would stain positive for the presence of RNA. **Choice D** is wrong because all bacteria and all viruses have proteins, and so both would stain positive for the presence of proteins.

161 **A**—Since all four of the microbes are bacteria, you're looking for the structure not found in bacteria. Bacteria are prokaryotes—unicellular organisms characterized by the lack of a true nucleus as well as the absence of all other membranous organelles. Bacteria have a single circular chromosome located in a region of the cell known as the nucleoid. So, **Choice A** is correct and **Choice B** can be eliminated. **Choice C** is wrong, since bacteria have cell walls. Likewise, bacteria contain all the necessary machinery for protein synthesis and reproduction, such as RNA, enzymes, ribosomes, and proteins, which is why **Choice D** is wrong. **FYI:** Prokaryotic ribosomes are structurally different from eukaryotic ribosomes, and this difference is often exploited in the development of effective antibiotics.

162 **B**—By culturing the four strains of bacteria on different nutrient plates, the epidemiologist was able to determine the nutritional requirements of each strain. A strain can grow only on those plates that contain all of the amino acids essential to that strain; if any of these amino acids are lacking, growth will not occur. Microbe Q grew on Plate 1 and Plate 3, both of which contain threonine and cysteine. Microbe Q did not grow on Plate 2 or Plate 4. Plate 4 is identical to Plate 1, except that tryptophan has been substituted for cysteine. Plate 2 is identical to Plate 3, except that phenylalanine has been substituted for threonine. Since growth occurred when threonine and cysteine were both present and was prohibited when either of them was absent, it can be deduced that both threonine and cysteine are essential amino acids for Microbe Q. Therefore, **Choice B** is correct.

Choice A and **Choice C** can be eliminated because neither of these amino acids is present in Plate 3, which supported Microbe Q growth. **Choice D** is wrong because proline can not be an essential amino acid for Microbe Q because it is missing from Plate 1, which also supported growth.

163 **A**—The phrase *pathogenic microbes* refers to Microbe Q and Microbe T only, since Microbes R and S were found to be non-pathogenic. To test whether the strains were affected by the antibiotics, the experimenter needed to use a medium that the strains could definitely grow on in the absence of antibiotics. With this in mind, you should have translated the question to read: Which of the four nutrient plates is capable of sustaining colonies of both Microbe Q and Microbe T? According to Table 1, Microbe Q grew on Plate 1 and Plate 3, while Microbe T grew on Plates 1, 2, and 4. Plate 1 is therefore the only plate that the epidemiologist could have used in the experiment illustrated in Figure 1. Thus, **Choice A** is correct and **Choice B**, **Choice C**, and **Choice D** are wrong.

164 C—An effective antibiotic is one that inhibits, if not completely prevents, bacterial growth. According to the passage, shaded areas in Figure 1 represent regions of good bacterial growth, and as can be seen, Microbe Q growth is inhibited by both Antibiotic Y and Antibiotic Z, while Microbe T is inhibited only by Antibiotic Z. Since Antibiotic Z inhibits both strains of bacteria, it makes sense that this drug would be the most effective in treating patients simultaneously infected with Microbe Q and Microbe T. Thus, **Choice C** is correct and **Choice A**, **Choice B**, and **Choice D** are wrong.

165 C—The best way to approach this question is by the process of elimination. **Choice A** can eliminated, since centrifugation separates substances on the basis of density and would therefore be of little use here, since all bacteria are so close in density that they would sediment into the same layer. **Choice B** sounds like a good idea—especially if you determined from Table 1 that cysteine and threonine are essential for Microbe Q, and that phenylalanine is essential for

Microbe T. You might therefore expect only Microbe Q to grow on the nutrient plate containing cysteine, and only Microbe T to grow on the nutrient plate containing phenylalanine. However, Microbe Q requires both cysteine and threonine for growth, and while Microbe T would grow on the phenylalanine plate, Microbe Q would not grow on either one. So **Choice B** is wrong. **Choice C** is similar to **Choice B**, except that one of the plates has all of the amino acids except cysteine, and the other has all of the amino acids except phenylalanine. This means that Microbe Q would grow on the plate lacking phenylalanine, but not on the plate lacking cysteine. Likewise, Microbe T would grow on the plate lacking cysteine, but not on the plate lacking phenylalanine. In this way, Microbe Q could be isolated from Microbe T, and so **Choice C** is correct. **Choice D** is obviously wrong, since clearly, a mechanism for isolating the two microbes does exist. **FYI:** The easiest way to isolate these microbes would be to use the original Plate 3 and Plate 4. As can be seen in Table 1, Plate 3 sustained only Microbe Q, and Plate 4 sustained only Microbe T.

Discrete Questions 166–170

166 A—Calcitonin lowers blood Ca^{2+} by promoting the incorporation of calcium ion into bone. A way to remember this is: cal*citonin tones* down the Ca^{2+}. Parathyroid hormone (PTH), on the other hand, increases blood Ca^{2+} concentration by promoting its removal from bone and its release into the bloodstream. PTH also decreases the excretion of Ca^{2+} from the kidneys and converts vitamin D_3 into its active form, which stimulates the absorption of Ca^{2+} in the intestines.

So, **Choice A** is the correct answer.

Choice B is wrong because prolactin is a hormone synthesized by the anterior pituitary gland, and stimulates the secretion of milk from female mammary glands. **Choice C** is incorrect because the function of ACTH, also synthesized and secreted by the anterior pituitary, is to stimulate the production of hormones from the adrenal cortex. **Choice D** is wrong because thyroxine (T_4) is a thyroid hormone involved in regulating metabolism.

167 **A**—The partial pressure of CO_2 in the blood is highest in those vessels carrying deoxygenated blood. Deoxygenated blood is returned to the right atrium of the heart via the inferior vena cava and the superior vena cava. From the right atrium the deoxygenated blood drains into the right ventricle, where it is pumped into the pulmonary arteries. The pulmonary arteries deliver the blood to the capillary beds surrounding the alveoli, which is where gas exchange occurs: CO_2 is traded for O_2. The now-oxygenated blood is returned to the heart via the pulmonary veins, that empty into the left atrium. The left atrium drains into the left ventricle, which pumps the oxygenated blood into circulation via the aorta. In addition, the heart is delivered its own supply of oxygenated blood via the coronary arteries that branch off the aorta. Thus, **Choice A** is correct and **Choice B**, **Choice C**, and **Choice D** are wrong, since these vessels carry oxygenated blood.

168 **C**—The three primary germ layers, which arise during the gastrulation stage of embryonic development, and from which all organ systems and structures are derived, are endoderm, mesoderm, and ectoderm. Endoderm is the innermost layer of cells, from which the following structures arise: the lining of the digestive tract, the lining of the respiratory tract, the liver, the thyroid, the pancreas, and the bladder. Mesoderm is the middle layer of cells, from which the following structures arise: skeletal muscle, dermis, bone, blood, the gonads, the kidneys, and the circulatory system. Ectoderm is the outermost layer of cells, from which the following structures arise: epidermis (including nail, hair, and the outer layer of skin), the lens of the eye, the pituitary gland, the lining of the mouth and nose, nervous tissue, and the adrenal medulla. Thus, **Choice C** is correct and **Choice A**, **Choice B**, and **Choice D** are wrong.

169 **B**—Blood type is determined by the antigens expressed on the surface of the red blood cells (RBCs). Type A blood has RBCs with the A antigen and will produce anti-B antibodies when exposed to the B antigen. Type B blood has RBCs with the B antigen and will produce anti-A antibodies when exposed to the A antigen. Type AB blood has RBCs with both the A antigen and the B antigen and will not produce anti-A or anti-B antibodies upon exposure to either antigen. Type O blood has RBCs with neither the A antigen nor the B antigen and will produce anti-A antibodies when exposed to the A antigen and anti-B antibodies when exposed to the B antigen. The Rh antigen is another RBC antigen. Rh^+ blood has the antigen and Rh^- blood does not. Rh^- blood produces anti-Rh antibodies only upon a second exposure to the Rh antigen. Rh^+ blood does not produce antibodies against Rh^- RBCs. The ideal blood transfusion occurs when donor and recipient blood types are a perfect match. The worst blood transfusion occurs whendonor and recipient blood types are a complete mismatch, resulting in severe agglutination and blood clotting.

Choice A is wrong because it would be a fairly good match, though not ideal, because donor and recipient are both type B, and the donor RBCs lack the Rh antigen. **Choice B** is correct because this blood type would cause severe agglutination in the recipient. Although they are a match in terms of the Rh antigen, the presence of A+ RBCs would elicit an attack by anti-A antibodies produced by the recipient's immune system. Since type O blood is known as the "universal donor" in the world of blood transfusions, it won't elicit antibody production against the A antigen or the B antigen, so **Choice C** and **Choice D** are wrong.

170 **B**—The most important factors determining the rate at which a compound diffuses through a membrane are the compound's size and its polarity, assuming there is no facilitated diffusion. Since Compound A and Compound B are the same size, and since there is no facilitated diffusion occurring, only polarity needs to be considered. Cell membranes are nearly impermeable to polar compounds because polar compounds are insoluble in the membrane's hydrophobic lipid bilayer. In contrast, nonpolar compounds (e.g., O_2) diffuse easily through the cell membrane. This implies that the transmembrane diffusion rate of a polar compound is likely to be fairly low and essentially independent of its concentration, which corresponds to the rate depicted by curve B. Likewise, the transmembrane diffusion rate of a nonpolar compound is likely to be fairly high and strongly dependent on its concentration, which corresponds to the rate depicted by curve A. Thus, Compound A is most likely a nonpolar compound and Compound B is most likely a polar compound, so **Choice B** is correct and **Choice A**, **Choice C**, and **Choice D** are wrong.

171 **B**—The contractile unit of a muscle fiber is called a sarcomere, and is composed of actin, myosin, troponin, and tropomyosin. When acetylcholine binds to receptors on the surface of a muscle fiber, it triggers the depolarization of the muscle sarcolemma, which in turn triggers the release of calcium ions from the sarcoplasmic reticulum. The calcium ions bind to troponin, causing a conformational change within the sarcomere that causes the tropomyosin strands to shift and expose the myosin-binding sites on actin. Myosin binds to actin and the sarcomere contracts. So, **Choice B** is correct. **Choice A** and **Choice D** are wrong since the calcium ions do not bind to either the sarcolemma or to actin. **Choice C** is wrong since the formation of permanent actin-myosin crossbridges occurs only in the absence of ATP and leads to the development of rigor mortis.

172 **D**—According to the passage, an incoming action potential triggers the release of acetylcholine via exocytosis, which means that the synaptic vesicles fuse with the membrane of the nerve terminal and release their contents into the synapse. Exocytosis is not a passive process and so requires ATP. The abundance of mitochondria in the nerve terminal supply the ATP, and so **Choice D** is correct.

Choice A is wrong because it doesn't account for the particularly high concentration of mitochondria in the nerve terminal. Furthermore, **Choice A** is not true; not all eukaryotic cells contain mitochondria, e.g., red blood cells. **Choice B** is wrong because while the fact that neurons are aerobic cells does account for the presence of mitochondria, it fails to explain why there is a high concentration of mitochondria in the nerve terminal. **Choice C** is wrong because diffusion is a passive process, which means that ATP is not required.

173 A—If the student's receptors for hot pain (the free nerve endings in the skin) had been severed, then the student would not have felt any pain and would not have withdrawn his hand from the hot plate. Thus, **Choice A** is right and **Choice B** is wrong. The sensation of pain is the result of an impulse being transmitted to the brain's sensory cortex via a sensory receptor and a sensory neuron. If one of these pathways were severed at any point, the impulse would not be sent to the brain, and the sensation of pain would not be felt. Thus, **Choice C** and **Choice D** must be wrong. **Note:** Though the sensation of pain is also conveyed to the sensory cortex via a different pathway, this pathway also begins with the stimulation of the hot pain receptors in the skin. So if these receptors were severed, the message would not be sent to the brain by this route either.

174 D—Touching a burning hot plate is more painful and dangerous than touching uncomfortably warm water. Thus, it's beneficial to withdraw a limb more rapidly from the hot plate than from warm water. The difference in reaction time corresponds to two factors: the distance the impulse must travel and the number of synapses the impulse must cross. The withdrawal reflex in response to hot pain is a reflex arc of two synapses: a sensory neuron synapses with an interneuron and the interneuron synapses with a motor neuron. Since this action is faster than the response to warm water, the nerve impulse triggered by the stimulation of the skin's "uncomfortably warm" receptors most likely travels through more than two synapses and does not bypass the brain by synapsing in the

spinal cord. This makes sense, since there isn't any real threat of injury. So, **Choice D** is correct.

Choice A is incorrect because an action potential is an all-or-nothing response; the quantity of acetylcholine released does not affect its magnitude. **Choice B** is incorrect because the withdrawal reflex in response to intense heat bypasses the sensory areas of the brain, synapsing directly in the spinal cord. In addition, the passage tells you that the sensation of pain is transmitted more slowly to the sensory cortex than to a motor neuron. **Choice C** is incorrect because, while it's true that epinephrine secretion does trigger the "fight-or-flight" response, acetylcholine is the only neurotransmitter secreted at the neuromuscular junction.

175 C—Since you're told that when one limb is withdrawn the opposite limb extends, the correct answer must have the left arm extending. According to the passage, to move the arm towards the shoulder, the biceps contract and the triceps relax. From this, it can be inferred that to straighten the arm, the biceps relax and the triceps contract. So, **Choice C** is correct, since when the left biceps relax and the left triceps contract, the left arm extends.

Choice A is incorrect because this would cause the right arm to extend, not to withdraw. **Choice B**, in which both the right biceps and the right triceps contract, is wrong because it's impossible. The muscles of the arm work in antagonistic pairs, so that when one muscle contracts the other muscle relaxes. **Choice D** is wrong, because if the left biceps contract, then the left triceps relax, which means that the left arm would be withdrawn. Likewise, the relaxation of the right biceps dictates the contraction of the right triceps, which would lead to the extension of the right arm, which is the opposite of what actually occurs.

Passage VI
Questions 176–180

176 D—Chlorination of butane results in the formation of 1-chlorobutane and 2-chlorobutane, since butane possesses two types of hydrogen that can be substituted. 1-chlorobutane is achiral, so statement III is correct. On the other hand, 2-chlorobutane possesses a chiral carbon, so statement I is correct:

Choice D is the only choice that contains both statements I and III so it is the correct response. Statement II is also correct because the reaction occurs through a free radical intermediate; the halogen can add to either side of the molecule forming a racemic mixture, which has no observed optical rotation.

177 A—The passage tells you that the order of reactivity of the halogens is fluorine, then chlorine, then bromine, then iodine. Bromine produces five times as much tertiary product than primary product, so it seems to be selective about which hydrogen it reacts with. However, with fluorine, equal amounts of product form, so it must be pretty unselective. Therefore, **Choice A** is correct: fluorine is the most reactive halogen, but it is the least selective, so there is an inverse relation between reactivity and selectivity. **Choice B** is wrong because fluorine is more reactive than bromine, so it will be a better halogenating agent. **Choice C** is also wrong because fluorine is simply more reactive than bromine: it doesn't matter which sort of hydrogen it is substituting. **Choice D** is true in that fluorine forms stronger bonds to primary carbons than bromine, but it doesn't account for the different products that are formed.

178 B—In free radical substitution reactions, only a small amount of initiator is required since a halogen radical is produced in the propagation step, which can drive the reaction without the help of the initiator (resulting in a chain reaction). Therefore, the reaction can be started by light of low intensity to produce a small concentration of halogen radicals; so **Choice B** is the correct response. **Choice A** is wrong because these reactions have high activation energies. **Choice C** is wrong because halogen-halogen bonds are quite strong. Finally, **Choice D** is wrong because alkanes are extremely unreactive molecules.

179 B—A chain termination step is one that ends the reaction chain. The chain in this reaction is kept going by the presence of free-radicals: to terminate the chain, the number of radicals must be reduced. This is shown in **Choice B**, where two radicals combine to form a neutral molecule. **Choice A** and **Choice D** are wrong because these are propagation steps; bromine radicals are generated, which assist the reaction, not terminate it. **Choice C** is wrong because no radicals are shown here at all. This is actually the overall reaction that occurs between bromine and the alkane.

180 D—The passage states that the most reactive type of hydrogen toward substitution is a tertiary hydrogen. Substitution of the tertiary hydrogen in 2-methylpropane will result in the formation of 2-bromo-2-methylpropane, **Choice D**. **Choice B** is wrong because it names the molecule as a butane, and the longest carbon chain has three carbons, not four. **Choice A** names the molecule as 2-bromomethylpropane. If this were true, propane would have a bromomethyl substituent, not a bromo and a methyl substituent.

Choice C is wrong because it states that the product has a 1-bromo substituent, not a 2-bromo substituent. This product would only be formed if the less reactive primary hydrogen was substituted.

Passage VII
Questions 181–186

181 **D**—According to the passage, eukaryotic cells contain genes known as proto-oncogenes, which normally code for proteins involved in the regulation of growth. If any of these proto-oncogenes become transformed into an oncogene, then that cell is said to be tumorigenic. A tumorigenic cell is one that gives rise to a tumor, and unlike normal cells, tumor cells don't obey the rules of normal cell growth and divide indefinitely. Thus, in a tumorigenic cell, you would expect to see an increase in all of the activities and processes associated with cell growth and division, such as mRNA synthesis (transcription) and ribosomal assembly. Likewise, cell division would also increase, since tumor cells replicate at an accelerated rate. Therefore, **Choice D** is the correct answer, and **Choice A**, **Choice B**, and **Choice C** are wrong.

182 **A**—A point mutation is the replacement of one nucleotide base pair with another pair of nucleotides in double-stranded DNA. A point mutation is also referred to as a base-pair substitution. Thus, a cellular oncogene activated by point mutation differs from the proto-oncogene from which it was derived by a single base-pair. So, **Choice A** is correct and **Choice B**, **Choice C**, and **Choice D** are wrong.

183 **C**—In order for a proto-oncogene to transform a cell, oncoproteins must be produced from proto-oncogene transcripts. But if there are complementary nucleic acid sequences present, the proto-oncogene mRNA will base pair with the nucleic acids before it can be translated and produce oncoproteins. So, **Choice C** is the correct answer.

According to the passage, cellular proto-oncogenes often become tumorigenic via a point mutation that leads to the formation of a defective protein, so **Choice A** is wrong. **Choice B** is wrong; you're told that a mutation that causes a proto-oncogene to produce an excess of its protein product, such as a chromosomal translocation, will convert the proto-oncogene into a tumorigenic oncogene. **Choice D** is wrong; you're told that a mutation that causes the proto-oncogene to undergo gene amplification would also cause an excess of protein product and convert the proto-oncogene into a tumorigenic oncogene.

184 **C**—A *c-onc* (proto-oncogene) is a cellular gene found in an organism's own genome. A *v-onc* is a gene found in the genome of transforming viruses. The *v-onc* is not normally part of the viral genome; it was incorporated into the viral genome from *c-onc* genes formerly found in a eukaryotic host cell. If the *v-onc* gene was captured from a host cell in the form of *c-onc* RNA, the *v-onc* gene will have a sequence similar to the sequence of *c-onc* RNA. The *v-onc* gene will be similar to the exons the *c-onc* gene spliced together. So **Choice C** is the correct answer.

Choice A is wrong, since if the *v-onc* gene contained only *c-onc* introns, the *v-onc* gene would code for nonsense, since it's the exons that contain the coding sequences. **Choice B** is wrong, because although it is true that a *v-onc* gene has a greater level of expression than its corresponding *c-onc* gene, expression level is independent of gene sequence. **Choice D** is wrong because although the *v-onc* RNA could be spliced after it had transcribed inside a eukaryotic host cell, it would not explain why the *v-onc* gene itself resembled the mRNA sequence of the *c-onc* gene.

185 **D**—The binding of a compound to a growth-factor receptor on the cell surface triggers a series of reactions that activate the protein *ras*, which in turn triggers another cascade of reactions. The end result is the activation of specific transcription factors and the expression of select genes. This is an example of signal transduction. Likewise, the second messenger system (as utilized by peptide hormones) is put into action by the binding of a molecule to a receptor on the outer surface of the cell membrane. This event triggers a cascade of events in which a signal is transmitted to the interior of the cell. On receipt of a signal from outside the cell, other reaction cascades are initiated inside the cell that result in a specific change in cellular activity. Typically, second messenger systems involve G proteins and cyclic AMP. Thus, **Choice D** is correct.

Choice A is wrong, since formation of an antibody-antigen complex occurs within the vessels of the circulatory and lymphatic systems, and involves the binding of proteins expressed on the surface of the antigen to the antibody-binding sites of the antibody itself. **Choice B** is wrong since the sodium-potassium pump transports sodium and chloride ions across membrane without any signal transduction. **Choice C** is wrong because the Krebs cycle, which is a part of cellular respiration, is regulated via a negative feedback mechanism. The synthesis of citrate from oxaloacetate and acetyl CoA is an important control point in the cycle. ATP inhibits citrate synthase, the enzyme that catalyzes citrate synthesis. As ATP levels increase, citrate synthesis is inhibited.

186 **B**—A promoter is a region of DNA involved in the binding of RNA polymerase to initiate transcription. The promoter region is located approximately 10–35 base pairs before the first coding base of the gene. The strength of a promoter describes the frequency at which RNA polymerase initiates transcription and appears to be related to the closeness with which its sequences conform to the ideal consensus sequences. So, a strong promoter increases the frequency with which RNA polymerase binds to the region and transcribes the gene. Based on this, **Choice B** is the correct answer.

Choice A is wrong since promoters are involved with transcription, not translation. **Choice C** and **Choice D** must be wrong since translocation and mutation typically lead to abnormal gene product, not to an excess of normal gene product.

Passage VIII
Questions 187–192

187 **A**—An animal's immune system produces antibodies in response to the presence of antigen—substances that are recognized by the animal as being "foreign," or "nonself." Healthy animals do not normally produce antibodies against their own circulating hormones. Since mice and rabbits are not normally exposed to human hormones, injecting them with extract from the human endocrine gland that synthesizes a particular hormone will elicit the production of antibodies specific for that hormone. The antibodies are then isolated from a blood sample for use in an RIA. Thus, **Choice A** is the correct answer.

Choice B is wrong because human endocrine gland cells produce hormones, not antibodies; the B-cells of the immune system produce antibodies. Furthermore, if human endocrine cells could produce antibodies, then they would be able to produce them *in vivo*. **Choice C** is wrong because it implies that human hormones will elicit an immune response only in mice and rabbits. Human hormones would do the same in most other mammals, too. Rabbits and mice are commonly used as test animals in laboratories because of certain similarities they share with humans, and because they are fast breeders. **FYI:** Exposing chimpanzees to a human hormone extract might not elicit antibody production by the chimp because both species share approximately 96 percent of their DNA. **Choice D** actually describes the principle behind vaccinations. Vaccination with a weakened or killed form of a pathogen elicits a mild immune response in the organism. This primary exposure to the pathogen results in B-cell proliferation and antibody production. Upon subsequent exposure to the pathogen, the immune response is typically faster and more efficient. What's wrong with **Choice D** is that immunization with a hormone extract will not cause an infection. Viruses and bacteria cause infections. Thus, **Choice D** is wrong.

188 D—ADH, or antidiuretic hormone, is the hormone secreted by the posterior pituitary gland in response to low blood volume or high plasma osmolarity. ADH restores plasma osmolarity or blood volume to normal levels by increasing water reabsorption in the kidneys. Therefore, you would expect the concentration of circulating ADH to be higher in a person suffering from severe blood loss than in a healthy person. Since the RIA for ADH in a healthy person yielded an ADH concentration of 3 pg/mL, then the only possible answer is 5 pg/mL, which is the only choice higher in value than the ADH RIA of a healthy person. Therefore, **Choice D** is the correct answer and **Choice A**, **Choice B**, and **Choice C** are wrong.

189 D—According to the passage, labeled and unlabeled hormone compete for binding sites on the antibody. If there is little unlabeled hormone in the sample, the percentage of antibody-bound radiolabeled hormone will be high; if there is a lot of unlabeled hormone, the percentage of antibody-bound radiolabeled hormone will be low. FSH (follicle-stimulating hormone) stimulates the maturation of an ovarian follicle during a typical menstrual cycle. During pregnancy however, the menstrual cycle is inhibited because progesterone, which is secreted by the corpus luteum during the first trimester of pregnancy and secreted by the placenta during the remainder of the pregnancy, inhibits FSH secretion. So, the concentration of FSH is very low during pregnancy. If an RIA for FSH were done on a woman before pregnancy and again in her 16th week of pregnancy, you would expect the percentage of antibody-bound radiolabeled FSH to be higher during pregnancy since the concentration of FSH in her body would be low. Thus, on Figure 1, the point that corresponds to the before pregnancy state must have a higher FSH concentration on the *x*-axis than does the pregnancy state. Therefore, **Choice D** is the correct answer.

Choice A, **Choice B**, and **Choice C** all show the FSH concentration to be greater during pregnancy than before pregnancy, and so are incorrect. Since all of the answer choices except for **Choice D** have a higher FSH concentration at the second point, you could have concluded that **Choices A**, **B**, and **C** all imply the same thing, and therefore must be wrong.

190 B—So long as the antibody binds to the radiolabeled hormone and the unlabeled hormone with equal affinity, then the concept of competition for the binding sites is valid, and so is the RIA. If the antibody preferentially bound the radiolabeled hormone, then the percentage of antibody-bound radiolabeled hormone would always be high, regardless of the concentration of unlabeled hormone in the blood sample being assayed. The standard curve generated from such data would be invalid, and therefore useless for calculating hormone concentrations. Thus, **Choice B** is correct and **Choice A** is wrong.

Choice C is wrong because if there was enough antibody in the solution to completely bind all of the radiolabeled hormone and unlabeled hormone, then the two couldn't compete for antibody binding sites. This competition is essential to RIA because the percentage of each of the hormones that binds to the antibody is directly proportional to its concentration in the solution. **Choice D** is wrong, because there is no evidence in the passage to support it. Antibodies can bind to antigens only at their antigen-binding sites.

191 **B**—Insulin is the pancreatic hormone that lowers blood glucose concentration mainly by stimulating the conversion of glucose into its storage form, glycogen. In response to high blood glucose, the pancreas secretes insulin, and blood glucose concentration decreases. Thus, one hour after an infusion of glucose, you would expect to find a higher concentration of insulin in a blood sample taken from the subject than before the infusion. And, in an RIA in which the concentration of unlabeled hormone is expected to be high relative to the concentration of radiolabeled hormone, the percentage of antibody-bound radiolabeled hormone is expected to be low. Thus, if Figure 1 were the standard curve for insulin, the point representing insulin after the glucose infusion must correspond to a higher hormone concentration than the point representing insulin concentration before glucose infusion. Therefore, **Choice B** is the correct answer and **Choice A**, **Choice C**, and **Choice D** are wrong.

192 **C**—That the precursor and active forms of a hormone are chemically and structurally similar implies that an antibody developed against either form of the hormone would be capable of binding to both, and would do so with equal affinity. The question stem states that the researcher wanted to measure the concentration of the active form of the hormone, since it's the active form that circulates and acts on target cells. However, the researcher used the precursor form to develop the antibodies and generate the standard curve used for the RIA. If the sample to be assayed contained only the active form, the results of the RIA would be valid. However, if the sample of unlabeled hormone to be assayed were somehow contaminated with the unlabeled precursor form, then the antibody would bind to both forms. Now there would be three competitors vying for the antigen-binding sites on the antibodies: the radiolabeled precursor form, the unlabeled precursor form, and the unlabeled active form. This means that the percentage of antibody-bound radiolabeled hormone would be atypically low. And since the percentage of antibody-bound radiolabeled hormone is inversely proportional to the concentration of unlabeled hormone in the sample, the calculated concentration of the active hormone would be greater than its actual concentration. Thus, **Choice C** is correct and **Choice D** is wrong.

Choice A is wrong for two reasons. First, the standard curve generated using the precursor form of the hormone would be valid, but only for calculating the concentration of either form of the hormone in a sample containing only that form. Second, according to the question, the researcher is looking to measure the concentration of the active form of a particular hormone, not its precursor form. **Choice B** is wrong since it proposes that the percentage of antibody-bound radiolabeled hormone would be greater than normal, while in actuality, it would be less than normal.

**Discrete
Questions 193–197**

193 **A**—Osmosis is the tendency of water to flow from regions of lower solute concentration to regions of higher solute concentration. Freshwater fish tend to gain water because of osmosis, and marine fish tend to lose it. If water is flowing into the freshwater fish, then the fish's environment must be hypotonic to its blood; that is, the freshwater has a lower concentration of dissolved solutes than the fish's blood. The marine fish is losing water to its surroundings, which means that its aqueous environment must be hypertonic to its blood. In both cases, the water is flowing from hypotonic regions to hypertonic regions. The term *isotonic* means that there is no difference in osmolarity between two regions; there is no net osmosis between isotonic regions. Thus **Choice A** is correct, and **Choice B**, **Choice C**, and **Choice D** are wrong.

194 **D**—Hemoglobin has four subunits, each with its own heme group, while myoglobin has only one unit and therefore one heme group. The sigmoid, or S-shape of hemoglobin's O_2-dissociation curve reflects the fact that the saturation of hemoglobin depends not only on the concentration of O_2 in blood, but also on the number of subunits that are occupied with O_2 molecules. Cooperative binding means that the binding of the first O_2 molecule to one of hemoglobin's subunits makes it easier for the second O_2 to bind. And the binding of the second makes it easier for the third, and so on. In other words, when the partial pressure of O_2 in the blood is low, it is more difficult for that first O_2 to bind, but because of the cooperativity after the first one does bind, it becomes much easi-

er for the other O_2 molecules to bind, which is why the curve rises steeply. Since myoglobin does not have multiple subunits, O_2 cannot bind to it in a cooperative fashion, which is why myoglobin's O_2 dissociation curve is not S-shaped. Its curve reflects the fact that the saturation of myoglobin is directly proportional to the concentration of O_2 in the blood. Thus, **Choice D** is correct and **Choice B** is wrong. **Choice A** is wrong because the Bohr effect is the term used to describe hemoglobin's decrease in O_2 affinity at high plasma concentrations of CO_2 and low pH. **Choice C** is wrong because while the difference in the partial pressure of O_2 between muscle tissue and arterial blood is the factor accounting for the diffusion of O_2 into O_2-depleted muscle tissue, it does not account for the difference in the shapes of the two curves.

195 **B**—All *meta* directors have a positive charge on the atom directly bonded to the ring or can be polarized to have a partial positive charge there. Most *ortho* and *para* directing groups have at least one pair of nonbonding electrons on the atom directly bonded to the ring. **Choice B** is correct because the nitrogen possesses a pair of nonbonding electrons. The carboxyl group in **Choice A** will certainly be a *meta* director since the carboxyl carbon is positively polarized. The same thing applies to the ketone group in **Choice C**: the carbonyl oxygen polarizes the bond so that the carbon has a slight positive charge. **Choice D** is also a *meta* director, since the electron withdrawing nature of the oxygens ensure that the sulfur atom is positively polarized.

196 **A**—When an amino acid reaches its isoelectric point, it is in the form of a zwitterion. In this state, the molecule is electrically neutral: the carboxylate group is negatively charged, and the ammonium group is positively charged. As a result, it will not migrate toward either the cathode or the anode when placed in an electric field. Since the amino acid migrates to the anode at pH 8.5, it must have a net negative charge. To attain neutrality and hence reach the isoelectric point, the ammonium group has to be protonated, which can be achieved by lowering the pH. Therefore, the isoelectric point must be lower than 8.5: **Choice A**.

197 C—Both LH and FSH are released by the anterior pituitary under the influence of their respective hypothalamic gonadotropin-releasing factors. However, male and female hormones differ in their pattern of release and physiological function. In males, the release of LH and FSH is relatively constant because they stimulate two continuous processes: testosterone synthesis and spermatogenesis. In females, the release of LH and FSH is strictly cyclic. Prior to ovulation, FSH and LH secretion continuously increase; the increase in FSH stimulates follicle development and the increase in LH stimulates the development of the corpus luteum following ovulation. The secretion of both hormones drops sharply following ovulation and does not begin to rise again until the onset of the next menstrual cycle. Therefore, the switch from cyclic production of gonadotropin-releasing factors to acyclic production during reproductive development would most certainly affect the release patterns of both of these hormones, and so **Choice C** is correct. **Choice A**, **Choice B**, and **Choice D** are incorrect.

198 D—Bacteria are often classified and named on the basis of their shape, of which there are three: spherical, rodlike, and helical (spiral). Spherical bacteria are know as cocci; rodlike bacteria are know as bacilli; and helical bacteria are known as spirochetes, or spirilla. Thus, if a sample from a CF patient infected with *Staphylococcus* were cultured and viewed under a microscope, the bacteria would appear spherical in shape. So, **Choice D** is the correct answer.

Helical bacteria are the least common of the three groups; rod-shaped bacteria include the common *E. coli*, as well as those bacteria responsible for causing lockjaw, diphtheria, and tuberculosis. So, **Choice A** and **Choice C** are wrong. **Choice B** is wrong since sickle-shaped bacteria do not exist; however, those individuals with the genetic disease sickle-cell anemia have red blood cells with an abnormal sickle shape.

199 C—CF patients suffer from pancreatic insufficiency because of abnormally viscous mucus secretions that block the ducts linking the pancreas to the small intestine. The pancreas synthesizes and secretes the following enzymes: trypsinogen, chymotrypsinogen, carboxypeptidase, amylase, and lipase. Lipase digests fats; amylase digests carbohydrates; carboxypeptidase, trypsinogen, and chymotrypsinogen all digest proteins. Trypsinogen and chymotrypsinogen are secreted into the small intestine, where enterokinase, an enzyme secreted by the glands of the small intestine, converts trypsinogen to its active form, trypsin. Trypsin then converts chymotrypsinogen to its active form, chymotrypsin. **Choice C** is therefore correct, since enterokinase—a product of the small intestine—would not be lacking in a CF patient. On the other hand, lipase, trypsin, and chymotrypsinogen would be included in an enzyme supplement administered to CF patients. Thus, **Choices A**, **B**, and **D** are all incorrect.

200 **B**—According to the passage, the gene for cystic fibrosis is autosomal recessive. Let F = the normal gene and f = the cystic fibrosis gene. Those individuals with CF have the genotype ff; those who are carriers have the genotype Ff; and normal individuals have the genotype FF. So in a cross between two heterozygotes: Ff × Ff, 25 percent of the offspring will have the genotype FF and will be normal; 50 percent will have the genotype Ff and will thus be carriers; and 25 percent will have the genotype ff and will have cystic fibrosis. Therefore, in a cross between two carriers, there is a 25 percent chance that their child will be affected by CF, and **Choice B** is the correct answer.

201 **D**—Since the CF gene codes for a defective transmembrane chloride channel, it would seem that this is the cause of the increased chloride and sodium in the sweat of CF patients. The chloride channel coded for by the CF gene must be unable to transport chloride from the sweat ducts into the surrounding epithelial cells. And due to the principle of electroneutrality, sodium would follow suit. So, **Choice D** is correct.

Choice A is incorrect because transporting less chloride into the sweat ducts would produce a lower concentration of chloride in the sweat. **Choice B** and **Choice C** are wrong because they suggest that the defective channel in CF patients transports sodium, contradicting the information in the passage.

202 **B**—The pancreas secretes trypsinogen, chymotrypsinogen, and carboxypeptidase, which are all involved in protein digestion; pancreatic amylase, which is involved in carbohydrate digestion; and lipase, which is involved in fat digestion. So, you might expect a CF patient to suffer from malabsorption proteins, fats, and carbohydrates. However, it is fat absorption that is the most severely impaired because lipase is the only enzyme that digests fat (in conjunction with bile). Carbohydrates, on the other hand, are digested by salivary amylase, maltase, sucrase, and lactase, in addition to pancreatic amylase. Likewise, proteins are digested by pepsin, aminopeptidases and dipeptidases, in addition to the pancreatic enzymes. Therefore, **Choice B** is correct and **Choice C** is wrong. Although pulmonary obstruction, is also a symptom of CF, it is caused by the thick mucus secretions of the respiratory epithelial lining, which often become infected by bacteria of the *Staphylococcus* family. So, **Choice A** is wrong. **Choice D** is wrong because although the passage implies that CF patients are susceptible to penicillin-resistant bacteria, this is not the result of pancreatic exocrine insufficiency, and is thus wrong.

203 **A**—According to the passage, CO_2 remains in the blood of CF patients longer than in the blood of healthy individuals. The CO_2 produced by cellular respiration diffuses out of the tissues and into plasma, where it reacts with water to form H_2CO_3, which dissociates into HCO_3^- and H^+. Most of the H^+ binds with hemoglobin. So, though there is an increase in plasma H^+ as a result of normal cellular function, the binding of the H^+ to hemoglobin maintains blood pH to within a fairly constant range. When the blood reaches the capillaries of the lungs, the reactions reverse: the H^+ and HCO_3^- reassociate to form of

H_2CO_3, which is then converted back into CO_2 and water, both of which are exhaled. However, in CF patients, the sticky, thick mucus interferes with normal gas exchange in the alveoli, causing the CO_2 to remain in the blood for a longer period of time in the form of HCO_3^- and H^+ before they reassociate back into H_2CO_3. An increase in plasma H^+ decreases blood pH, since the two are inversely related. Since a decrease in blood pH is just another way of saying an increase in acidity, **Choice A** is the correct answer, and **Choice B**, **Choice C**, and **Choice D** are wrong.

Passage X
Questions 204–208

204 **D**—In Figure 2, H^+ bonds with the oxygen of the carbonyl group. It is then lost in step 4 to regenerate H_3O^+ and the α-halo ketone. A catalyst is a material that increases the rate of a reaction but remains unchanged itself, so the hydrogen ion does fit this definition.

On the other hand, the hydroxide ion is a reactant. In Figure 1, the hydroxide abstracts an α-hydrogen from the ketone in the first step to produce water and the enolate ion. Since the hydroxide anion is used up, and not regenerated, it is a reactant and not a catalyst. Therefore, **Choice D** is the correct response.

205 **A**—Tautomers are compounds that differ in the arrangement of their atoms, but exist in equilibrium with each other. The most common type of tautomerism is that in which molecules differ in the attachment of a hydrogen and the placement of a double bond, namely, keto-enol tautomers. In Figure 2, the reactant, acetone, is in its keto form. It becomes proto-

nated by acid to form an intermediate which then slowly isomerizes to produce the enol form of acetone.

Enantiomers are a subdivision of stereoisomers, so they differ in their spatial arrangement, not their atomic connectivity. The product and reactant in step 2 do differ in their atomic connectivity, so **Choice C** and **Choice D** are wrong.

Geometric isomers are also another type of stereoisomer and are defined as compounds that differ in the position of groups around a double bond. The product and reactant do not fit this definition either, so **Choice B** is wrong.

206 **A**—Alpha halogenation in basic solution usually doesn't stop at the mono-halogenated product stage because the halogen on the alpha carbon is highly electronegative: it pulls electron density towards it, so the two remaining protons are highly acidic. Since the conditions are basic, these hydrogens can be easily abstracted and the anion that is formed can attack the positively polarized region of another halogen molecule, resulting in multiple halogenations. Therefore, **Choice A** is the correct response. **Choice B** is true in that the base is strong and will abstract protons, but it is not the reason why multiple halogenations occur. **Choice C** is incorrect because α-halo ketones are not unstable compounds: they can be isolated quite easily. **Choice D** is wrong because abstraction of a proton will result in the formation of a carbanion not a carbocation, and a halogen would destabilize a carbocation, not stabilize it.

207 **C**—This question can be interpreted as, "What reactants are involved in the rate limiting step?" Remember that the rate-limiting step is the slow one. Therefore, in Figure 1, the rate depends upon the abstraction of an α-proton from acetone. The two species involved in this reaction are acetone and OH⁻; roman numerals I and III, making **Choice C** correct. Bromine has nothing to do with the slow step; it is involved only with the fast step, which does not affect the rate. Hence **Choice B** and **Choice D** are wrong. **Choice A** is wrong because the rate of the reaction does not solely depend upon the concentration of acetone.

208 B—In this reaction, a ketone reacts with a Grignard reagent to form an alcohol:

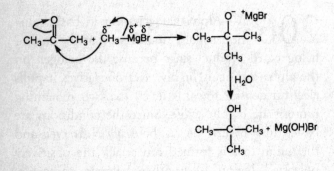

Therefore, the molecule formed is *tert*-butyl alcohol: **Choice B**. **Choice A**, **Choice C**, and **Choice D** can be eliminated because none of these functionalities are formed in the reaction. In addition, **Choice A** and **Choice D** do not contain the *tert*-butyl group.

Passage XI
Questions 209–214

209 C—Synapses are neural junctions that transmit depolarization waves from one neuron to another. Once a depolarization wave has reached the presynaptic knob, vesicles containing a neurotransmitter, in this case acetylcholine, merge with the presynaptic membrane and diffuse across the synaptic cleft to bind with receptors of the postsynaptic membrane. This results in depolarization of the postsynaptic membrane and thus initiates the transmission of another nerve impulse. After depolarization, acetylcholine remains bound to the postsynaptic receptors, and thus no more neural impulses can be transmitted unless acetylcholine is removed from the receptors. Acetylcholinesterase restores the excitability of the postsynaptic membrane by cleaving acetylcholine; therefore, **Choice C** is the correct answer. **Choice B** is wrong, since the passage states that acetylcholinesterase doesn't work until after acetylcholine has been released by the presynaptic membrane. **Choice D** is wrong because a plausible mechanism to restore full excitability to the presynaptic knob would be to replace acetylcholine. However, ACE breaks down acetylcholine, so it does cannot affect the activity of the presynaptic membrane. **Choice A** is true in that the reaction of ACE with acetylcholine will prevent the transmitter being reabsorbed by the presynaptic membrane, but it is the reactivation of the receptors which is the most important consequence of the action of ACE.

210 B—Since a carboxylate group (designated as CO_2^-) is negatively charged, and the quaternary nitrogen atom of acetylcholine is positively charged, they will be attracted by electrostatic interaction; so **Choice B** is correct. **Choice A** is wrong because there is no hydrogen in the carboxylate group or the quaternary nitrogen that can take part in hydrogen bonding. **Choice C** is wrong because a hydrophobic interaction is an attraction between nonpolar groups. The attraction between the carboxylate group and the quaternary nitrogen is the opposite of this: it is a polar interaction. **Choice D** is wrong because London forces are weak attractive forces between instantaneous and induced dipoles occurring in nonpolar molecules.

211
D—In the imidazole ring, the double bonded nitrogen has five valence electrons, three of which are used in bonding. The remaining lone pair of electrons are donated to form an N-H bond, leaving a positive charge on the nitrogen. A Lewis acid is an electron pair acceptor and a Lewis base is an electron pair donor. Nitrogen, therefore, acts as a Lewis base by donating its electrons to form a bond to hydrogen; **Choice D** is therefore the correct answer. **Choice A** and **Choice B** are wrong because they give the wrong definitions for Lewis acids and bases. **Choice C** is incorrect because nitrogen doesn't have any room in its valence shell to accept electrons, so it definitely won't act as a Lewis acid.

212
D—In Figures 1 and 2, the tyrosine residue of the enzyme donates a proton which becomes bonded to the carbonyl oxygen in acetylcholine. This gives the ester carbon a positive charge. In Figures 2 and 3, an esterification reaction occurs: the oxygen in the serine group nucleophilically attacks and adds to the positively charged carbon in acetylcholine to form an ester (acetylserine) and an alcohol (choline). Therefore, protonation of the carbonyl oxygen in acetylcholine results in an increased positive charge on the carbon attached to it, increasing its susceptibility to nucleophilic attack. The increased positive charge on the carbon causes it to be attracted more strongly to the negative charge on serine's hydroxyl oxygen so it will diffuse towards serine more quickly, and the reaction will proceed at a faster rate. Therefore, **Choice D** is correct. ACE is a catalyst, whose function is to increase the rate of reaction, not to affect the equilibrium or the extent of the reaction, so **Choice B** is wrong. Protonation does not affect the leaving ability of the choline group, so **Choice A** and **Choice C** are wrong.

213
B—Acetylcholine undergoes nucleophilic attack by the hydroxyl oxygen of serine. Since the carbon-oxygen single bond of acetylcholine is broken (resulting in the loss of choline) and replaced by a new carbon-oxygen single bond to serine, the reaction is a nucleophilic substitution. The oxygen of serine attacks the positively charged carbon while at the same time, the choline group leaves. This is characteristic of an S_N2 reaction, so **Choice B** is the correct answer. **Choice A**, S_N1, is wrong, since the first step in an S_N1 reaction is loss of the leaving group to form a carbocation. In this reaction, loss of the leaving group would place a double positive charge on the central carbon atom, making it a very unfavorable step. **Choice D** is wrong because if serine were a better leaving group than choline, the reaction would not proceed. Although **Choice C** is true, there is nothing in the passage or the diagrams that state this. In addition, none of the reactions involve competition between OH^- and CH_3^-.

214
A—Just as esterification occurs in Figures 2 and 3, so the ester that is formed is basically cleaved by OH^-. This is exactly what happens in Figures 6 and 7:

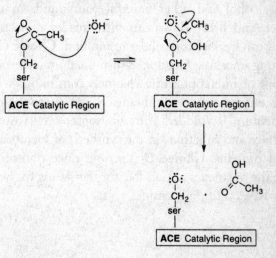

This process fits the definition of an ester being hydrolyzed by a base, the only key difference being that in this situation, the ester is not free—it is attached to the ACE catalytic region. Therefore, **Choice A** is correct. **Choice B** is incorrect because acetylserine does not contain an ether functionality. **Choice D** is incorrect because a carboxylic acid is formed, not reacted. **Choice C** is wrong since there is no alcohol functionality present to oxidize.

Discrete
Questions 215–219

215 **A**—Lysosomes are membrane-bound organelles containing hydrolytic digestive enzymes, which work best at a pH of 5—well below the pH of the cytosol. Lysosomes fuse with endocytotic vesicles and digest their contents; also, lysosomes recycle the cell's own organic material by engulfing an organelle or chunk of cytosol, dismantling it, and returning the organic monomers to the cell for reuse. Thus, **Choice A** is correct. **Choice B** is wrong because peroxisomes are organelles that contain enzymes that transfer hydrogen from various substrates to oxygen, producing hydrogen peroxide. Through these reactions, peroxisomes detoxify alcohol and other harmful compounds in the liver, and break down fats into smaller molecules that can be used for cellular respiration. **Choice C** is wrong since rough endoplasmic reticulum is the network of interconnecting channels continuous with the outer nuclear membrane. Rough endoplasmic reticulum is studded with ribosomes on its outer surface and functions in the synthesis of membrane and proteins. **Choice D** is wrong since ribosomes are the organelles responsible for translating messenger RNA into polypeptides.

216 **C**—The four bases found in DNA are adenine, thymine, guanine, and cytosine. The four bases found in RNA are adenine, uracil, guanine, and cytosine. Adenine binds with uracil or thymine and guanine always binds with cytosine. In double-stranded nucleic acid, the quantity of adenine equals the quantity of thymine (if it's DNA) or the quantity of uracil (if it's RNA). In single-stranded nucleic acid, the quantity of base does not matter, as long as they add up to 100 percent. The viral genome is most likely single-stranded RNA, since the amount of adenine does not equal the amount of uracil and the amount of cytosine does not equal the amount of guanine. So, **Choice C** is correct and **Choice D** is wrong. **Choice A** and **Choice B** are wrong since DNA doesn't contain uracil.

217 **C**—**Choice C** is the correct answer for two reasons. Firstly, $(CH_3)_3COH$ will form a tertiary carbocation; $(CH_3)_3C^+$. Here, there are three alkyl groups that, by electron donation through sigma bonds, can stabilize the positive charge. Secondly, the polar protic solvent H_2SO_4 is used. This drives the formation of the carbocation, since it can stabilize the transition state that forms. **Choice B** is wrong because even though $(CH_3CH_2)_3COH$ would form a tertiary carbocation, acetone is a polar aprotic solvent that would not be able to stabilize the transition state as effectively as a polar protic solvent. **Choice A** and **Choice D** would form secondary and primary carbocations, respectively. These are not as stable as the tertiary carbocation, since they possess fewer alkyl groups to stabilize the positive charge on the carbocation.

218 **B**—Pepsin is the protein-digesting enzyme secreted by the gastric glands of the stomach. The environment of the stomach is very acidic; it has a pH of approximately 2, due to the continuous secretion of HCl by the stomach's parietal cells. In contrast, the lumen of the small intestine is alkaline, due to the secretion of bicarbonate ion from the pancreas. Pepsin requires the highly acidic environment of the stomach for optimal function. Therefore, a graph representing the optimal activity of pepsin as a function of pH would be centered around and have its peak at a pH of 2, and so **Choice B** is correct and **Choice A**, **Choice C**, and **Choice D** are wrong.

219 **D**—Mammalian fetal circulation differs from mammalian adult circulation in a number of very important ways. The ductus arteriosus and the foramen ovale are the two shunts in fetal circulation that divert blood away from the lungs, and the ductus venosus is the shunt that diverts blood away from the liver. In the fetus, gas exchange occurs in the placenta, not in the lungs, which are nonfunctional prior to birth. The combined effect of these factors is that there is a mixing of oxygenated and deoxygenated blood in a majority of the blood vessels of the fetal circulatory system; this mixing stops at birth, when the lungs become functional. Likewise, with two atria and only one ventricle in the amphibian heart, there is a mixing of oxygenated and deoxygenated blood. Thus **Choice D** is correct.

Choice A is wrong since gas exchange in the fetus occurs in the placenta, and gas exchange in the adult amphibian occurs in its lungs when it's on land, and in its gills when it's in water. **Choice B** is wrong because placentas are unique to mammals. **Choice C** is wrong, because the amphibian heart has only three chambers, while the mammalian fetal heart always has four.

LAST-MINUTE TIPS

Last-Minute Tips

And Now for the Real Thing . . .

Is it starting to feel like your whole life is a buildup to the MCAT? You've known about it for years, worried about it for months, and now spent at least a few weeks in solid preparation for it. As the test gets closer, you may find your anxiety is on the rise. You shouldn't worry. After the preparation you've received from this book, you're in good shape for Test Day.

To calm any pretest jitters you may have, though, let's go over a few strategies for the days before and after the test.

The Week Before the Test
- Study hard. It's your last few days to work on MCAT material!

- Do one last assessment of areas that still need work.

- Review your content notes.

- Check your admission ticket for accuracy.

- Visit the testing center if you can. Sometimes seeing the actual room where your test will be administered and taking notice of little things—like the kind of desk you'll be working on, whether the room is likely to be hot or cold—may help to calm your nerves. And if you've never been to the campus or building where your test will be given, this is a good way to ensure that you don't get lost on Test Day. Remember, you must be on time—the proctors won't wait for you.

- Avoid great emotional turmoil—not a good time to break up with your boyfriend/girlfriend.

COUNTDOWN TO TEST DAY

The tendency among students is to study too hard during the last few days before the test, and then to forget the important practical matters until the last minute. Part of taking control means avoiding this last-minute crunch.

A WIN-WIN OPPORTUNITY

Read the newspaper daily, either just for the weeks before the test, or preferably as part of your permanent routine. You'll benefit greatly. You'll have practice at overcoming the hurdle of reading unfamiliar or difficult material, you'll have impressive examples for your essays, and you'll sound intelligent and connected during interviews.

KNOW WHEN TO FOLD 'EM

Don't try to cram lots of studying into the last day before the test. It probably won't do you much good, and it could bring on a case of test burnout.

PACK A SURVIVAL KIT

On the night before the test, get together an "MCAT survival kit" containing the following items:

- a watch
- a few No. 2 pencils (pencils with slightly dull points fill the ovals better)
- erasers
- two ball-point pens (black), for the Writing Sample
- photo ID Card
- your admission ticket
- snacks for the breaks and a lunch
- aspirin and tissues (nothing is worse than an unexpected headache or case of the sniffles)

The Day Before the Test

- Minimize MCAT studying! Light review only.
- Put together some snacks to take with you to the test.
- Get a normal night's sleep.
- Don't drink any alcohol.
- Think through your route to the test site again.
- Make sure you have everything you need.
- Make sure you set an alarm (or two).

Morning of the Test

- Eat a healthy breakfast.
- Get your brain turned on. Read something—a newspaper, book, or a magazine.
- Don't review MCAT material!
- Dress in layers so you can adjust to temperature changes during the day.
- Leave early so you won't be rushed.

During the Test

- Relax. Be cool and calm.
- If you start to get anxious, stop what you're doing and take a few deep breaths.
- Focus. Try not to be distracted by people around you.
- Don't obsessively check the time. You'll actually waste time, and make yourself nervous.
- Don't get flustered if they fingerprint you as you enter the testing room. This is standard operating procedure and is not intended for your FBI file. If you're on the up and up, you'll have nothing to worry about.
- Bring your own timing device—a watch or a stopwatch—so long as it doesn't make any noise (devices that beep on the hour or sound an alarm at specified times are prohibited from the testing site). Most test centers have a clock on the wall that the proctor will use to time the test, but don't take anything for granted—your test center may not (stranger things have been known to happen). After the test booklets are handed out, and you've filled out all of the required information, the test will begin. Your proctor may write the starting

and ending time of each section on a blackboard in front of the room, and may announce the time remaining at specified intervals.

- Read each question stem carefully, and reread it before making your final selection. Also, to make sure your answer sheet is gridded accurately, say the question number and choice to yourself (silently, of course) as you grid.

- Don't get bogged down in the middle of any section. At the end of every section are questions that may be really easy and feasible. Make sure that you get to them! Conversely, don't be alarmed if you run across extra-tough questions at the beginning. It happens. Skip past tough ones and come back to them later, making sure to circle them in the test booklet so you can find them fast.

- Try not to think about how you're scoring. It's like a baseball player who's thinking about the crowd's cheers and the sportswriters and his contract as he steps up to the plate: There's no surer way to strike out. Instead, focus on the question-by-question task of picking (A), (B), (C), or (D). The correct answer is there: You don't have to come up with it; it's sitting right there in front of you! Concentrate on each question and each passage and you'll be much more likely to hit a home run.

After the Test

Suppression versus Cancellation

Unlike many things in life, the MCAT allows you a second chance. If at the end of the test you feel you've really not done as well as you can, you always have the option either to suppress your scores, or to void your test—as long as you do one or the other immediately following the test. Choosing to suppress, to not release your scores, means the scores are still computed—you still get to know your scores—but they're not reported to any medical schools. Schools are informed, though, of the total number of nonvoided MCATs taken and may ask about the results of unreported scores. If at any time in the future you decide you want the scores reported, you can request that the scores be released. If you thought you bombed and thus suppressed your scores, only to happily discover that you did great, you can still have the scores reported. If, however, you fail to request a "no release" at the time of the test, you cannot go back and suppress the scores after test day.

If you void, or cancel your test, it means that no scores are ever computed. No one will ever know how well or poorly you did—not even you. Unless you're certain you did poorly, say you really mixed up answers on the grid, you should choose "no release," not cancellation. This way you at least get an assessment out of the test taking experience, and, hey, you

I AM NOT A CROOK

No, they don't fingerprint you because they expect you to cheat. They do it to have some way of making sure you're who you say you are.

PROCTOLOGY

Hey, proctors are usually nice people, but nobody's perfect. Be your own timer.

OPPORTUNITY KNOCKS ONCE

You must decide whether you're going to cancel or suppress scores on test day itself. Once you leave the testing room, the opportunity is gone.

never know. Keep in mind that test takers historically underestimate their performance, especially immediately following the test. They tend to forget about all of the things that went right, and focus on everything that went wrong.

Post-MCAT Festivities
After all the hard work you've done preparing for and taking the MCAT, you want to make sure you take time to celebrate afterwards. Plan to get together with friends the evening after the test. Don't discuss the test—it's over, history, kaput. Have fun, let loose. After all, you've got lots to celebrate: You prepared for the test ahead of time. You did your best.

APPENDIX

MEDICAL SCHOOL ADMISSIONS
Dwight Warren, Ph.D.
Admissions Consultant

An Introduction to the Admissions Process

Over the last six years, the number of applicants to medical schools has increased astronomically. For the class entering medical school in the fall of 1997, there were 47,060 applicants. This represented a 1 percent increase over the previous year and a staggering 73 percent increase over the 1989 entering class. And while the number of candidates seems to have levelled off in the past year, the number of medical school positions remains a mere 16–16,500. That means that there are close to three times as many applicants as there are spots in medical school. The bottom line: The present environment for getting into medical school is as competitive as it has ever been.

To be a successful applicant, you need to treat your quest for admission as a strategic campaign. You must put your best foot forward—first on paper, then in person. The more you understand about the application process, the more time and care you dedicate (both in research and preparation) to approaching this process, the better your chance of gaining admission into medical school. Think about it. If you've spent countless hours studying organic chemistry in order to get into medical school, you can definitely spend some time investigating the admission process.

Consider this section as your game plan. We're your coaches. But the hard work is up to you. Let's get started.

Great Candidates, Mediocre Applications

Being a strong candidate isn't enough to ensure admission to the medical school of your choice. You have to show the admission officers how well-qualified you are—by conducting an effective, meticulously organized campaign for admission.

FIRST THINGS FIRST

Most likely you'll be focusing on applying to med school for the year and a half before matriculation. And it's during those intense 18 months that you'll take the MCAT, solicit letters of recommendation, complete the application paperwork, and be invited to medical school interviews. It's possible that you're already in that period as you read this, and if that's the case, feel free to skip to the next chapter. If you're not there yet (and congratulations for being forward-thinking enough to read this book early), you need to focus on what you should do now—before the home stretch—in order to maximize your chances of acceptance.

REVIEW ACADEMIC REQUIREMENTS

Not everyone can get up one morning and decide to apply to medical school this year. All medical schools have a set of academic prerequisites for admission. Most medical schools require a minimum of **one year each of biology, general chemistry, organic chemistry, and physics.** These classes should have a laboratory component. You should be aware that in addition to these core requirements, more than half of medical schools require a year of English and about a third require college math or calculus. You should refer to the latest edition of *Medical School Admission Requirements*, a publication we'll discuss in depth later, to research requirements of the individual schools you're considering.

It's probably not a coincidence that the subject requirements for admission are the very same ones needed in preparation for the MCAT. These are important classes for you to concentrate on. You need to do whatever you can to do your best in these subjects. That probably means avoiding overloading your schedule with two toughies simultaneously (orgo + physics = trouble unless it's all you're taking). You may need to

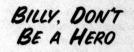

READY, SET ...

Do your homework before you jump into the application process.

BILLY, DON'T BE A HERO

There is no need to take all your prerequisites at once. You need to do well in these courses—consider spreading them out over a longer period of time.

consider taking longer to fulfill your requirements rather than rushing and possibly suffering some debilitating grades.

If you're a "nontraditional" applicant, you may need to go back to school to fulfill your premedical science requirements. You can take individual classes at a local college, or you may want to consider a premedical postbaccalaureate program designed specifically for nontraditional candidates. Contact the career center at a local college or the premed advisor at your alma mater to research your options.

Science versus NonScience Majors

There's no question that medical schools in the '90s are looking for students with broad-based undergraduate backgrounds. The days of "only science majors need apply" are long gone. Your choice of a major should be made based on your own academic interests; not what you think medical schools want. That being said, medical schools still take a hard look at your undergraduate/graduate scientific performance. They'll evaluate both your science GPA and your cumulative GPA. So, if you're not a science major, these core sciences courses can become even more crucial, because you'll have fewer additional science grades in your science GPA. This can work to your advantage if you did very well in the core courses, or it can hurt you if you did poorly.

GET TO KNOW YOUR PREMED ADVISOR

Most undergraduate institutions have one or more professionals whose job it is to help students interested in pursuing careers in medicine and the allied health professions. It's very important that you get to know your premed advisor. Your premed advisor can help you decide if you should apply to medical school and where you should apply. Only your premed advisor will have institution-specific data: how students from your school, with your academic record and MCAT scores have fared in the past. Don't consider this book (or any book for that matter) a substitute for your premed advisor.

In many undergraduate institutions, the premed office handles the letters of recommendation. In some cases, they simply relay the letters to the medical schools. In other cases, the premed advisor or committee write a letter to the admission offices on your behalf. This letter can take the form of a "composite letter" that excerpts your recommendations, or it may simply be a cover letter that accompanies the recommendations. Either way, it is imperative that you get to know the people who are going to be writing letters on your behalf. In most such cases, the advisor(s) will require a certain number of meetings with advisees. You should take these meetings very seriously.

BACK TO SCHOOL?

More and more applicants are choosing medicine as a second career. To get a complete listing of postbaccalaureate programs in the U.S. call Medpath at Ohio State University College of Medicine: (614) 292-3161.

GOING IT ALONE

Naturally, you can choose to apply to medical school without the help of the premed office. But you do so at your own risk. Medical schools are usually familiar with the procedures of different undergraduate institutions. If they know you had access to a premed advisor, they will almost certainly call into question why you chose to bypass the premed office.

With the number of applications to medical school at an all-time high, prehealth advisors are a harried bunch these days. It's possible that if you're not a particularly strong candidate, you may find your advisor less than enthusiastic about your applying to medical school. He or she may have legitimate concerns about your competitiveness and may try to dissuade you from applying. Then it's up to you. You may have to go it alone without the full support of the premed office. Be realistic. If everyone agrees your chances are slim, make sure you have a backup plan just in case you're not admitted.

EXPOSE YOURSELF (TO MEDICINE, THAT IS)

In the Preface (you didn't skip the Preface, did you?), we talked a little about exposing yourself to the practice of medicine before you decide whether or not you want to pursue medical school. It's equally as important that you continue to be active in health care activities for as much of your premedical career as possible. How important? Well, a recent survey* of medical schools asked them to rate 45 preadmission variables. Only these five variables (in no particular order) were chosen as "very important" to student selection:

- Medical school interview ratings
- GPA
- MCAT scores
- Letters of evaluation
- Knowledge of health care issues and commitment to health care

Medical schools aren't easily fooled. They know there's a difference between a two-year commitment to a health-care related project and an eleventh hour decision to become a hospital volunteer.

In the next chapters we'll go through the admission process step-by-step, from application to interview, so you'll get off on the right foot and benefit from every advantage.

* Academic Medicine, *Vol 69 (5), pp. 394–401, May 1994.*

BACKUP PLAN

If you're not accepted to medical school, strategize, gain relevant experience, and try again. Perseverance is viewed positively.

NO GUTS, NO GLORY

Not all volunteer work is equal in the eyes of the admissions committees. Wheeling patients to X-ray is not the same as volunteering in an AIDS hospice or nursing home.

WHAT ABOUT OSTEOPATHIC MEDICINE?

There are two types of medical degrees, allopathic (MD) and osteopathic (DO). Like allopaths, Doctors of Osteopathic medicine are fully trained to diagnose illness, prescribe medications, and perform surgery. The American Medical Association and the Federal Government recognize MDs and DOs as equals, and both are licensed to provide comprehensive medical care in all 50 states.

Osteopathic physicians differ from allopathic physicians in their approach to medicine. Osteopaths view medicine more holistically, seeing the human body as a single organism with all body systems interrelated, and using manipulative techniques in the diagnosis and treatment of their patients. Approximately 64 percent of the 38,000 DOs currently practicing are primary care physicians.

There are sixteen colleges of osteopathic medicine in the United States. Over 10,000 students applied to osteopathic medical schools in 1996. All osteopathic medical schools require all applicants to complete the MCAT and its academic prerequisites.

The American Association of Colleges of Osteopathic Medicine (AACOM) provides a centralized application service, AACOMAS, that forwards applicant information to each of the sixteen osteopathic schools designated by the applicant. AACOMAS allows students to submit one application, a single set of academic transcripts, and one set of MCAT scores. AACOMAS works similarly to the allopathic medical colleges' application service, AMCAS.

For more information on osteopathic medicine, contact AACOM:

American Association of Colleges of Osteopathic Medicine
6110 Executive Boulevard
Suite 405
Rockville, MD 20852
(301) 468-0990
http://www.aacom.org/

DIFFERENT BUT EQUAL

Doctors of Osteopathic Medicine (DOs) are fully licensed physicians with medical privileges equal to those of allopathic physicians (MDs). Osteopathic medicine was founded by an allopathic physician.

YOU CAN RUN

All accredited osteopathic medical schools require applicants to take the MCAT.

WHERE TO APPLY

Choosing which medical schools to apply to is a major decision. If you take the time to research medical schools, you'll be in a better position to match their criteria with yours. By reviewing this chapter you'll be prepared to start drafting your list.

RESEARCHING SCHOOLS

Unfortunately, many applicants know very little, if anything, about the medical schools they apply to. They enter the application process blindly, and base their decisions on "common knowledge" or "school reputation." This is a naive way of planning a future. So before plunging into the actual logistics of the application process, let's review some of the main criteria for selecting schools.

Accredited versus Nonaccredited Schools

First, we must make the important distinction between the 141 American and Canadian medical schools accredited by the AAMC's Liaison Committee on Medical Education (LCME) and the remaining medical schools around the globe (foreign medical schools).

In general, we advise that you don't apply to foreign medical schools the first time around. Aside from the obvious barriers such as language and culture, the conventional wisdom is that the quality of instruction and resources available at many foreign medical schools are inferior. These schools can vary wildly in quality since they don't need to adhere to any accreditation standard. In general, graduates of foreign medical schools have a harder time passing their licensing exams and gaining acceptance into U.S. residency programs. You probably shouldn't consider a foreign medical school unless you've been rejected from an American

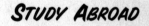

BOTH EYES OPEN

Do your research; you'll make a more informed decision and you'll sound impressive in your interviews.

STUDY ABROAD

For information on foreign Medical Schools, check out the book *Foreign Medical Schools for U.S. Citizens* by Carlos Pestana, M.D., Ph.D., P.O. Box 790617, San Antonio, TX 78279-0617

or Canadian school at least once (if not twice). Then, you should speak to your premed advisor and do extensive research on the quality of the schools you're considering.

For a complete listing of LCME-accredited schools, buy a copy of the annually published *Medical School Admission Requirements* by contacting:

Association of American Medical Colleges
Attn: Membership and Publication Orders
2450 N Street, NW
Washington, DC 20037-1129
(202) 828-0416
http://www.aamc.org

O.F.A.: OUR
FAVORITE
ACRONYMS

AAMC: *Association of American Medical Colleges*

LCME: *Liaison Committee on Medical Education*

MSAR: *Medical School Admission Requirements*

EDP: *Early Decision Program*

AMCAS: *American Medical College Application*

MCAT: *Medical College Admission Test*

YOU AND YOUR MSAR

There are currently 122 accredited medical schools in the United States, three in Puerto Rico, and 16 in Canada. *Medical School Admission Requirements*, which is published every April and is affectionately called the "MSAR," provides comprehensive information on all of these schools. This resource is the closest thing to a premed bible that exists. The information in this book comes from the horses' mouths—the schools themselves. It isn't second-hand accounts or student opinions. It's the official stuff.

The first part of the MSAR includes over 100 pages relating to the admissions process. The second part includes profiles of all the LCME-accredited schools in the United States and Canada. Let's take a guided tour through the structure of these school profiles so that you can know what to look for when you peruse your MSAR (yes, you should shell out the $15 and purchase your own copy). This information can help you decide where to apply.

All the school profiles in the MSAR include the following divisions:

- General Information
- Curriculum
- Requirements
- Selection Factors
- Early Decision Program
- Tuition
- Financial Aid
- Application and Acceptance Policies
- Information on Previous Year's Class

General Information

Medical schools use this section to describe themselves and any affiliates (feeding hospitals). They'll indicate whether the school is public or private. Often there will be a paragraph describing the program's central hospital.

Curriculum

There are currently three different curricula used in medical schools. In this section, the medical school typically identifies which curriculum it employs or if there is more than one curriculum available. The three curricula can be broadly classified as Traditional (Discipline-Based), Traditional (Systems-Based), and Problem-Based Learning. We'll review the differences among these later in this section.

Requirements

While this section is typically pretty standard in terms of prerequisite premedical coursework and taking the MCAT, requirements can vary from school to school. For example, there are over 70 schools that have a one-year English requirement, while approximately 14 schools require a year of humanities. Skip this section of the MSAR at your own risk; you may not have all the requirements for your dream school.

Selection Factors

This section of the MSAR is important because it lists the mean grade point average and MCAT scores for the most recent entering class. This can be used as a crude indicator of school competitiveness. A school whose students have a mean GPA of 3.6 and double-digit MCAT scores is probably more competitive than a school whose numbers are 3.3 and 8s, respectively.

Early Decision Program (EDP)

Does the school have one, and if yes, what are the deadlines? This section also gives information on: earliest dates for acceptance notices; the time applicants have to respond to acceptance; whether or not deferrals are offered; and the starting date of classes.

A little more than half of the medical schools in the United States offer Early Decision Programs. For an EDP, you file only one application to the one medical school you wish to attend. Most schools accept these special applications around mid-June. You would be prohibited from applying to any other schools until the school has rendered a decision. If you're accepted, then you must attend. Most schools will notify candidates by October 1.

MAKING YOUR FIRST CHOICE YOUR ONLY CHOICE

Apply Early Decision only if you feel strongly about your first choice, and only if you're certain that if you're accepted you'll attend. If you apply Early Decision but don't get in, you'll be playing application catch up.

Early Decision Programs are appropriate only for very competitive applicants who have a strong preference for one particular school. These applicants benefit in that they save considerable money on applications, interviews and travel. In addition, they know where they're going to med school by October.

If you apply Early Decision but are not accepted, you'll be behind your peers in the application process. It's not a decision to be taken lightly. You should definitely sit down with your premed advisor and decide if this option is appropriate for you.

Tuition

This should be a big consideration as you apply to medical school. Scholarships to medical school are few and far between. A word about loans: you have to pay them back! (You can look up *loan* in the dictionary if you don't believe us.) This leads into our next category . . .

Financial Aid

This section of the MSAR will inform you whether the school offers any need-based or merit-based scholarships. Often the school will list what percentage of the student body receives financial aid.

Application and Acceptance Policies

This section provides you with some key pieces of data:

- *AMCAS Deadline*
  Traditionally AMCAS schools have one of the following deadlines:
  October 15
  November 1
  December 1
  December 15

- *School Application Fee*
  This fee refers to the amount the applicant will need to pay in addition to the AMCAS fee. This fee is usually requested at the time that the secondary application is submitted, as will be discussed later. There is a useful piece of information hidden in this section. Some schools have an "application fee to all applicants." This means that they'll send secondaries to all AMCAS applicants. In contrast, other schools, such as all the University of California programs, have an "application fee after screening." This means that they'll send secondaries only to selected applicants. So if you receive a secondary application from a school it can mean either a) nothing; they send one to everyone with a pulse or b) you've made the first cut. Your MSAR can help you distinguish between these two possibilities.

THE AMCAS

The AMCAS is a centralized application processing service. They process, duplicate, and send your application, transcript, and MCAT scores to all AMCAS-member schools.

WHAT ARE SECONDARIES?

After schools receive your initial paperwork, you'll most likely be forwarded another application. This secondary application may ask for more biographical information and additional essays.

- *Oldest Acceptable MCAT Scores*

  Most schools currently accept scores up to two to three years old, but be on the lookout for the few schools that will not. For example, in 1995 the following schools did not accept pre-1994 scores: UCLA, UC San Francisco, USC, E. Carolina, Universidad Central del Caribe, and Ponce School of Medicine. On the other end of the spectrum, there are only a handful of schools that will allow pre-1991 scores, including Johns Hopkins, which doesn't require the MCAT at all. Always review the most recent MSAR for your top choices' requirements.

Information On Previous Year's Class

This final section of each school entry in the MSAR is an important area for you to study carefully as you create your list of schools. In particular, this section will alert you to whether or not the school accepts large numbers of out-of-state applicants.

State-supported medical schools are required to give preference to in-state applicants. Some medical schools actually have quotas for specific regions of the state. Some medical schools will try to accept more people from underserved areas of their state in the hope that they will return to practice there. Obviously, this could be a big advantage for you if you are from an underserved or underrepresented area of your state, but can work against you if you are from an overrepresented area.

You can also use this section to study the breakdown for private schools to which you wish to apply. Some private schools will offer more positions to in-state applicants. In some instances this is because these private schools receive some state funding.

OTHER RESOURCES

School Catalogs

In addition to studying the MSAR, another excellent way to research medical schools is to read their catalogs. These catalogs provide lots of pertinent information—history of the school, curriculum, size and make-up of student body, feeding hospitals, etcetera. You should be aware that medical schools are trying to sell themselves and that they use their catalogs as marketing tools.

School Rankings

Now that you're acquainted with some key ways of researching schools, you should have a better idea of how to go about compiling your list. Of course, people always want to know which are the "Top Ten" schools, and

HAVE YOUR MCAT SCORES EXPIRED?

Don't assume your scores are still valid or are stale; check the MSAR to see the age of scores schools will accept.

MAIL ORDER MEDICAL SCHOOLS

Gather catalogs. You'll get an overview of a school for just the cost of a postcard or phone call (phone numbers are listed in the MSAR).

the most often quoted source is *U.S. News & World Report* Graduate Issue (published every March).

NARROWING DOWN YOUR LIST

At some point, you're going to have to bite the bullet and narrow down your list of schools. While there is no magical number of schools to apply to, the average is now around twelve schools (California applicants, however, apply to nearly twice as many schools.) Naturally, if you're going to apply to lots of very competitive schools, you may need to construct a more extensive list. Work with your premed advisor to select schools that make sense for you. Check to see where students from your college with your GPA and MCAT scores have been accepted. Also, inquire whether your school has a historical feeder relationship with a particular medical school.

While you're agonizing over which schools to keep on your list, consider the following issues:

- Competitiveness
- Cost
- Curriculum
- Teaching Hospitals
- Location

Competitiveness

As we mentioned in the Introduction, competition for medical school is very intense. You need to be realistic about your chances of getting in. There are many qualified applicants who won't be accepted. Don't take anything for granted; it's best to apply to schools of varying degrees of competitiveness.

The entire notion of ranking schools is, of course, a highly subjective and controversial exercise. However, rankings can provide an idea of how competitive a school is. For instance, so-called Top Ten medical schools (e.g., UCSF, Hopkins, Harvard, Stanford) are very competitive. For a more objective method of evaluating a school's competitiveness, you can refer to the MSAR's GPA and MCAT data as noted above.

So, when applying, it is helpful to view schools in categories: for instance, highly competitive schools; middle-tiered schools; and finally, the backup or "safety" school (though these days there really is no such thing as a safety school). Don't take the risk of applying to only the most competitive schools—the outcome may be rejection from all of them.

By the way, don't get too hung up about a school's "reputation." All LCME-accredited schools provide a solid medical education and no matter where you go, you get the magical MD after your name.

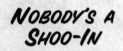

DON'T LIMIT YOURSELF

Don't skimp on the number of applications you make. Yes, it's expensive, but this is an important decision. It pays to give yourself as much of a choice as possible.

NOBODY'S A SHOO-IN

Clearly, the numbers (GPA and MCAT) are important factors in the admission decision. But even a candidate with stellar numbers can be rejected if he/she makes a tactical blunder on the application.

Cost

You may have already taken out loans to pay your undergraduate education, or have mortgages or high rents to pay. Tuition to medical school will only add to your financial burden. Of the 122 LCME-accredited medical schools in the United States, 52 are private institutions and the rest are state-sponsored. The difference in cost between attending a state and a private medical school can be striking. For example, let's consider the tuition at a state institution such as the University of Nevada/Reno Medical School. In 1996 tuition for a resident was $6,821, as opposed to $17,976 for a nonresident. While the cost for a non-resident is by no means pocket change, compare this to a private institution such as Georgetown Medical School. Tuition at Georgetown ran $21,625 in 1996.

Remember, we're comparing only tuition. This doesn't figure in cost of living (room, board, entertainment). It is safe to say that the cost of living in Reno, Nevada is significantly lower than in Washington, D.C. If you were a resident of Nevada, you are talking about a difference of at least $20,000; that's $80,000 in four years.

The solution seems all too obvious, right? Everyone attend state schools! The problem: limited slots and strict residency requirements. State schools will strongly favor those applicants who are state residents (i.e., those who are already paying taxes to support the existence of the school). Unfortunately, residency requirements differ from state to state, so there is no one set way of establishing residency. Nonetheless, when considering the economics of going to medical school, state residency may become a vital issue. It is important that you decide which state schools are feasible for you and that you clear up any misconceptions concerning residency requirements.

Curriculum

Although most medical schools offer four-year programs, uniformity among medical school curricula no longer exists. At present, there are three general types of medical school curricula available:

1. Traditional (Discipline-Based)

2. Traditional (Systems-Based)

3. Problem-Based learning

ARE STATE SCHOOLS FOR EVERYONE?

Attending a state school may seem like the answer, but make sure that you meet the state's residency requirement, and keep in mind that state schools are traditionally more competitive because they're financially attractive.

FUND YOUR FUTURE

KapLoan, The Kaplan Student Loan Information Program, can help you get information and guidance about educational loans for medical school. For more information, call 1-888-KAP-LOAN.

Traditional (Discipline-Based)

Until recently, most medical schools offered variations of the same basic curriculum. It consisted of a comprehensive review of basic sciences (anatomy, biochemistry, physiology, pharmacology, pathology, etcetera) in the first two years of medical school. A typical day involved attending lectures from early morning to late afternoon for the four or five courses being taken concurrently. At the end of the second year, a student would take the National Boards Exam Part I (now called the U.S. Medical Licensing Examination), a competency exam testing knowledge of all the basic science material covered in the first two years. Finally, in the third and fourth years, clinical rotations began.

Traditional (Systems-Based)

Several years ago, many medical schools began to tinker with the standard traditional curriculum. Instead of presenting the basic sciences in a segmented, topical organization, some schools began to design their curriculum around the human organ systems. Therefore, instead of having students take broad basic science topics such as anatomy, biochemistry, histology and physiology concurrently, students would concentrate on one system at a time. So while studying the cardiovascular system, a student would learn all the relevant anatomy, histology, pathology, etcetera, involved. It is believed that the system curriculum provides a more integrated approach to learning medicine. Many schools are heading in this direction and the National Board exam currently has a greater interdisciplinary approach as well.

Problem-Based Learning

The most avant-garde curricular approach was introduced in McMaster Medical School in Ontario, Canada. They instituted a revolutionary change in their medical school curriculum—one based on small-group, problem-based learning (PBL). The University of New Mexico School of Medicine was also an early proponent of the PBL approach. In 1987, Harvard Medical School adopted this problem-based curriculum, deeming it the "New Pathway." What these innovations addressed were several perceived problems in the traditional curricula. First of all, in the traditional curricula, the first two years of medical school seemed to perpetuate the so-called "premed mentality" with students subjected to a didactic/lecture-based program with an emphasis on factual recall and continual assessment and ranking.

The new curriculum proposed the following changes:

- Reduce the amount of lecture time drastically (i.e., only three hours per day).

- Base the entire curriculum on large tutorial groups and problem-based learning. Typically, groups of five to seven students meet with a faculty group leader (usually a Ph.D. or MD) and discuss a particular clinical case that elucidates the basic science ideas and concepts that they are currently studying. For instance, when studying cardiac physiology, they might investigate a case of a 45-year-old man who presents with chest pain and shortness of breath—most likely a case of angina. As the case unravels, the students not only begin to learn the basics of clinical medicine (the vocabulary, normal lab values, etcetera), but they're challenged to understand the basic physiology, pathology, and pharmacology of the disease as well.

- Introduce clinical courses early on (e.g., a class on how to interview patients and take a medical history). With a problem-based curriculum, the last two years of medical school are identical to those in traditional curricula.

Determining which curriculum type is "better" than the other is difficult, though there are some obvious pluses and minuses. The biggest criticisms of the traditional method are those voiced by the designers of the problem-based route: pressure-cooker atmosphere; failure to promote cooperation among colleagues; perpetuation of didactic lecture method of teaching instead of self-study techniques. The problem-based curriculum is not without its critics as well. In an environment in which self-direction is promoted, there is a significant concern that students will not learn all that they need to. That is, some students need to be directed, told what to study in order to pass the first part of the National Boards and become physicians. In addition, in order to run a problem-based curriculum, an incredible number of faculty members must be involved and the faculty must be trained to be effective small-group facilitators.

A final curriculum issue of interest: grading. Some schools use pass-fail grading, some pass-fail-honors, and some prefer traditional A through F assessment. This may be of interest to you. It is relatively safe to assume that pass-fail schools have a less "cutthroat" environment than those with grades. A word of caution: Don't ask about grading during your faculty interviews (save this question for the students).

Do your research! You should know what type of curriculum is being offered at the school that you wish to attend. You should weigh the pros and cons of the different types of curricula available to you and select one appropriate to your learning style. A great benefit of all this research:

MATCH GAME

Don't wait to worry about a school's curriculum until you're on campus. Find a school with a curriculum that's compatible with your preferences.

you'll sound really smart at your medical school interviews.

Another resource: the AAMC's *Curriculum Directory*. Contact the AAMC just as you will to obtain your MSAR.

Teaching Hospitals

Just as important as the basic science curriculum that a medical school offers are its affiliated teaching hospitals. You must understand that you'll be doing your clinical rotations only in those hospitals that are designated as teaching hospitals of your medical school. Your first clinical experiences will be shaped, in large part, by the type of hospitals to which you are exposed. For example, if a medical school is primarily associated with city hospitals, you'll probably be exposed to a disproportionate amount of trauma and emergency medicine. Likewise, if Veteran Administration hospitals predominate, you may encounter many cases of emphysema, heart disease, and post-traumatic stress disorder. What you experience during your clinical rotations may greatly influence your choice of specialty.

Location, Location, Location

Location is another important consideration in deciding where to apply to medical school. Most premedical students, however, are so concerned about whether or not they'll be accepted by a school that they fail to consider if they'll be happy spending four years in that locale. Applicants tend to evaluate the medical schools lists based on reputation and prestige, rather than location and lifestyle.

While there are obviously innumerable factors to be considered, a few major ones include:

Safety

Many medical centers are located in inner cities with associated high crime rates. It's obviously an added stress to be in area where you feel unsafe. Some medical centers will provide escorts and other security services. Keep this in mind when you're visiting schools and inquire about safety issues. If you're really concerned, you can call the local police station and ask for crime statistics.

Housing

Remember that in addition to tuition, you'll also have to pay for housing, food, and transportation. Unfortunately, due to the location of some schools, nearby housing is either unsafe or unaffordable. In some inner-city schools, the majority of the student body resides in dormitories. These dorms are often expensive and have inadequate kitchen facilities. Nonetheless, they may be truly the best alternatives given the location of some medical schools.

HIT THE ROAD

The best way to research locations is to visit as many schools as possible.

READ ALL ABOUT IT

If you're considering a particular locale, get your hands on its newspaper. This will give you a handle on cost of living, available transportation, and local issues.

In contrast, students who decide to attend equally good programs in small towns or communities may be pleasantly surprised to find inexpensive housing near the school itself. In addition, crime will not be as big a problem in these areas.

Transportation

This is obviously important as it pertains to housing and community shops. If there isn't housing near the medical center or its affiliated hospitals, then you'll need to have a car. If you don't, it is important that there be adequate public transportation, whether it be a bus line or subway system.

Affiliation With an Undergraduate Institution

It's of great benefit to you if your medical school is part of a larger institution. Typically, the undergraduate institution allows the graduate students to enjoy the same privileges as the undergrads. This will include gym facilities, movies, libraries, clubs, and other organizations. In addition, if the institution has strong athletic teams, then graduate students have access to tickets and can enjoy this diversion from classwork.

Proximity to Family and Friends

If there are special people in your life with whom you enjoy spending time, it may be important for you to live nearby. Medical school does not afford you much free time and the time it takes to travel can easily make frequent or lengthy visits difficult.

The bottom line: You should choose a school where you'll be happy and comfortable for four years. Medical school has enough stressors with the long hours and hard work. Don't complicate matters by choosing a school in a place where day-to-day living will be a chore.

PEOPLE WHO NEED PEOPLE

Long-distance relationships are tough enough without medical school tossed into the mix. If this is an issue for you, carefully balance it with your other location considerations.

HOW TO APPLY

After you've made the decision to apply to medical school and have chosen where to apply, your next move is to start working on your applications. This is your opportunity to sell yourself, to show yourself as something more than grades and scores. You should prepare carefully. Use the worksheets in the Appendix to help keep you organized at all times.

THE APPLICATIONS

Probably the most important thing to keep in mind about your medical school application is that it is your single best opportunity to convince a group of strangers that it would be a huge mistake if you were not admitted to their school. Remember, every person who applies will have strengths and weaknesses. It's how you present those strengths and weaknesses that counts.

So what's the best way to present yourself on the application? We all know that some people are natural self-promoters in person, but until the interview stage, this process is written, not spoken. The key here is not natural talent but rather organization—carefully planning a coherent presentation from beginning to end and paying attention to every detail in between.

AMCAS versus Non-AMCAS

AMCAS (American Medical College Application Service) is a centralized application processing service that lives in Washington, D.C. The AMCAS people do not make any admission decisions. They simply process, duplicate, and send your application, transcript and MCAT scores to all AMCAS member schools that you designate. The AMCAS application is a godsend—it greatly simplifies the initial stages of the

DEVELOP A THEME

Start thinking early about what theme you want your application to convey. Decide what your real purpose is in applying to medical school, and make sure that this sense of purpose comes through in all aspects of your application. For instance, is your goal to pursue a career in pediatrics? If so, do some volunteer work on a pediatric cancer ward (and make sure to discuss it on your application); ask a physician on the ward to write a recommendation for you; use the personal statement to discuss your contact with the patients. All of these efforts will give your application coherence and a sense of purpose— and help it stick in the minds of the admissions officers.

Non-AMCAS Schools

In 1996, the following schools had to be contacted individually for applications (schools not listed participated in the AMCAS program):
- Baylor College of Medicine
- Brown University School of Medicine
- Canadian Schools of Medicine (16 schools)
- Columbia University College of Physicians and Surgeons
- Harvard Medical School
- Johns Hopkins University School of Medicine
- New York University School of Medicine
- Texas A & M University Health Science Center College of Medicine
- Texas Tech University Health Sciences Center School of Medicine
- University of North Dakota School of Medicine
- University of Rochester School of Medicine and Dentistry
- University of Missouri/ Kansas City School of Medicine
- University of Texas System (Southwestern, Galveston, Houston, San Antonio)
- Yale University School of Medicine

application process. Instead of having to complete individual applications for every single school, you complete just one application (AMCAS application). All but sixteen of the LCME-accredited medical schools in the United States are AMCAS schools. Either get an AMCAS application from your premed advisor or career center or contact:

AMCAS
Section for Student Services
Association of American Medical Colleges
2450 N Street, NW, Suite 201
Washington, DC 20037-1131
(202) 828-0600
http://www.aamc.org

Schools that don't participate in AMCAS (a.k.a., non-AMCAS schools) have their own individual applications that you'll need to complete. This must be done for each of the non-AMCAS schools that you apply to, and the applications can differ significantly. Do not send the AMCAS application to a non-AMCAS school; they won't be amused. We'll explore non-AMCAS applications a little later.

The AMCAS Application: An Overview

AMCAS applications become available in April for the class entering in the fall of the following year. AMCAS begins accepting applications on June 3. The sooner you obtain the application, the sooner you can complete it; the sooner you can send it in, the better off you'll be. (But don't send it before June 3—it will be returned.) Remember, always try to get a jump on the game. Medical schools will want to see an application form, your transcripts, your MCAT scores, and letters of recommendation before they inform you that your application is complete. Until they receive all the components of your application folder, they will not consider you for a personal interview. Use the AMCAS application checklist and tracking sheet in the Appendix to keep track of every step.

Many schools institute a rolling admission system. Those applicants who are reviewed first will be given the first interviews, and subsequently, be granted admission before other candidates. There is seldom a downside for getting your application in as soon after June 3 as possible. Even if you're taking the August MCAT, you should try to get your application in early so medical schools can open a file for you. You'll look eager and organized. That being said, if you can't send it in June or early July, and you find that working on it really cuts into your MCAT prep time—put it away until after the test. You really need to focus on getting your best possible MCAT scores, and it isn't detrimental to get the AMCAS application in a little later (but no later than September), since schools won't consider your application until they have your August MCAT scores anyway.

Although some schools don't employ rolling admission, they nonetheless begin assessing applications as soon as they are received, and consequently, will begin to offer interviews to those who they feel are qualified candidates. This is a major advantage: If you send your materials in too late, you will be given an interview later in the application season. You don't want to be among the herd of late interviewees at a school. Not only will the admission committees have less time to consider your application, but it will also be harder to stand out in the crowd. Again, the moral of the story is to be prepared. *Do not procrastinate.*

AMCAS-E

Last year, AMCAS began offering an electronic application form. Titled AMCAS-E, it allows you to complete your application on computer and submit your data on disk. AMCAS-E also automatically converts your school grades into AMCAS grades based upon college codes. In addition, you can use the electronic application to prepare transcript requests, apply for fee waivers, and obtain information on med school addresses. Although AMCAS will continue to accept paper applications in 1997, most students will probably find the electronic form much easier to deal with.

AMCAS Application: Up Close and Personal
The AMCAS application consists of three sections:

1. General Information (Education, Work, Activities, Honors)

2. Personal Statement

3. Coursework and GPA calculations

1. General Information
The information requested is similar to what you find in almost any kind of application. Avoid the "kitchen sink" mentality. You want to spotlight those activities and honors that are most important to you and the ones that you hope will distinguish your application. Always list in order of decreasing priority. You may also want to highlight health-related activities, public service work, science- or medicine-related research experience. Common sense will serve you well here.

AMCAS GOES ELECTRONIC

Last year, med school applicants had to submit their AMCAS applications on paper, which often meant typing on unwieldy forms. AMCAS-E changes that: Now you can complete your application on your computer and send the disc to AAMC, which then prints your application and forwards it to your schools of choice. It's a great innovation in the application process.

AAMC ON THE NET

Check out the AAMC's Web page:
http://www.aamc.org

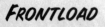

FRONTLOAD

List your most important undergraduate activities or honors first.

NOW IS NOT THE TIME TO WRITE A HAIKU

Don't be too creative. Remember—the medical establishment is still a conservative one.

2. Personal Statement

The Personal Statement is the one area on the AMCAS application where you can infuse a little bit of personality. As with all creative outlets, there is no single correct way to go about this, no simple formula to follow. Yet there are some pitfalls that you want to avoid when writing your essay:

- The Personal Statement is not the time to recount all your activities and honors in listlike fashion. Avoid writing the rehashed résumé or typical biographical essay ("I was born in a small fishing village . . . .").
- Make it "personal." This is your opportunity to put a little panache into the application. Show the admission committee why you decided to go into medicine. Was it an experience you had in school? Was there a particular extracurricular that changed your way of thinking? Did you find a summer lab job so exhilarating that it reconfirmed your love for science? Try to use vignettes and anecdotes. Weave a story, and make this essay a pleasure to read.
- You probably want to avoid delving into any controversial topics (e.g., abortion, euthanasia, etcetera). If you do, definitely avoid being dogmatic or preachy. You don't want to take the risk of alienating a reader who may not share your politics.
- Try not to make apologies for your past. For instance, if you received a C in physics (hey, it could happen), you may feel compelled to justify it somehow. Unless you believe that the circumstances truly do merit some sort of mention, do not make excuses. You don't need to provide them with a road map to your weaknesses; they'll probably find them just fine without your help.
- You can't take liberties with margins or fonts with AMCAS-E, since margins will be preset and fonts will be standardized. That means that you'll have to write a personal statement of the appropriate length—no rambling on for pages, or trying to turn a paragraph into a page. If you're submitting a paper application, stay within preset borders, and type in a font no smaller than a point size of 12.

Because the Personal Statement is such an important part of your application, it shouldn't be done overnight. A strong Personal Statement may take shape over the course of weeks or months and require several different drafts. Write a draft and then let it sit for a few weeks. You may find (to your astonishment) that your first instincts were good ones; on the other hand, you may shudder at how you could ever have considered submitting such a piece of garbage. Either way, time lends a valuable perspective.

Allow at least a month or so to write your statement, and don't be afraid to take it through numerous drafts or overhaul it completely if you're not satisfied. Most important, get several different opinions. Ask close friends or relatives to scrutinize it to see if it really captures what you want to convey. Be sure to ask them about their initial reaction as well as their feelings after studying it more carefully. Once you've achieved a draft that you feel comfortable with, try to have it read by some people who barely know you or by people who don't know you at all. Such people may include advisors at your school, professors not familiar with your work, or friends of friends. A stranger or semistranger often provides a better perspective on your work. Since they haven't heard the story before and don't know the characters, they're often better able to tell you when something is missing or confusing.

The bottom line is to let a reasonable number of people read the essay and make suggestions. If certain criticisms are consistently made, then they're probably legitimate. But don't be carried away by every suggestion every reader makes. Stick to your basic instincts because, after all, this is *your* Personal Statement.

One final note about procedure. Proofreading is of critical importance. Again, don't be afraid to enlist the aid of others. If possible, let an English teacher review the essay solely for spelling and grammar mistakes. If English is not your first language, this is especially important. Nothing grabs an admission officer's eye quicker than a misspelled word.

Please be aware that interviewers often use your Personal Statement as fodder for questions. They may focus on a couple of key points mentioned in your essay and use these as springboards for discussion. Now, if you have included experiences and ideas that are dear to you, that you feel strongly about, you will have no problem speaking with passion and confidence. Nothing is more appealing to admission folks than a vibrant, intelligent, and articulate candidate. If you write about research you conducted five years ago, you'd better brush up before your interviews. Play it smart: Stack the deck in your favor.

If letters of recommendation serve as outside endorsements (as we'll discuss later), then the Personal Statement is your own personal pitch. Remember, you're up against thousands and thousands of qualified candidates. You have to make yourself stand out from the crowd. Everyone has a story to tell. The key lies in how you tell it.

Non-AMCAS Applications

Not surprisingly, most of the non-AMCAS schools provide applications similar in content to the AMCAS application. These applications also contain general information pages and of course, an essay (or essays). The major difference may be that a non-AMCAS school requests a copy of your transcript, rather than making you compute yearly and subject GPAs, as is the case with the AMCAS application. Since there is so much

TIME LENDS PERSPECTIVE

Start drafting your Personal Statement early on, so that you'll be able to put it aside for a few weeks or even months. You'll be amazed at how different it will look when you go back to it.

GREAT EXPECTATIONS

Remember, med schools fully expect these essays to be good; a shoddy Personal Statement is a major red flag.

IT WILL COME BACK TO HAUNT YOU

If you engage in hyperbole in any part of your application, you risk running up against an interviewer who will see through your exaggerations. It could result in the denial of your application. It's just not worth the risk.

overlap, once you have completed the AMCAS application, you shouldn't have much difficulty cranking out the non-AMCAS applications. You probably can take most of your Personal Statement from the AMCAS application. Use the non-AMCAS application checklist and tracking sheet in the Appendix to stay organized.

Secondaries

So you finally finish your AMCAS application. You relax and congratulate yourself on completing all that hard work. You put away the checkbook and sit back to await your interview invitations. Well don't get too comfy, because there is more paper on the way! Nearly all schools will forward a secondary application after they receive your AMCAS paperwork. As noted earlier, some schools will send secondaries to all applicants, while others will screen before sending secondaries. What do the secondaries entail? Well, they can vary from demanding just a little more biographical information, to requesting full-fledged essays. The one thing they almost uniformly request: more money (surprise, surprise). Check out the tracking sheets in the Appendix to help organize your application paperwork. It's usually at the secondary application stage that you'll be asked to forward your letters of recommendation. Which brings us to our next topic . . . .

Recommendations

We've chosen to discuss recommendations at this point since these letters are typically submitted with the secondary applications. Nonetheless, you need to think about and solicit your letters long before you reach this stage of the process.

Remember the purpose of these letters: they serve as outside endorsements of your medical school candidacy. The more personal the letter, the better off you are. Many premeds feel compelled to have their letters written by big-name professors or high-profile faculty members who hardly know them. Chances are these letters will be no more than glorified form letters and will be written with very little insight or care. You should select someone who knows you well to write the letter. If this happens to be a professor of a class, that's great. But don't hesitate to have a teaching assistant, advisor, or work supervisor write you a letter as well. These people have gotten to know you in the academic, extracurricular, or work environment and can fully attest to your abilities. If a T.A. or class assistant writes the letter, ask them to have the professor cosign it.

How many letters should you solicit? Three seems to be the minimum number. You probably want two from science professors. You may wish to receive the third from an academic in a humanities course, from someone involved in a particularly important extracurricular activity, or from a superior in the workplace. You should avoid obtaining letters from friends, relatives, clergy, or politicians.

FOLLOW DIRECTIONS

Admission officers are amazed at how many applicants simply refuse to follow directions. Don't think that you're an exception to any rules. If the application asks for X, give them X, not Y.

AND YOU ARE...?

Beware the impersonal recommendation. It is a definite red flag to the admission officer.

When you approach someone to write a letter of recommendation, don't hesitate to ask whether he or she can write you a strong letter of support. If the person hesitates in any way, look elsewhere. Although this may be embarrassing, it will hurt you a lot more in the long run to have someone write you a lukewarm or unenthusiastic letter.

The schools expect these letters to be glowing endorsements. Anything less is a red flag. Once you have garnered a positive response, be sure to provide your recommendation writer with a résumé of your activities to provide a more complete picture of you as a person. If you have a strong academic record, you may want to include a copy of your transcript to showcase your academic prowess and consistency. Any articles or papers that you think may be helpful should also be offered. Finally, always provide the writer with addressed and stamped envelopes to either your premed advisor/committee or the school in question. (Ask your premed advisor how the letters should be handled.)

Don't wait until the fall to ask for letters of recommendation! Those premeds who procrastinate will be scrambling to get recommendations, and science professors will be overwhelmed with requests. You don't want to be crushed in the fall rush. You can imagine the quality of these letters. Again, don't procrastinate!

Keep track of the status of your letters. If they're late, call and check on their progress. But don't harass your recommendation writers; if you make a pest of yourself, it could negatively impact what they end up writing about you. Once you've confirmed that your letters have been sent, thank-you notes to the writers are a nice touch. Personal visits are in order after you've been accepted.

Use the recommendation organizer that appears in the Appendix to stay on top of everything.

INTERVIEWS

There is a fair amount of mythology surrounding the medical school interview. Much of the fear stems from the legacy of the "stress interview." One of our favorite tales is this classic passed from one generation of premeds to the next: the interviewer asks our unsuspecting candidate to open a window. As hard as he tries, he can't open it. Why? Because it's nailed shut! We believe that this story is apocryphal. Or maybe it happened once and became legendary.

You can rest assured that stress interviews are now the exception, not the rule. But the interview is an assessment of your composure and maturity. You may be asked a question that makes you uneasy. If something weird or stressful does happen—just keep your cool. (For example, if the

WHEN FILLING OUT YOUR APPLICATIONS:

- Don't use application forms from previous years. Most applications change from year to year.

- Always double- and triple-check your application for spelling errors. You lose a certain amount of credibility if you write that you were a "Roads Scholar."

- Check for accidental contradictions. Make sure that your application doesn't say you worked in a hospital in 1990 when your financial aid forms say you were driving a cab that year.

- Prioritize all lists. Let the admission committee know that you realize what's important—i.e., always list significant scholastic accomplishments first.

- Don't mention high school activities or honors. Unless there's something very unusual or spectacular about your high school background, don't mention it. Yes, this means not taking note of the fact that you were senior class president.

QUALITY TIME

One way to make sure your recommendation writer is familiar with you and your background is to talk face-to-face. Make an appointment with your recommendation writer to discuss your candidacy.

DO THE WAIVE

Conventional wisdom dictates that you waive your option to review your recommendations. Med schools usually prefer that you not have any hand in what is written about you in these letters.

window thing happened to you, an appropriate response would be to say: "It appears to be stuck." An inappropriate response would be to throw a tantrum or a chair.) However, if the interviewer behaves in an inappropriate manner, consider contacting the Dean of Admissions; doing so is in your best interest and the school's.

The Interview and Admissions

Because medical schools are inundated with thousands of applications, most admission committees use the interview as a major cut. They'll screen applications with an eye to the GPA and MCAT scores. They'll then invite candidates that they are interested in for a personal interview.

Whereas the initial step in the admissions process (reviewing your numbers) may seem cold and calculating, the interview introduces the element of humanity into the admission process. Here is where you can let your personality and charm shine through. You should remember that these days, medical schools are looking not only for intelligent, motivated candidates, but also kinder and gentler ones.

Once you have reached the interview stage, you should realize that everyone's numeric credentials are probably close to comparable. The quality of your interview may make the difference. Knowing what takes place during an admission committee meeting might bring this home, so take a look:

A group of approximately ten people huddle around a circular table. The head of the committee opens up the first folder, from a stack of many, and reads aloud the name "John Smith." "Did anyone here have the pleasure of interviewing John Smith?" If a committee member has, he or she begins to speak on his behalf. Usually the comments run the gamut from the very specific, "I found him to be incredibly bright and well-spoken, in particular about his research concerning . . ." to the very nebulous, "I can't really put my finger on it, but I have this feeling that John will make an excellent doctor. I highly endorse this candidate!" In any case, positive endorsements keep the folder alive and maybe even garner admission at this particular meeting.

Remember, once granted an interview, your fate is in your own hands. So by all means, be prepared (along with don't procrastinate, one of the two leitmotifs of this book)!

Preparing for Interviews

Many students go into their first few interviews completely unprepared, hoping to see what it's like and maybe getting the hang of it. Now nobody in their right mind would attempt to run a marathon untrained (or take the MCAT), just to see what it was like. The same principle applies here. You want to be able to anticipate the questions that they will ask and formulate the essence of your responses. You want to minimize the potential for disaster.

Current Events

More often than not, the interviewer will base his or her questions on your Personal Statement and your application. (This is especially true if you have an "open file" interview, when the interviewer sees your application beforehand.) But on occasion, an interviewer may ask you to comment on a medicine-related current event or ethical issue: "What are your feelings on current health care reform proposals?" "Do you agree with Kevorkian's actions?" "What are your views on abortion?" Since you are planning to become a doctor, these questions are fair game. It is not expected, however, that you be an expert on these topics—just that you have thought about these issues and have something reasonably intelligent to share.

Common Interview Questions
In addition to medicine-related questions, you should also review classic interview questions:

Personal
- Tell me about yourself.
- Why have you decided to pursue medicine as a career?
- When did you decide that you wanted to be a doctor?
- Do you have any family members who are physicians?
- What is your greatest strength/weakness? Success/failure?
- If you don't get into medical school, what will you do?
- What did you like about college?
- What is your favorite book? What are you reading now?
- How do you spend your free time?
- What area of medicine are you interested in?
- Where do you see yourself in ten years? (Hint: don't say, "prison.")
- Where else have you applied? Why do you want to go here?
- What leadership roles have you assumed?
- What clinical experience have you had?

Ethical
- What are your views on abortion?
- Do you have an opinion on fetal-tissue research?
- How would you feel about treating a patient infected with HIV?
- Do you agree with Dr. Kevorkian's actions?

STAY ON TOP OF CURRENT EVENTS

You should read the newspaper and keep up on current events. Go through some back issues of a news weekly and read all the pertinent medicine-related articles.

ARE YOU SERIOUS ABOUT MEDICINE?

Be specific about why you want to go to medical school. Try to articulate good, solid reasons.

ONE BEST ANSWER

If you're asked what you'll do if you don't get into medical school, don't say, "go to law school" or "work in the family business." By all means, say you'll apply again. Be committed.

FLASHBACK TO FLASHCARDS

You may want to write some sample questions on index cards and jot some notes or thoughts on the back of the card. Remember, practice analyzing the issues, but don't memorize the answers.

Hypothetical Situations
- You are treating a terminally ill patient who is being kept alive by life support. You feel that he should be taken off the machines. What do you do?
- A pregnant teenager comes to you to discuss her options. She hasn't told her parents about her pregnancy. What do you do?

Health-Care Issues
- What do you think the role of the government should be in health care?
- Do you think health care is a right or a privilege?
- Have you been following the health-care debate? Where do you stand?

Obviously, you won't encounter all of the above samples. Additionally, there may be others that you're asked that aren't on this list. That's OK. If you take the time to examine these issues, you'll have the confidence to answer most questions that come your way. Practice answering these questions, but do not memorize answers or practice monologues in front of the mirror. An interview is a conversation; you're not auditioning for Hamlet. Nothing is worse than answers that sound canned. You must be able to improvise and think on your feet.

Mock Interviews

Mock interviews are invaluable trial runs. You finally have a chance to answer some of those practice questions. You can have someone evaluate your speaking style, the content of your answers, your body language, and your overall presentation.

Some colleges offer mock interviews, and you should check the availability by consulting your premed advisor or career center. In any case, even if a formal mock interview isn't available, you can always have a friend or relative act as the interviewer and evaluate your performance. You may even want to videotape your interview for a more detailed critique. Regardless of which route you take, you must solicit feedback. Only then will you realize if you speak too quickly; if you should enunciate more clearly; if you have a tendency to shake your leg when nervous; if you start every sentence with "like," "ummmm," or "you know." You want to work out all the kinks before, not during, the actual interview!

Scheduling

Your interview offers all usually arrive at approximately the same time. Remember, the sooner you have your interview with the school, the sooner you'll be considered for acceptance. So schedule the interviews as early as possible. Many students will try to schedule those interviews at "less desirable" schools earlier—to gain interview experience and overcome early jitters. However, do not delay your other interviews too long, as it may significantly delay completion of your application.

Financial reasons may compel you to schedule groups of interviews in particular geographical regions. For instance, you may want to set up a West Coast interview tour and visit several schools in the same area during one trip. Don't hesitate to request alternate dates if available; this can save you considerable time and money.

Travel and Accommodations

Traveling to interviews is a significant expense that many students overlook. In an ideal world, you would schedule different "interview tours" to minimize the amount of traveling. In the real world, however, this is often not possible, due to school scheduling limitations or inflexibility. You may find yourself having to travel to the same region a number of times. This can add up to a hefty amount of change, so be prepared. Some airlines offer discounts to medical students traveling to interviews, so it's well worth your while to do your homework. And try to limit your travel to one airline so you can accrue frequent flier miles.

Always call the admission office in advance to find out whether parking is available or to inquire as to the most economical means to reach the medical school from the airport. In addition, you should ask about accommodations. Most medical schools have programs that enable you to stay with a medical student for free. Although a free room may be economically enticing, remember that it is more important for you to be comfortable. If sleeping on the floor of a medical student's apartment is going to stress you out, maybe you should try to locate the nearest budget motel.

Finally, you should always try to arrive the night before the interview, in order to familiarize yourself with the area and the school. This will also give you the opportunity to unwind and get a good night's sleep. Nothing is more underwhelming than an inattentive and dreary-eyed applicant.

Dress

The interview is not the time to make a fashion statement. Whether you like it or not, your physical appearance will be the first impression you make on the interviewer. You want to be remembered as the self-confident candidate with loads of charm and wit, not the one with the funny hat or braided facial hair.

Men should opt for a dark suit (blue, gray, black) and an attractive, but not too flashy, tie. Facial hair should be groomed and you should probably forgo the earring even if you normally wear one (but it's up to you). Oh yeah—no sneakers (or tennis shoes for you Westerners).

YOU'RE ON CANDID CAMERA

If you are able to videotape yourself in a mock interview, try playing the tape back in fast forward. Any nervous gestures you display will seem even more obvious (and comical) when they repeat every two seconds.

FREE TO BE YOU AND ME

It may seem ridiculous to worry about appearance, about such personal expressions as jewelry or facial hair. But is it worth taking a chance when medical school is on the line?

Women should wear a suit or dress coordinates. Skip the too-high heels and go easy on the jewelry and makeup. You're vying for a place in medical school, not a role on *Melrose Place*.

Finally, one suit or dress is usually enough. You don't have to change outfits for every interview. In fact, when you go to your interviews, you'll begin to recognize certain of your fellow candidates by their "interview outfit." It doesn't matter. Remember, you're trying to impress your interviewer, not your competition. If you have a bunch of interviews in a row, make arrangements for dry cleaning your beloved interview outfit.

Interview Day
Before the Interview
Arrive a little early and a lot prepared.
- Nothing is worse than being late to an interview, so make sure to give yourself a healthy cushion of time to get there. Don't be rushed. On the other hand, don't show up too early.
- Don't bring family members or girlfriends/boyfriends to the interview. Drop them at the mall; give them movie money. Just don't take them to your interview!
- Be sure to review your application and your Personal Statement before you arrive. The interviewer may ask you specific questions concerning your application and Personal Statement. Bring a copy with you as well.

Treat support staff courteously.
- After arriving at the admission office, be sure to be polite to the receptionist or other support staff. A rude comment or inappropriate behavior can quickly be passed on to admission committee members and interviewers.
- Treat every interaction as if it were an integral part of the interview.

The Interview
Introduction
- Acknowledge the interviewer by name ("Hello, Dr. X"), introduce yourself.
- Shake hands (firm but not bone-crunching).

Open versus Closed interview
There are commonly two types of medical school interviews, open and closed. They're differentiated by whether the interviewer has seen your file.
- Open Interview: If the interviewer has already reviewed your application and Personal Statement, he or she will often begin the interview by referring to the application or a particular section of your Personal Statement.

DON'T PULL AN EDDIE HASKELL

Be respectful, but not overly ingratiating.

- Closed Interview: If the interviewer has never seen your application folder, he or she may begin with a very open-ended question such as, "So, tell me a little about yourself."

Answering questions
- Avoid being arrogant or dogmatic. Remember you're not a doctor yet. You don't know what medical school or medicine is really like. At the same time, do not compromise your views in order to please the interviewer. Be firm but flexible.
- If the interviewer is being antagonistic, do not answer in kind. Think before you speak. Do not raise your voice. Speak slowly. Be cool and composed.
- If you don't know the answer to a specific question, don't be afraid to say that you don't know. Often, if you try to make something up, the interviewer will see right through you. This could simply be a composure test. It takes a great deal of maturity to simply say, "I don't know." (Of course, you can't answer "I don't know" if the question is, "Tell me about yourself.")

Length
- There is no standard length to a medical school interview. It can be as short as fifteen minutes or over an hour long.
- Interview duration is not indicative of the quality of the interview.

After The Interview
Closure
- Shake hands and say good-bye.

Lunch and tour
- Many schools schedule prospectives for two interviews. Usually an interview is held during the morning, followed by lunch and a student tour. The second interview is usually scheduled for the afternoon. Though you may be relieved that the first interview is over, you should not let your guard down. The medical students who are conducting the tour may be evaluating you as well. Remember to treat every interaction as if it were part of the interview.
- Watch your suit or dress during lunch; you don't need the added stress of wondering whether the interviewer can spot the newly acquired mustard stain on your tie or blouse. (Or worse, something stuck between your teeth! Be safe; drop by the rest room before the next interview.)

INTERVIEW REMINDERS

- Maintain eye-contact
- Don't fidget
- Don't cross arms
- Don't fondle items on the interviewer's desk
- Try not to speak too quickly
- Smile at appropriate times

The Waiting Game

Waiting to hear from medical schools can be agonizing, and you may be tempted to pester the admissions officers for progress reports. Go through official channels to contact the offices, and make contact for a *legitimate* reason, such as a new letter of recommendation or grade.

Remember, don't get too discouraged if you're not accepted your first time around. You may have been the next name on every waiting list. Reapply with improved MCAT scores, a more carefully prepared application, additional experience, stronger recommendations, or something else that shows a change. Admission officers will appreciate that you're serious about medical school and medicine.

CONCLUSION

We hope that this section on medical school admission has helped you appreciate the multitude of steps required to gain admission to medical school. A strong application requires substantial planning and a great deal of time and effort on your part. As we discussed earlier, if you're not ready to make a total commitment, you should reconsider entering this challenging process.

But if you are prepared to follow this book's advice, you can be sure that you'll be making the most of your chance to impress your top-choice medical schools. The stakes are high. So are the rewards.

THE APPLICATION ORGANIZER

As you can see, you have a lot of details to stay on top of during the application process. The more organized you are, the more you'll be rewarded with completed applications and early interviews and acceptances. We'd like to help. Throughout this book we've made references to worksheets in the Appendix. We know what you're thinking—the appendix is a vestigial organ with no important function. Well, not in this book. In addition to vital admissions information, the Appendix consists of an application organizer to keep you on track.

TAKE CONTROL

You can't afford to procrastinate or miss a single opportunity in the application process to make yourself seem desirable as a medical student. A key step is getting organized.

APPLICATION CHECKLIST

❏ Get to know your school's premedical advisor(s).

❏ Complete 1 year each of biology, general chemistry, organic chemistry, and physics prior to taking the MCAT.

❏ Register to take the MCAT. (Registration materials become available every February for both administrations.)

❏ Obtain an AMCAS application (available starting in April for admission the following year).

❏ Refer to a copy of *Medical School Admission Requirements* for information about individual medical schools (new edition published every April).

❏ Request letters of recommendation (as early as feasible). Find out if your premedical advisor(s) writes a composite letter.

❏ Request catalogs from individual schools (AMCAS and non-AMCAS).

❏ Obtain passport-sized color photos. (Secondary applications may require a photograph.)

❏ Create a separate folder for each school you're applying to.

For AMCAS Schools

❏ Arrange for a copy of transcripts from all undergraduate and graduate schools you have attended to be forwarded to AMCAS (AMCAS accepts transcripts starting March 15).

❏ Complete AMCAS application, copy for your files, and send to AMCAS.

❏ Complete all secondary applications sent by individual AMCAS schools. Copy and submit by deadlines.

NOTE: At the MCAT administration, if you agree to release your results to the AAMC, then there will be no need to arrange for your scores to be forwarded to AMCAS schools. (The AAMC will distribute your scores to the AMCAS schools you're applying to.)

For Non-AMCAS Schools

❏ Arrange for a copy of your transcript(s) to be sent to each non-AMCAS school you are applying to.

❏ Complete individual applications, copy and submit by deadlines.

❏ Have your MCAT scores forwarded to each non-AMCAS school you are applying to.

NOTE: When taking the MCAT, you will have the opportunity to designate up to six non-AMCAS schools that will receive your MCAT scores. For additional score reports, and for pre-1991 scores, you will need to complete an Additional Score Report Request Form.

AMCAS Schools

To receive an AMCAS application, call or write to:

AMCAS
Section for Student Services
Association of American Medical Colleges
2450 N Street, NW, Suite 201
Washington, DC 20037-1131
(202) 828-0600
http://www.aamc.org

Non-AMCAS Schools

In 1996 the following schools required that you contact them individually for applications. All schools not listed below participated in the AMCAS program.

• Baylor College of Medicine
• Brown University School of Medicine
• Canadian Schools of Medicine (16 schools)
• Columbia University College of Physicians and Surgeons
• Harvard Medical School
• Johns Hopkins University School of Medicine
• New York University School of Medicine
• Texas A & M University Health Science Center College of Medicine
• Texas Tech University Health Sciences Center School of Medicine
• University of North Dakota School of Medicine
• University of Rochester School of Medicine and Dentistry
• University of Missouri/Kansas City School of Medicine
• University of Texas System (Southwestern, Galveston, Houston, San Antonio)
• Yale University School of Medicine

MCAT / AMCAS Tracking Sheet

❏ Sent for MCAT Registration Packet on _____
  MCAT Program
  P. O. Box 4056
  Iowa City, Iowa 52243
  (319) 337-1357

❏ Mailed MCAT Registration form on _____ Check #_____

Make a copy of the MCAT registration form and AMCAS application before you send them, and when you do send them, do so by certified mail, return-receipt requested.

❏ Received MCAT Admission Ticket on _____

❏ At MCAT administration, designated the following non-AMCAS schools to receive scores *(six maximum).*

_____ _____ _____

_____ _____ _____

❏ Received MCAT scores on _____
  Verbal Reasoning _____ Physical Sciences _____
  Writing Sample _____ Biological Sciences _____

MEANWHILE . . .

❏ Sent for AMCAS Registration Packet on _____

❏ Received AMCAS Packet on _____
  (if not within two weeks, call AMCAS)

❏ Mailed AMCAS application on _____
  (AMCAS will return applications received before June 3)

❏ Requested that the following institutions send official transcripts to AMCAS:

Institution_____ Request date_____ Received by AMCAS _____

Institution_____ Request date_____ Received by AMCAS _____

Institution_____ Request date_____ Received by AMCAS _____

Obtain an unofficial copy of each transcript to help you accurately complete your applications.

❏ Received Missing Official Transcript form on _____
  Contacted institution for missing transcripts on _____

❏ Received Transmittal Notification on _____ Cycle/form #_____

If transmittal notification isn't received within three weeks of the acknowledgment card, call AMCAS.

Tracking Sheet—AMCAS Schools

Medical School	Secondaries				Letters of Rec.		Application	Interview	Outcome
	Date Received	Date Due	Date Sent	Receipt Acknow-ledged	Date Due	Date Sent	Date File Complete	Date of Interview	A/WL/R
1.									
2.									
3.									
4.									
5.									
6.									
7.									
8.									
9.									
10.									
11.									
12.									
13.									
14.									
15.									
16.									
17.									
18.									

TRACKING SHEET—NON-AMCAS SCHOOL

NAME OF MEDICAL SCHOOL_____

ADDRESS _____
        Street   *City*   *State*   *Zip Code*

CONTACT PERSON_____Phone

- ❏ Catalog/application   Requested_____ Received _____
- ❏ Duplicated all forms for work on drafts
- ❏ Ordered MCAT scores to be sent if not done at MCAT administration*   Date_____ Check #_____
- ❏ Completed final draft of application and essay   Date_____
- ❏ Typed and copied application   Date_____
- ❏ Mailed application and essay**   Date_____ Check #_____
- ❏ Requested transcripts   Date_____
- ❏ Letters of recommendation sent
- ❏ Completed any secondary paperwork   Date_____
- ❏ Received notification that application is complete   Date_____
- ❏ Interview   Date_____
- ❏ Notification of acceptance, rejection, or wait-list   Date_____ Status_____
- ❏ Final decision   _____

*   You must do this for all pre-1991 scores.

** Certified mail return receipt requested; or include a self-addressed postcard for school to mail back.

TRACKING SHEET—NON-AMCAS SCHOOL

NAME OF MEDICAL SCHOOL_____

ADDRESS_____

             Street   *City*   *State*   *Zip Code*

CONTACT PERSON_____Phone_____

- ❑ Catalog/application   Requested_____ Received_____
- ❑ Duplicated all forms for work on drafts
- ❑ Ordered MCAT scores to be sent if not done at MCAT administration*   Date_____ Check #_____
- ❑ Completed final draft of application and essay   Date_____
- ❑ Typed and copied application   Date_____
- ❑ Mailed application and essay**   Date_____ Check #_____
- ❑ Requested transcripts   Date_____
- ❑ Letters of recommendation sent
- ❑ Completed any secondary paperwork   Date_____
- ❑ Received notification that application is complete   Date_____
- ❑ Interview   Date_____
- ❑ Notification of acceptance, rejection, or wait-list   Date_____ Status_____
- ❑ Final decision   _____

*   You must do this for all pre-1991 scores.

**   Certified mail return receipt requested; or include a self-addressed postcard for school to mail back.

LETTERS OF RECOMMENDATION ORGANIZER

NAME_____TITLE_____

ADDRESS_____

BUSINESS ADDRESS_____

PHONE #: HOME_____BUSINESS_____

SENT THANK-YOU NOTE_____NOTIFIED OF FINAL OUTCOME_____

NAME_____TITLE_____

ADDRESS_____

BUSINESS ADDRESS_____

PHONE #: HOME_____BUSINESS_____

SENT THANK-YOU NOTE_____NOTIFIED OF FINAL OUTCOME_____

NAME_____TITLE_____

ADDRESS_____

BUSINESS ADDRESS_____

PHONE #: HOME_____BUSINESS_____

SENT THANK-YOU NOTE_____NOTIFIED OF FINAL OUTCOME_____

NAME_____TITLE_____

ADDRESS_____

BUSINESS ADDRESS_____

PHONE #: HOME_____BUSINESS_____

SENT THANK-YOU NOTE_____NOTIFIED OF FINAL OUTCOME_____

After you've completed this sheet, duplicate it and place a copy in the file folder of each school you are applying to.